American Superrealism

The Wisconsin Project on American Writers

Frank Lentricchia, General Editor

American Superrealism

NATHANAEL WEST AND THE POLITICS OF

REPRESENTATION IN THE 1930S

Jonathan Veitch

THE UNIVERSITY OF WISCONSIN PRESS

The University of Wisconsin Press
2537 Daniels Street
Madison, Wisconsin 53718

3 Henrietta Street
London WC2E 8LU, England

Library of Congress Cataloging-in-Publication Data

Veitch, Jonathan.
American superrealism: Nathanael West and the politics of
representation in the 1930s / Jonathan Veitch.
204 pp.   cm. — (The Wisconsin project on American writers)
Includes bibliographical references (p. 139) and index.
ISBN 0-299-15700-8 (cloth: alk. paper).
ISBN 0-299-15704-0 (pbk.: alk. paper).
1. West, Nathanael, 1903–1940—Criticism and interpretation.
2. Capitalism and literature—United States—History—20th century.
3. Politics and literature—United States—History—20th century.
4. Literature and society—United States—History—20th century.
5. National characteristics, American, in literature.   6. Surrealism
(Literature)—United States.   7. Depressions in literature.
8. Economics in literature.   9. Mimesis in literature. I. Title.
II. Series.
PS3545.E8334Z9   1997
813'.52—dc21   97-14031

For my father, John P. Veitch, who went west . . .

Contents

Acknowledgments

If it takes a village to raise a child, it also takes one to write a book. I have been blessed with a warm and generous village of family, friends, mentors, and colleagues who have helped me to do both over the last few years. My deepest debt of gratitude is to my father and mother—John and Carol Lee Veitch—who taught me the things that matter most in life and embodied them with grace and style. Their extraordinary love has provided my sister, Jonna, and me with the foundation that has enabled us both to lead happy and productive lives.

I also wish to thank Al and Barbara Gelpi, who encouraged my intellectual ambitions, first as mentors at Stanford and later as dear friends. Other friends and family have also lent me their support: John and Jonna Carls, Kathy L'Amour, Kevin Goodman, Keith Bloom, Jeff Stockwell, Chet Olsen, Anthony Grumbach, and Doug Sortino. Not only did they insist that I tell them what I was working on, they listened intently to the answer (or at least they acted as if they did) and affirmed its worth.

Sacvan Bercovitch first suggested to me that I write a book on Nathanael West and the 1930s, and he has remained unfailingly supportive throughout its gestation. From the beginning I have tried to hold his high standard of critical excellence before me as both a model and a source of inspiration. Several others were willing to look over portions of the manuscript at various stages of undress, and they were kind enough to do so without blushing: among them, Leo Marx, Werner Sollors, and Daniel Aaron. Helen Vendler has been particularly generous with her time, giving me both advice and enouragement when I most needed it. Dickran Tashjian and Miles Orvell served as readers for the University of Wisconsin Press. Their encouraging response and helpful commentary not only improved the manuscript, they also breathed new life into its tired author. I am grateful to all of them.

No project of this sort can come to fruition without an immense amount of institutional patronage. I am indebted to David Donald and the American Civilization program at Harvard University, the Whiting Foundation, the Huntington Library, and the University of Wisconsin in Madison for grants that enabled me to complete my work. At Madison I have been fortunate enough to enjoy the company of an exceptional group of colleagues: Joe Wiesenfarth, Tom Schaub, Eric Rothstein, Gordon Hutner, Dale Bauer, Lynn Keller, Don Rowe, Sarah Zimmerman, and most of all, Heather Dubrow. They have remained steadfast in their support despite the considerable demands I sometimes made on them. I have received far more from them, the department, and the university than I shall be able to repay.

Finally, I wish to thank Lenore and Peter Mott, who frequently interrupted their own busy professional lives to help me with mine. They graciously (and eagerly) consented to take care of Margaret and Alexander so their father could, as Margaret explains it, "do his homework." Last but not least, there is one person for whom thank you is simply not enough. That is my wife, Sarah. More than anyone else, she has been my partner in this arduous process: listening to my ideas, encouraging me when I doubted their merits, always giving me just the right advice. On more than one occasion, Sarah has encouraged her moody husband to "be breezy." Now that I am finished with my homework, perhaps I can. I confess that I have spent far too many late nights at the computer when I should have been curled up beside her.

Preface

Nathanael West holds something of an anomalous place in American literary history. Often mentioned in studies of the thirties, his place within that decade—and within American literature more generally—is poorly understood. West has been endowed with the "power of blackness" (by Harry Levin), hailed as "a poet of darkness" (by Harold Bloom), and described as an apocalyptic writer (by just about everyone).[1] But few have ventured to explain the precise nature of his distinctive method of negation. Similarly, West has been identified as a homegrown surrealist (by Edmund Wilson), a "writer on the left" (by Daniel Aaron), the predecessor of Bernard Malamud, Joseph Heller, John Hawkes, and others (by Bernard Malamud, Joseph Heller, John Hawkes, and others).[2] But here too there has been little attempt to expound on these provocative affiliations. More recently, West has begun to receive the critical attention he deserves. Thomas Strychacz has written a chapter on both *Miss Lonelyhearts* and *The Day of the Locust* in *Modernism, Mass Culture, and Professionalism,* and Rita Barnard has devoted the final third of *The Great Depression and the Culture of Abundance* to West's critique of the culture industry. As illuminating as these critics are—and at times they can be very illuminating indeed—they tend to treat West's fiction as an illustration of their own theoretical interests (i.e., the professionalization of literature and literary study, and the cultural critique of Walter Benjamin and the Frankfurt School, respectively).

None of this confusion would come as a surprise to West himself. During his own day, he lamented the lack of understanding with which his fiction was greeted: "Somehow or other I seem to have slipped in between all the 'schools' [of writing]. . . . The radical press, although I consider myself on their side, doesn't like my 'particular kind of joking,' and think [it] even fascist sometimes, and the literature boys whom I detest, detest me in turn. The highbrow press finds that I avoid the big significant

things and the lending library touts in the daily press think me shock-
ing."[3] These comments offer a useful place to begin if we are to understand West's ambiguous position both within the thirties and within
American literature. For, as I will argue, that ambiguity is largely derived
from a confusion over both his own politics and the politics of representation. Nowhere is this seen more clearly than in his attempt to carve out
a middle ground between "radical press[es]" like the *New Masses* on the
one hand and the "literature boys" at *Partisan Review* on the other.

Although West never joined the Communist Party, he did share many
of its political convictions and on occasion worked actively on its behalf.
In 1935, for example, he signed his name to a manifesto circulated by the
American Writers' Congress that read in part: "The capitalist system
crumbles so rapidly before our eyes that . . . today hundreds of poets, novelists, dramatists, critics and short story writers recognize the necessity of
personally helping to accelerate the destruction of capitalism and the establishment of a workers' government."[4] In Southern California, West
became involved with the plight of migrant workers and supported the
attempts of studio employees to organize and affiliate with the CIO during 1937–38. He was an active member of the Screenwriters' Guild during a critical juncture in its history, when it fought and won recognition
from the studios.[5] And he participated in the activities of the communist-
inspired Anti-Nazi League in Hollywood, which was, at the time, the
most powerful antifascist group in the nation.

Signing manifestos and joining progressive organizations was one
thing; finding a way to incorporate those political concerns into his fiction was quite another. In a letter to Malcolm Cowley, West comments
on the problems he had doing just that in *The Day of the Locust*:

> I'm a comic writer and it seems impossible for me to handle any of the
> "big things" without seeming to laugh or at least smile. Is it possible to
> contrive a right-about face with one's writing because of a conviction
> based on a theory? I doubt it. What I mean is that out here [in Holly-
> wood] we have a strong progressive movement and I devote a great
> deal of time to it. Yet . . . I find it impossible to include any of those
> activities in [my novel]. I made a desperate attempt before giving up. I
> tried to describe a meeting of the Anti-Nazi League, but it didn't fit
> and I had to substitute a whorehouse and a dirty film. The terrible sin-
> cere struggle of the league came out comic when I touched it and even
> libelous. Take the "mother" in Steinbeck's swell novel—I want to be-
> lieve in her and yet inside myself I honestly can't. When not writing a
> novel—say at a meeting of a committee we have out here to help the

migrant worker—I do believe it and try to act on that belief. But at the typewriter, by myself, I just can't.[6]

West's difficulties with the communist left are articulated quite nicely here. Unable to submit to the dictates of proletarian culture during the early thirties (which demanded, so West felt, writing "based on a theory"), he was equally unable to believe in Steinbeck's Ma Joad (the echt symbol of the Popular Front's populist ideology). Instead, West substitutes "a whorehouse and a dirty film." It was precisely this "particular kind of joking" that prompted his critics to dismiss him as a dandy who preferred tweaking the pieties of the bourgeois to the earnest give-and-take of political struggle.

West's particular kind of joking masks a profoundly different reading of Depression America from the one promoted in the pages of the *New Masses*. For one thing West was less interested in the masses than in the phenomenon of "mass man." One searches in vain among the heartsick contributors to Miss Lonelyhearts' advice column or the desperate retirees who have "come to California to die" for a single factory worker or union leader. Their absence is attributable to the fact that West kept his sights resolutely trained on an emerging consumer economy and the apparatus that supported it. Meanwhile, his contemporaries were preoccupied with scrutinizing a production-oriented economy for signs of its imminent collapse. (As we shall see in the chapter on *The Day of the Locust,* whorehouses and dirty films have far more to tell us about the emerging economic order than even the most instructive meeting of the Anti-Nazi League.) To be sure, West was not immune to the pull of the Communist Party; as his letter to Cowley shows, his inability to write to its concerns caused him a great deal of consternation. But his decision to explore an entirely different subject matter not only represented a self-conscious break from the fiction of the left, it constituted a subtle criticism of its interpretation of American society as well.

That difference in interpretation continued after 1935, well into the era of the Popular Front, when the communists replaced the heroic factory worker with all-American figures like Ma Joad. Not only was Ma Joad, as West intimates, too good to be true, there were other problems with her as well. West suspected her of incipient fascist tendencies; or rather, he suspected that the pretensions to innocence, the return to a populist provincialism that she represented, harbored the seeds of a homegrown fascism (the subject of *A Cool Million*). Thus, instead of following the official line of the Popular Front, which saw fascism as "contamination from abroad" or "conspiracy from above," West's narratives suggest that if fascism were to emerge in America, it would most likely emerge from below, from the people themselves, or in the case of *The Day of the Locust,* from the sadomasochistic rage of mass man—the result of his disenchantment from the spell of commodity fetishism. Such a reading was so thoroughly at odds with the prevailing opinion of the day—except, of course, for that of the Frankfurt School—that few appreciated its significance. What did come through loud and clear, however, was West's loss of faith in the masses as a revolutionary agent of history, and that rightly troubled those on the left who took the time to read him.

If West has been accused of dandified politics, he has also been accused—then and since—of a pessimism so severe that it borders on nihilism. It is this, more than anything else, that seemed to separate him from his contemporaries on the communist left. As Daniel Aaron has observed, "It was all well and good to depict the hells of bourgeois capitalism . . . but in the last reel, the glow of the Heavenly City ought to be revealed."[7] There is no Heavenly City in West's fiction unless one counts the thwarted, utopian aspirations that lie buried in the cheap artifacts of mass culture: the "bright shawls, exotic foods, [and] outlandish costumes" of the El Gaucho restaurant in *Miss Lonelyhearts* or the "Samoan huts, Mediterranean villas, Egyptian temples" that line the Hollywood hills in *The Day of the Locust.*[8] Rita Barnard has argued that while the utopian energies mummified in these artifacts are for the most part beyond the reach of their consumers, they do possess a dialectical potential that is capable of unleashing the "anarchic and frightening, but certainly also liberatory" riot with which *The Day of the Locust* concludes.[9] This is a provocative argument, and it is one to which I will return at various points throughout the course of the book. For now it is enough to observe that in substituting the consumer for the producer or worker, West essentially abandons the teleological faith of his communist contemporaries. This results in a Brave New World of "anarchic and frightening" energies that may ultimately prove to be more reactionary than "liberatory."

Given West's differences with the communist left—his rejection of proletarian culture as well as the latent if not the explicit politics of the Popular Front, his deep skepticism about the revolutionary potential of the masses, and so on—one would think that he would have found a more sympathetic hearing from the critics at *Partisan Review* who shared many of those same views. But West's fiction was resolutely ignored by Rahv, Philips, and company during the thirties—this, despite the fact that they claimed to be beating the bushes for an American alternative to the writers championed under the banner of Proletcult and the Popular Front. How can that be explained? It may be that in a milieu that was infamous for turning ideological quarrels into vicious personal antagonisms, West's friendship with many of *Partisan*'s enemies on the communist left was enough to damn him. Or perhaps it was because West refused to abandon his communist sympathies in the histrionic manner that had become the order of the day (typified by writers like Rahv and Farrell). Certainly, West's own characterization of the writers and critics associated with *Partisan Review* as "literature boys" suggests that his hostility toward them lay in their increasing inclination to dissociate literature from politics.

 Ironically it was on these very grounds that West was eventually rediscovered by a second generation of critics at *Partisan Review*.[10] (I am thinking here primarily of Daniel Aaron, Norman Podhoretz, and Leslie Fiedler, who are probably more responsible for establishing West's literary reputation than anyone else.) Indeed, the history of West's reception and much of the misunderstanding associated with his fiction have, to a large extent, been bound up with the odyssey of these intellectuals. As they migrated from the communist left to the "vital center" in the forties and fifties, they took West and a number of other writers with them, depoliticizing their fiction in the process.[11] Podhoretz's commentary on West is typical in this regard:

> Nothing could be further from the spirit of his work than a faith in
> the power of new social arrangements or economic systems to alleviate
> the misery of the human condition. West was one of the few novelists
> of the 30's who succeeded in generalizing the horrors of the Depres-
> sion into a universal image of human suffering. His "particular kind of
> joking" has profoundly unpolitical implications; it is a way of saying
> that the universe is always rigged against us and that our efforts to
> contend with it inevitably lead to absurdity.[12]

This "profoundly unpolitical" construction of West is in accord with a broader reading of literary modernism promulgated by a number of New York Intellectuals who sought to provide a refurbished and chastened postwar liberalism with a critical awareness of what Lionel Trilling described as the "hell within."[13] For Trilling, Podhoretz, et al., this emphasis on the "hell within" offered a necessary counterbalance to liberalism's naive faith in social perfectibility which had made it so susceptible to the ideological "excesses" of the thirties. Whatever may have motivated this agenda, it has had the unfortunate effect of transforming a deeply political writer like West into a "universal satirist" for whom, in Aaron's words, "the real culprit is not capitalism but humanity."[14]

As I suggested earlier, West's pessimism would seem to sanction this sort of reading. But Podhoretz is mistaken if he attributes that pessimism to existentialist despair over the "human condition"; for West, the ubiquity of the "culture industry" is such that "humanity" is inseparable from the capitalist forms that "produce" it. Instead of "generalizing the horrors of the Depression into a universal image of human suffering," as Podhoretz suggests, West particularizes those horrors within the quite specific historical milieu of the Depression, when an emerging mass culture began "standardizing its products and consolidating itself as a vast oligopoly (the Hollywood studio system being the most obvious instance)."[15] West understands, even if his critics do not, that under these conditions the liberal faith of the New York Intellectuals in the "humanity" of the bourgeois subject (conceived as a free and independent agent capable of ethical decisions under the guidance of the accumulated wisdom of Western culture) is no longer imaginable except as a form of nostalgia. To suggest otherwise leaves these critics open to the very same charge they leveled at so many others, i.e., of failing to appreciate the complexity of modern reality, a reality that is, as they should well know, "always already" constituted by the practices of advanced capitalism. To reverse Aaron, then, in West's fiction the real culprit is not humanity, but capitalism. In fact, one might say that his fiction offers one of the most insightful critiques of the inhumanity of capitalism during the thirties (an era known for some biting critiques).

It is a testament to the power of the thirties—a decade whose symbolic importance in the national imagination may only now be coming to an end as a result of the fall of the Soviet Union and the dismantling of the American welfare state, the usurpation of a monologically defined class struggle by the politics of multiculturalism, and indeed, with the death of so many of its noteworthy participants—that one of the period's most virulent and protracted arguments should cloud our understanding of West's fiction for so many years afterward.

2

My purpose in writing this book is not to burnish Nathanael West's reputation in order to secure his place on the minor slopes of Parnassus. Instead, West provides the occasion for an investigation into three related fields of interest. First and foremost, I hope to offer a fresh reading of the

1930s, a reading that puts the problem of representation at the center of the decade's concerns. With the collapse of the American economy, many Americans discovered to their dismay that they did not understand the nature of the debacle that was so deeply affecting their lives. This prompted a wide variety of attempts to reconstruct the "hidden" logic of an elusive social reality. Indeed, there was an unprecedented commitment within the arts to the production of what might be described as "social knowledge." Case studies, reportage, documentary photography, proletarian literature, and "social problem" films investigated areas of experience that had heretofore been denied "official" recognition.[16] (In some cases, those investigations were conducted by officials themselves, notably those of the New Deal.) Despite the merits of their respective approaches, they all tended to share a similar faith in a reality that is, as Lionel Trilling once described it, "always reliable, always the same, always easily known."[17] That is not to say that these various approaches did not recognize the need for a "little digging," a "trip across the country," "scientific" conclusions based on "empirical" evidence. But for the most part, those who employed these techniques did so with confidence that in the end reality can be made fully visible.

Nathanael West did not share the same faith. Instead, he recognized that the dissolution of the familiar world under modern capitalism had resulted in a cultural sargasso of the first order. In contrast to those who ignored this state of affairs in order to mine reality for a specific "content" that could be put to persuasive purposes, West problematized the status of reality by exploring the way that "content" is shaped through various strategies of representation. Almost alone among his contemporaries, then, Nathanael West took representation as his subject. This enabled him to reject the usual stances of opposition that were operative during the thirties in favor of a resistance that is more highly mediated— that focuses on mediation itself. In fact, I will argue that West's self-reflexive approach—grounded as it is in the anti-aesthetic strategies of Dada and surrealism—offers what is probably the most insightful means of understanding the particular obstacles to the pursuit of social knowledge in a society increasingly dominated by the obfuscating spectacles of advanced capitalism.

This line of argument leads me to the second major concern of the book before you: the possibilities and limitations of Dada and surrealism as modes of social criticism.[18] "Surrealism," Hal Foster observes, has become "a retroactive point of reference for postmodernist art, especially for its critique of representation." But that critique has been largely ignored within the context of Anglo-American modernism.[19] That is because up until recently few critics were prepared to concede the existence of a vital avant-garde in America, much less explore its critical possibilities.[20] Roger Shattuck, a guide *sans pareil* to the European avant-garde, utterly fails us here:

> One can put together an impressive array of exchanges between European surrealists and Americans. On leaving Russia in 1931, E. E. Cummings translated Aragon's *Red Front*. . . . William Carlos Williams served as the American correspondent for Ribemont-Dessaignes' *Bifur* in 1930, and Gertrude Stein carried on a lively correspondence with René Crevel. . . . But every one of these items stands for little more than a fleeting engagement in the course of a full career. . . . Insofar as one can trace effects of surrealism on the . . . arts in this country, they crop up along the trajectory that carried abstract-expressionist painting into action painting and more recently into pop art.[21]

Comments like these have tended to obscure the rich and varied influence of Dada and surrealism in America long before the advent of abstract expressionism and pop. Inspired by the examples of Gertrude Stein, the Armory Show, Picabia and *291*, Duchamp and his readymades (in the teens), the surrealist exiles and *View* (during World War II), a diverse group of American artists made Dada and surrealism integral to their work: among them, Man Ray, Joseph Stella, Charles Demuth, Peter Blume, Morton Schamberg, Djuna Barnes, the Arensberg circle, Wallace Stevens, Mina Loy, Charles Henri Ford, William Carlos Williams (Shattuck's comments notwithstanding), and last but not least, Nathanael West.

Even where critics acknowledge an avant-garde presence in America, they have tended to dismiss it as a largely depoliticized phenomenon. Andreas Huyssen, for example, has argued that "the lack of political perspective in the [American avant-garde] is a function of the altogether different relationship between avant-garde art and cultural tradition in the United States, where the iconoclastic rebellion against a bourgeois cultural heritage would have made neither artistic nor political sense. In the United States, the literary and artistic heritage never played as central a role in legitimizing bourgeois domination as it did in Europe."[22] Huyssen is certainly right to observe that in America art does not play the same legitimizing role that it does in Europe. But it is precisely for that reason that some American artists are able to look beyond their "literary and artistic heritage" in order to engage a much broader range of issues. Where the European avant-garde can seem obsessed with thumbing its nose at the "grand tradition" of art and the institutions that support it, American artists like Nathanael West have managed to fashion that anti-aesthetic stance into a fruitful mode of criticism. Indeed, I will argue that West takes the traditional motifs, strategies, and concerns of Dada and surrealism—its scatological humor, its use of the readymade, its fascination with human machines and "exquisite corpses," its systematic substitution of artifice for nature—and extends their capacity for social criticism in groundbreaking ways.

Third and finally, I am interested in exploring the complicated presence of mass culture in America during the 1930s, at once this country's raison d'être and bête noire. West was one of mass culture's earliest and shrewdest critics. Although he was deeply critical of mass culture, it is important to note that West did not share the mandarin disdain of the Frankfurt School. Placed as he was in the ambiguous position of fabricating the dream life of the crowd (as a screenwriter in Hollywood) while he was busy savaging it in his fiction, West was never able to sustain the cultural divide between high culture and low that Adorno took for granted. In West's hands, high culture and low, avant-garde and kitsch, became hopelessly intertwined, making their vexed relation a much more complicated phenomenon than many of his contemporaries or critics imagined.

By that I do not mean to limit myself to the fairly obvious observation that his novels are filled with a variety of forms drawn from mass culture, including everything from B-movie plots to old vaudeville routines and schmaltzy Tin Pan Alley tunes. These "readymades" do not merely appear in West's fiction, they literally constitute the world of his fiction. That is why West is able to describe *Miss Lonelyhearts* as " 'a novel in the form of a comic strip.' The chapters to be squares in which many things happen through one action. The speeches contained in the conventional balloons."[23] West not only transforms all his novels into comic strips, he grants body to the results, asking us to accept the absurd limitations of his "funny pages" as constitutive. Moreover, he is alive to the pathos—more often, bathos—of Being as it is grotesquely contorted within the cartoonish dimensions of mass culture and its various forms: "the dough of suffering . . . [stamped] with a heart-shaped cookie knife," as the narrator of *Miss Lonelyhearts* puts it.[24] The result: Dostoevski as Roy Lichtenstein might have translated him.

It would be inaccurate to argue, as some critics have, that West's "concessions" to mass culture merely "replicate . . . the reifying processes of commodity production."[25] To the contrary, West's fiction offers one of the most thorough critiques of that process available in American literature. In effect, West's "comic strip fiction" explores the ideological grid through which representations of American society are created, accepted, and codified. In addition, he was attentive to the specific cultural domain in which these representations were reproduced and disseminated—the advice column in an urban newspaper (*Miss Lonelyhearts*), the dime novel (*A Cool Million*), Hollywood itself (*The Day of the Locust*). Despite the claim of these media to be dispensing nothing more than "advice" or "entertainment," West took them as the loci for a persuasive ideological authority during the thirties and the sites upon which some of the decade's major issues were powerfully articulated: the emergence of therapeutic culture, the suzerainty of the culture industry, the deleterious effects of commodity fetishism, the rise of fascism, the politics of representation.

West, of course, was not immune to the conditions he describes. His fiction was subject to the same commodifying pressures that it criticizes so trenchantly. In this, his own fate as a writer becomes emblematic of the larger problem that bedeviled the avant-garde in the thirties and has led to (premature?) pronouncements of its "death" ever since: namely its appropriation and subversion by the very culture it presumes to challenge. Nowhere is this conundrum dramatized more tellingly than in the fate of West's novels as they underwent the substantial revision necessary to make them "acceptable" for the screen. In epilogues to the chapters on *Miss Lonelyhearts* and *A Cool Million*—both of which were bought by movie studios during the thirties—I examine the painful and sometimes comic process by which these texts moved from a criticism of American society to an affirmation of its most cherished values. The screen adaptation of these novels offers what I hope will prove to be a fascinating case study of the culture industry's capacity to absorb even the most inhospitable "counternarratives" and put them to "good" use.

American Superrealism

Closed bank, Haverhill, Iowa, 1939, photograph by Arthur Rothstein. Library of Congress, Prints & Photographs Division, FSA/OWI Collection, [707117 F34-28362-D]

Who Can We Shoot?
The Crisis of Representation
in the 1930s

American life is a powerful solvent. (George Santayana)

In the opening pages of *The Grapes of Wrath* (1939)—the text that has, more than any other, come to symbolize the wrenching experience of the Depression—there is a revealing exchange between a tenant farmer and a young man on a tractor. The young man has been sent to knock down the farmer's house and evict him from his land. The farmer stands in the doorway, rifle in hand, prepared to make one final, desperate stand:

> "It's mine. I built it. You bump it down—I'll be in the window with a rifle. You even come too close and I'll pot you like a rabbit."
> ". . . You're not killing the right guy."
> "That's so," the tenant said. "Who gave you orders? I'll go after him. He's the one to kill."
> "You're wrong. He got his orders from the bank. The bank told him, 'Clear those people out or it's your job.'"
> "Well, there's a president of the bank. There's a board of directors. I'll fill up the magazine of the rifle and go into the bank."
> The driver said, "Fellow was telling me the bank gets orders from the East. The orders were, 'Make the land show profit or we'll close you up.'"
> "But where does it stop? Who can we shoot?"[1]

In many ways, the conundrum of the Depression can be found right here, in the tenant farmer's absolute befuddlement before the layers of mediation that threaten to dissolve individual responsibility—indeed, that seem

3

to dissolve individuals altogether. The lines of authority responsible for the tenant farmer's fate end in holding companies and their subsidiaries—the elusive abstractions of monopoly capitalism. Muley Graves explains to a disenfranchised Tom Joad, "The Shawnee Lan' an' Cattle Company"—the owner of his family's land—"ain't nobody. It's a company." And getting "mad" at that can make "a fella crazy."[2] As this exchange amply demonstrates, for many Americans the causes of the Depression defied representation, making it impossible to know how to respond, or rather, who to shoot. Among the many deleterious effects of the Depression (hunger, joblessness, degradation), this vertiginous loss of the capacity to represent social reality was among the worst.

There were many during the 1930s who shared the farmer's bewilderment over the causes responsible for such disenfranchisement. The narrator of Tennessee Williams' *Glass Menagerie* likened the pain of that bewilderment to "having [his] fingers pressed forcibly down on the fiery Braille alphabet of a dissolving economy."[3] The great chronicler of the Depression, Arthur Inman, adopted a different metaphor. He compared the experience to being trapped in a darkened theater during a change of scenes: "The lights gradually grew dim, then dark. While you strained to see and could not, the scenery was shifted. You could hear the people moving, the shuffling feet of the stage hands, the sound of rollers."[4] But, Inman tells us, it was impossible to make out anything more than that. He was right. The scenery had shifted. However, it had shifted many years before the Depression itself. The collapse of the American economy was not responsible for the change of scenery; it merely forced people to reckon with changes in American society that had been a long time in the making.

Those changes have been described in many ways by many different historians of modernity. But the description that comes the closest to defining the specific circumstances of the farmer's predicament can be found in Robert Wiebe's *The Search for Order*. In his study of social change during the Progressive Era, Wiebe outlines the process by which nineteenth-century America was transformed from a "society of island communities" into a "regulative, hierarchical . . . bureaucratic order." Needless to say, that transformation did not take place without a great deal of trauma, the chief source of which was a radical loss of individual autonomy. According to Wiebe, America's island communities operated under the assumption that they could literally "harness the forces of the world to [their own] destiny."[5] If that was largely an illusion, it was no doubt an empowering one. It became increasingly apparent, however, that it was the individual herself who was harnessed to the forces of the world rather than the other way around. And by any standard those forces have to be counted as overwhelming. In Wiebe's estimation, "No age"—by which he means the fifty years that preceded the Great Depression—"lent itself more readily to sweeping, uniform description: nationalization, industrialization, mechanization, urbanization. Yet to almost all of the people who created them, these themes meant only dislocation and bewilderment."[6]

Even a New Dealer like Thurman Arnold—who, as a member of Roosevelt's "Brain Trust," might be expected to serve as a guide to the capitalist order he was attempting to preserve—confessed to a certain measure of bewilderment. "We were—and are—in everyday contact with invisible empires," Arnold wrote.

> The map of no one of them is to be found in an atlas, but a match, a package of borax, a diamond, a storage battery, a radio set is a link between each American and this series of corporate world estates. You wish to light a cigarette. The match is almost certain to bear the name of the Diamond, Universal, Ohio, or Lion Match Company. But all of these are satellites of Diamond. And Diamond is connected with Bryant and May of London and with the company known as Swedish Match. . . . It is easy to add other examples: . . . Pick up a movie ticket, examine a tin can, take a look at a parking meter, call for an anti-malarial compound, send a cable to Mexico City . . . and you find yourself in personal contact with an invisible *imperium* which transcends the United States.[7]

In this account, matches, diamonds, and storage batteries become the ciphers of an "invisible *imperium*" that elude the cryptography even of someone as knowledgeable as Arnold himself. If his attempt to locate this Orientalized empire beyond the borders of the United States sounds disconcertingly like the exclusionary, ultranationalist rhetoric deployed by protofascist organizations of the twenties and thirties, it is a measure of the extent to which the crisis of representation affected liberals and reactionaries alike.

As a result of these enormous transformations, Americans awoke to find themselves in a world that was altogether different from the one into which they had been born.[8] According to Alan Brinkley's influential study of the thirties, "many of [these] changes had occurred almost unnoticed—small, incremental alterations in surroundings to which most people could easily and unthinkingly adjust. In the absence of a sudden, cataclysmic jolt, few had connected this halting evolution with any broader sense of process or structure. The Great Depression provided that jolt."9 Indeed, the severity and scope of the Depression forced Americans to undertake an unprecedented rite of self-examination. And when they did, they found to their chagrin that they lacked a language with which to understand the social world they had wrought at the very moment when understanding that world was most crucial. Without such a language, the Depression was rendered inexplicable, and hence, without redress. The opening lines of Archibald MacLeish's Depression-era poem *Land of the Free* could easily serve as a refrain for much of the nation: "We don't know/We aren't sure."10

In the absence of a viable explanation, Americans were forced to resort to a variety of metaphors (some of which were more illuminating than others): The Depression was a marathon (Horace McCoy's *They Shoot Horses Don't They*); a prison sentence (Mervyn LeRoy's *I Am a Fugitive from a Chain Gang*); a natural disaster (Pare Lorenz's *The River*); the wrath of an angry God imposed on a wayward nation (the sermons of Father Coughlin and Sister Aimee Semple McPherson); a prison sentence, a natural disaster, *and* the wrath of an angry God (Steinbeck's *The Grapes of Wrath*). Each of these conceits calls for the same social posture of submission and endurance. In the end all one could do was wait while Roosevelt tinkered. The iconography of the period is filled with images of people waiting—waiting on street corners, in broken-down cars, in breadlines. For what? No one appeared to know.

For those who had the misfortune to find themselves in one of those breadlines, surely one of the most confusing aspects of the Depression was the presence of want in the midst of so much plenty. Economists have labeled that phenomenon "underconsumption." Whatever its merits as an explanation for the cause of the Depression, the results defied common sense. One farmer summed up the absurdity of the situation by observing that he expected to make a fortune by *not* raising hogs. An unemployed man—sounding very much like Alice in a Depression-era Wonderland—gave this testimony to a congressional subcommittee in 1932:

> In the State of Washington I was told that the forest fires raging in that region all summer and fall were caused by unemployed timber workers and bankrupt farmers in an endeavor to earn a few honest dollars as fire fighters. . . . A number of Montana citizens told me of thousands of bushels of wheat left in the fields uncut on account of its low price that hardly paid for the harvesting. In Oregon I saw thousands of bushels of apples rotting in the orchards. . . . At the same time, there

are millions of children who, on account of the poverty of their
parents, will not eat one apple this winter.[11]

During the thirties that crisis was compounded still further by the
symbology associated with the Depression itself. The 1929 stock market
crash may have been more a symptom than a cause of economic instability, but its dramatic role as a harbinger of the Depression gave finance a
centrality in the American imagination that it had not had since the cur-
rency debates of 1896. This had the effect of focusing attention on one of
the most arcane features of monopoly capitalism. "Unlike the bulky
power of manufacturing and commerce," Wiebe explains, "finance functioned invisibly. With fugitive slips of paper, men in hidden offices seemed
capable of moving the universe."[12] It was not just that "power lay elsewhere, in 'alien' hands"; for most Americans, to confront finance capitalism was to confront an economic system that was in some fundamental
ways no longer intelligible.[13] Nowhere is this situation dramatized more
effectively than in the photograph (shown at the beginning of this chapter) taken by Arthur Rothstein, a Farm Security Administration photog-
rapher. There is nothing particularly special about Rothstein's "Closed
bank, Haverhill, Iowa, 1939." So many pictures were taken of shuttered
banks like this one that the subject has become something of a cliché. But
for those who lived through the Depression, this was a scene of great
trauma: the dead end to the bewildered farmer's attempt to secure an explanation for his travails. In Rothstein's photograph the bank is simply
closed, the money withdrawn. This hard fact is reenforced by the pho-
tographer's static, closely cropped gaze, which offers no alternative to the
empty building's mute presence. The ironies of the scene are inescapable.
The solid masonry of the bank, meant to suggest the permanence and sta-
bility of the country's basic institutions, has fallen into ruin, while
ephemeral, cardboard handbills announce the arrival of a thriving circus.
But there is more than irony here. Rothstein's photograph points to the
maddening surrealism of the Depression itself, which seemed to meet all
efforts to explain its causes with the laughter of a jeering clown.

To return, then, to the scene from *The Grapes of Wrath* with which we
began: Steinbeck's attempt to represent the "unrepresentable" offers a revealing glimpse not just into the plight of the Joads, but into the evasions,
misperceptions, and fears of millions who enthusiastically embraced this
novel in their search for the causes behind the unprecedented breakdown
in their economic system. Steinbeck might have explained the farmer's
dispossession as a function of complex social forces: the ongoing ratio-

nalization of the agricultural sector during the twenties and thirties, in which small plots of land were subsumed into larger parcels in order to capitalize on widespread mechanization and efficiencies of scale—a process of reorganization that was accelerated by bad weather, the depletion of the soil, the volatility of overseas markets, and a severe credit crunch caused by the financial panic of the thirties. But such explanations would hardly offer the farmer much solace, or even much sense of control over his fate.[14] Instead, Steinbeck chooses to adopt a rhetorical strategy that reveals more about his own representational impasse than the farmer's situation:

> The tractors came over the roads and into the fields, great crawlers moving like insects. Snub-nosed monsters, raising the dust and sticking their snouts into it, straight down the country, across the country, through fences, through dooryards, in and out of gullies in straight lines. They did not run on the ground, but on their own roadbeds. They ignored hills and gulches, water courses, fences, houses. . . . The driver could not control it—straight across country it went, cutting through a dozen farms and straight back. . . . He could not see the land as it was, he could not smell the land as it smelled; his feet did not stamp the clods or feel the warmth and power of the earth.[15]

In this scene the tractors serve as a synecdoche for the vast and impersonal forces of modernity itself. They move across the land without touching it, without being affected by it. Indeed, they seem to possess an ominous, relentless logic of their own, an "artificial" logic of "straight lines" that is opposed to the "natural" topography of "hills and gulches, water courses, fences, houses." We have come across this scene many times before. It is the old, familiar scene of the machine in the garden.[16] Against the overwhelming abstractions of the machine, Steinbeck poses the claims of the particular, the local, the existential, the historical. For Muley, the land that is being plowed under is still quite fertile—if not with nutrients, then with memory:

> "I been goin' aroun' the places where stuff happened. Like there's a place over by our forty; in a gully they's a bush. Fust time I ever laid with a girl was there. Me fourteen an' stampin' an' jerkin' an' snortin like a buck deer, randy as a billygoat. So I went there an' I laid down on the groun', an' I seen it all happen again. An' there's the place down by the barn where Pa got gored to death by a bull. An' his blood is right in that groun' right now. Mus' be. Nobody never washed it out.

In the face of his dispossession all Muley can do is reconnoiter the places where "stuff happened." But the memories he invokes must submit to an economic calculus ("a margin of profit") that appropriates them without recognizing their true (use) value: "What'd they get so their 'margin a profit' was safe?" Muley asks. "They got Pa dyin' on the groun' . . . an' me jerkin' like a billygoat under a bush in the night."[17]

Muley's longing for presence in the midst of absence results in a romantic critique of monopoly capitalism that pits the particularity of lived experience against the abstract forces of modernity. That critique contains a resonance that is not easy to dismiss. But its power comes at the cost of rewriting a complex historical moment into a hypostasized and unsustainable opposition between nature and culture. While that opposition may have had its uses as a provisional strategy, it ultimately obscured rather than illuminated the social forces at work during the thirties. In the process, an immensely complicated social, cultural, and economic structure was reduced to an undifferentiated, and ultimately unreadable entity, or as Steinbeck would have it, "a snub-nosed monster."

Steinbeck was certainly not alone in formulating the problem this way. As we shall see, this static and unproductive opposition between nature and culture—the defining feature of pastoralism—stands behind much of the fiction, photography, and filmmaking of his contemporaries. Indeed, one might go further and argue that pastoralism in its myriad forms constitutes the dominant mode of social criticism during the decade, encompassing everything from the movies of Frank Capra to the documentary photography of the Farm Security Administration, from the agrarianism of the Fugitives to the proletarian literature of the left (which William Empson has aptly described as a "covert pastoral").[18]

One might cite any number of instances by way of example, but perhaps the purest and most sustained manifestation of the pastoral impulse during the Depression (and certainly the supreme aesthetic achievement of the decade) can be found in the photographs taken of tenant farmers, small towns, and other rural subjects under the auspices of the FSA. "In our entire collection," Roy Stryker, the head of the photographic section, boasted, "you'll find no record of big people or big events. . . . There are pictures that say Depression, but there are no pictures of sit-down strikes, no apple salesmen on street corners, not a single shot of Wall Street and absolutely no celebrities"—which is to say, the "pictures that say Depression" do not include America's industrial workforce, its citadels of finance, or its mass media.[19] The FSA's account of the Depression, in short, does not include any of the forces that might be attributed to modernity.

That is the case even where those forces are ineluctably tied up with the "rural" subject matter of the photographs. "In am under no illusion about state fairs," Stryker observed in a letter to Arthur Rothstein. "They have become very smart and have a decided urban tinge. . . . Keep your camera pointed at the rural side of it."[20] One can, of course, argue that the FSA was doing no more than it was charged to do: photograph rural subjects. But as the foregoing example shows, it was not easy to distinguish, much less divorce, the rural from the urban, folk culture from mass culture, tradition from modernity. The fact that the FSA did so in such a surgical fashion and that the results were embraced by most Americans—then and now—as the official story of the Depression, indicates that the pastoral possessed a symbolic resonance that went far beyond the needs of the particular moment.[21]

That should come as no surprise. For the pastoral allows Americans to indulge in a fictive return to Wiebe's "island communities" where, as Lawrence Levine explains, it is still possible to believe "in the individual; in voluntary cooperation; in a harmony of interests; in the virtues of the agrarian/small-town way of life; in the future; in the possibilities of peaceful, progressive reform; in the superiority and primacy of the American Way."[22] And perhaps most important for our purposes, it allowed Americans during the thirties to believe that the crisis of representation was, in fact, no problem at all, that the obfuscating spectacle of capitalist modernity could be dispelled by nothing more than the authenticating presence of people like the Joads, whose strength, probity, and capacity to endure promised a return to first principles.

For Steinbeck, the reliance on pastoralism as a mode of criticism merely limited the scope and effectiveness of his efforts to represent social reality. But for others, this uncritical opposition between rural and urban, traditional and modern, nature and culture left them susceptible to a virulent form of antimodernism that posited a realm of innocence outside the inevitable complications and differences of a thoroughly mediated society.[23] During the thirties this reactionary quest for innocence manifested itself in a variety of ways. Muley's attempt to reclaim the innocence of the particular or the local can be found in everything from the saccharine celebrations of the American village in plays like *Our Town* to the more dubious antimodern sentiments of the Southern Agrarians. Meanwhile, Muley's determination to measure everything against his own experience finds its analogue in the demagoguery of Father Coughlin, Huey

Long, and Francis Townsend, who constantly invoked the self-validating experience of the common man in their war against size, concentration, complexity, and mediation. In its most extreme form this quest for innocence and purity resulted in the demonizing of the racial and ethnic Other by protofascist organizations like America First, the Ku Klux Klan, and the Silver Shirts (of which more later).

Part I

Chapter One

American Superrealism

The title of this book—*American Superrealism*—is an archaism, drawn from a brief moment in American cultural history when the critical possibilities of European surrealism were exploited by a handful of homegrown writers and painters in the early thirties.[1] Superrealism is the way that *surréalisme* was first "translated" when it made its U.S. debut in, of all places, Hartford, Connecticut—the home of the American insurance industry. It was there, at the Wadsworth Athenaeum in 1931, that the subversive canvases of De Chirico, Ernst, Masson, and Picasso were displayed together for the first time under the title *Newer Super-Realism.* The term remained in circulation for a while during the early thirties before becoming subsumed in its French variant. Although superrealism never constituted a separate movement, I have chosen to retain the original translation in order to distinguish it from the depoliticized phenomenon that surrealism eventually became in America through the "accidentalism" of action painting, the commercialization of its strategies and motifs in fashion photography, the "outrageous" antics of Salvador Dali (justly dubbed by his critics with the anagram AVIDA DOLLARS).[2]

Superrealism has other descriptive advantages as well. While both *sur* and *super* can be used almost interchangeably to mean "on," "upon," "over," the latter has assumed a special place in the American lexicon that speaks to the country's preoccupation with size, speed, and quantity—as in supermarket, superhighway, superpower, Superman. In short, it is embedded in American life and commerce (much the way Kurt Schwitters' *merz* is embedded in "komMERZiel"). In addition, superrealism is a compound word, the first part of which acts as an intensifier that, in West's hands at least, caricatures-burlesques-deconstructs the mimetic codes and conventions upon which more traditional forms of realism rely. It is, as its name implies, an "excessive realism" that aspires to turn its particular kind of joking into a distinct mode of social criticism.

As I noted earlier, the importance of surrealism in West's fiction has often been remarked upon, but it has been insufficiently understood, or more often, simply misunderstood. That is a confusion for which West himself is partly to blame. In his fiction doorknobs bleed, flower, speak; horses languish at the bottom of swimming pools; can openers turn into hairbrushes and flowerpots into victrolas, while revolvers dispense candy that turn out to be buttons.[3] And yet West could declare in all seriousness and with some accuracy, "I am not a surrealist." What could he possibly mean? In the case of this particular disavowal, West may have been attempting to distance himself from surrealism because he feared its popular reputation among American book buyers for whom the epithet was, as one critic has described it, "equivalent to incomprehensibility."[4] Even so, there is an element of truth in his denial. In many ways West is opposed to the goals and practices of surrealism, or at least to the goals and practices of a very specific kind of surrealism.

Beyond the dramatic example of his fiction, the closest West ever came to articulating his affiliation with surrealism is in a blurb written by the author himself for the dust jacket of *The Dream Life of Balso Snell* (published in the same year as surrealism's inaugural American exhibition): "In his use of the violently disassociated, the dehumanized marvelous, the deliberately criminal and imbecilic," West observes, "he is much like Guillaume Apollinaire, Jarry, Ribemont-Dessaignes, Raymond Roussel, and certain of the surrealists."[5] Prompting the question, which surrealists? Apollinaire, Jarry, and Roussel were frequently invoked as patron saints by a range of avant-garde artists in their attempt to provide themselves with what André Breton described as an "initiatory tradition."[6] Beyond their mutual interest in "the dehumanized marvelous, the deliberately criminal and imbecilic," West was clearly attracted to Apollinaire's fascination with forgeries, hoaxes, and the second-hand; Jarry's penchant for slapstick and scatological humor, his preoccupation with what he once described as *l'horrifiquement beau*; Roussel's "dead-pan" method of describing the most fantastic and improbable scenes.[7] But perhaps the best clue to West's orientation within the historical avant-garde lies in his attempt to associate his work with that of Georges Ribemont-Dessaignes. A close collaborator of Tristan Tzara's, Dessaignes produced a number of Dada paintings, poems, critical essays, and novels, *Celeste Ugolin* [1926] being the most famous. There is nothing in Dessaignes' work in particular that would link him to West; rather, it is the *jeu d'esprit* of Dada itself that West hoped to claim for his fiction by invoking his name. Dessaignes described that spirit as a rebellion "not only against the bourgeois order but against all order, all hierarchy, all sacralization, all idolatry."[8]

That will do as a preliminary description of the kind of negation that lies at the heart of West's fiction, particularly the self-consciously dadaesque *Balso Snell*. After that first volume, however, West sought to imbue Dada's anarchic style of rebellion with a more focused, socially conscious orientation. Consequently, his subsequent fiction has far more in common with the politicized "interventions" of Berlin dadaists like Hannah Hoch, George Grosz, and John Heartfield than with those of Dessaignes and French Dada.[9] Indeed, one might say of West what Louis Aragon said of Heartfield: "As he was playing with the fire of appearances, reality took fire around him . . . John Heartfield was no longer playing. The scraps of photographs that he formerly manoeuvred for the pleasure of stupefaction, under his fingers began to *signify*."[10] West would ultimately take the signifying practices of Depression-era America for his subject. But Heartfield's brand of political satire, while close to West's fiction in many ways, does not provide the point of departure for either his method or his peculiar insight.

For that we must look, as West puts it, to "certain of the surrealists."[11] But which ones? One might expect West to be the most sympathetic to the surrealism of committed leftists like Aragon. The elaborate *pas de deux* between surrealism and communism is a story that has been told many times before and need not be repeated here.[12] Suffice it to say that in 1931, when West wrote the blurb for *Balso Snell*, the surrealists were split between those like Aragon who insisted that the movement be subordinated to the needs of the Communist Party (i.e., that the liberation of the mind was impossible without liberation from the oppressive circumstances of capitalism) and those like Breton who, while recognizing the necessity for revolution, nevertheless insisted that surrealism possessed the same importance and stature as communism. West's discrimination among surrealisms may have been an attempt to disassociate himself—however vaguely—from what were taken to be the reactionary tendencies of the latter.

Perhaps the best example of West's attempt to cast his own surrealist inclinations in an explicitly politicized mode can be found in this short poem:

> The spread hand is a star with points
> The fist a torch
> Workers of the World

Ignite
Burn Jerusalem
Make of the City of Birth a star
Shaped like a daisy in color a rose
And bring
Not three but one king
The Hammer King to the Babe King
Where nailed to his six-branched tree
Upon the sideboard of a Jew
Marx
Performs the miracles of loaves and fishes

The spread hand is a star with points
The fist a torch
Workers of the World
Unite
Burn Jerusalem

These lines are excerpted from a longer poem called "Burn the Cities" that includes similar scenes of conflagration involving Paris ("warehouse of the arts") and London (center of empire).[13] The imprecatory tone of the poem, along with its rhetoric and imagery, is clearly inspired by the *Communist Manifesto*. But the more immediate model is Aragon's "Red Front," the controversial poem (published in 1931) that contributed to the widening division between surrealists along the lines adumbrated above.[14] Cummings' translation of "Red Front" was published in *Contempo* a few weeks before West published his version of the poem in the same journal (although West was probably familiar with it and the issues it raised well before then).[15] Aragon's attempt to put *le surréalisme au service de la révolution* might have satisfied the Communist Party, but it did not ultimately satisfy West. To paraphrase Breton's tepid "defense" of "Red Front," the poem tends to substitute "social drama" for "poetic drama" and in the process reduce surrealism to a matter of surface technique. West's politicization of surrealism would eventually take a different approach from that of "Red Front" or "Burn the Cities," an approach that would prove to be much richer and far more insightful.

In order to explain what I have in mind, I want to turn to an essay by Clement Greenberg entitled "Surrealist Painting" (1944). In that essay Greenberg offers an illuminating distinction between two very different kinds of surrealism—a distinction largely grounded on the use of the technique of automatism. As Greenberg observes,

> The difference between automatism as a primary and as a secondary
> factor is responsible for the two different directions in which surrealist
> painting has moved. On the one side are Miró, Arp, Masson, Picasso,
> and Klee. . . . On the other side are Ernst, Tanguy, Roy, Magritte,
> Oelze, Fini, and a myriad more. . . . With the first group automation
> may be relatively complete or incomplete, but in either case it is pri-
> mary as a rule and intervenes decisively. . . . The other direction of
> surrealist painting can best be charted by fixing the almost invariable
> point at which the automatic procedure stops.[16]

Greenberg's attempt to define surrealism in relation to the technique of
automatism helps to distinguish between two radically different approaches toward art and ultimately, as we shall see, toward the problem
of representation itself. For Miró, Arp, Masson, and Klee, automatism is
presumed to offer a privileged entrée into the realm of the unconscious,
which is seen as a quasi-mystical source of creative energy. As Arp himself rhapsodized, "Spiritual reality bestows rich gifts on him who does
not close himself to it. In the depths, the abscesses of festering reason dissolve without trace. Apes and parrots are the greatest enemies of art and
dreams. Men with their reason seek the key that will open the gate of
mystery, the gate of life. Never in this way will they penetrate to the infinite, peacock-colored halls, in which the golden flames dance and embrace one another."[17]
   Greenberg surely would have found such rhetoric embarrassing, if not
irrelevant to the "real" contribution these artists made to modern art. As
far as he was concerned automatism is valuable only insofar as it provides
the means (or at very least, an excuse) to circumvent the restrictive conventions of painting as it has traditionally been defined: i.e., as a window
to be looked through, rather than a flat surface to be looked at. In casting aside the artist's traditional obligation to represent the visible world
faithfully, automatism "serves to lift inhibitions which prevent the artist
from surrendering, as he needs to, to his medium." And anyone who
knows anything about Clement Greenberg knows that for him surrendering to one's medium is the supreme discovery of modern art, which,
Greenberg claimed, "restored painting to itself and enabled the modern
artist to rival the achievements of the past."[18]
   In contrast to those who rely on automatic techniques in order to create "art for art's sake," Greenberg identified another group of artists (to
which we might add the names Marcel Duchamp and Nathanael West)
who were indifferent to automatism as well as to its psychological implications. If that is the case, then what is the status of the unconscious for

these particular artists? Does automatism, to quote Roger Shattuck, "dredge up profound, suppressed thoughts closely connected to childhood and primitive knowledge? Or a store of clichés, trivia, and drivel mostly of cultural origin?"[19] Ernst, Magritte, Duchamp, and West were united in their insistence that the roots of the unconscious are "mostly of cultural origin." For these artists the unconscious could never become what Arp once described as a world of "unlimited freedom";[20] rather, the unconscious reveals itself to be a world that is, as Rosalind Krauss puts it, "already filled, already—to say the word—readymade."[21] This by no means trivializes its importance for them. They recognized that the unconscious is a reflection of the possibilities and limitations that a particular culture makes available to it at any given historical moment. Consequently, these artists sought to create an art that returns us to—indeed, never lets us forget—the contested terrain out of which our fantasies, dreams, and ideas emerge. If that means drawing on "clichés, trivia and drivel," to borrow Shattuck's pejorative description, these artists did not hesitate to do so. In fact they created an art almost entirely composed of these and other, similar readymades.

This reading of the unconscious as nothing more—or to be more accurate, nothing less—than a cultural artifact has important aesthetic implications that challenge the very foundation of the modernist art Greenberg espoused. Instead of "surrendering to their medium," as Greenberg tells us they should, these artists drew on a repertoire of imagery that offered itself up *"before* they pick their brushes up" (italics mine).[22] As far as Ernst et al. were concerned, the rest is digestion. Magritte, for example, disliked being called a painter at all, preferring instead to be received as a thinker whose medium of communication happened to be paint. Duchamp concurred. He had nothing but disdain for what he described as "retinal" painting: "The great merit of surrealism [or rather, Duchamp should have said, 'certain of the surrealists'], "is to have rid itself of retinal satisfaction."[23] Given this disdain for painting, it should come as no surprise to find that when the time comes to execute their ideas on canvas, these artists adopted, in Greenberg's words, the most conventional "modalities of three-dimensional vision" derived from the mummified canons of "nineteenth-century academic art." Painting as such ceased to present a problem, "and where all problems have been solved," Greenberg insisted, "only academicism is possible."[24]

Greenberg's critique of "academic" surrealism helps us to understand—even if Greenberg does not—its latent critical potential. For as we shall see, the very qualities that contributed to academic surrealism's weakness as "art" made for its strength as a mode of social criticism. In Greenberg's account, the motive for a naturalistic technique is plain: "The more vividly, literally, painstakingly the absurd and the fantastic are represented, the greater their shock."[25] There is no doubt some truth to this. But more is at stake here than a desire to *épater le bourgeois.* What Greenberg failed to realize—or more likely, chose to ignore—is a thoroughgoing critique of representation implicit in this "dependence" on the seemingly untroubled illusionism of nineteenth-century academicism. Instead of arguing that the fantastic has been rendered in literal form in order to increase its shock value, it would be more accurate to say that the fantastic has been rendered in literal form in order to deflate the pretensions of the unconscious and ground them in their point of origin: the "prosaic" world of culture. And if that is true, then one might also reverse Greenberg's argument and say that the literal has been endowed with fantastic or "hallucinatory vividness" (Greenberg's phrase) in order to expose its essentially phantasmagoric nature. Either way, these alternating strategies of deflation and hallucination subject representation to a thorough deconstruction.[26]

This is essentially the argument that Michel Foucault makes in *This Is Not a Pipe,* his homage to Magritte. As Foucault explains it, traditional representation depends on both "affirmation" and "similitude." But with the emergence of modernism that unity begins to break down. This makes for two very different kinds of aesthetic responses, which Foucault associates with many of the same artists that Greenberg did. On one hand we find the abstract art of Klee and Kandinsky, which affirms a higher, spiritual reality but forfeits any claim of similitude; on the other hand we find the illusionistic art of Magritte filled with likenesses to a reality it is unable or unwilling to affirm.[27] The former, as Hal Foster puts it in his gloss of Foucault, is "far less subversive to both traditional mimesis and transcendental aesthetics than is usually thought. . . . In its cancellation of representation abstraction preserves it, whereas simulation unfounds it, pulls the real out from underneath it. Indeed, simulation confounds the entire opposition of representation and abstraction conventionally considered to control modern art."[28]

It is on this ground—or lack thereof—that I would like to situate my investigation of Nathanael West. Like Magritte, Ernst, and other academic surrealists, West was fascinated by the problem of representation. In his fiction, reality reveals itself to be thoroughly and inescapably coded or written. As we have seen, it is this more than anything else that distinguishes him from other surrealists for whom this was taken as a regrettable state of affairs.[29] Unlike his counterparts on the left (such as Heartfield and Aragon), West refused to offer a master narrative that would expose the political reality or "truth" *behind* those signifying practices. (Indeed, one might say that West's fiction is deeply politicized without being overtly political.) And unlike the artists that Greenberg appropriated for high modernism, West was unwilling to move *beyond* representation to embrace pure aestheticism or affirm a higher spiritual reality. For West representation or similitude constitutes the sum total and limit of what can be known. If this position deprived him of the immediate political satisfactions of the former and the aesthetic or spiritual satisfactions of the latter, it did nevertheless allow him to explore the ways that reality is constructed—literally and figuratively—under capitalist modernity.

Chapter Two

Euclid's Asshole
The Dream Life of Balso Snell

PROLOGUE

In an unpublished short story entitled "The Fake," Nathanael West recounts the adventures of Beano Walsh, a would-be American artist living the life of a bohemian in Paris during the twenties. Despite his extravagant claims for his art, Beano is really more of a con artist than anything else. He has managed to convince a well-heeled philanthropic organization to fund his dubious aesthetic ambitions largely on the basis of his manic energy and charisma. Although the philanthropists are quite willing to indulge the whims and idiosyncrasies of their artists, as good burghers they also want to make sure they are getting their money's worth. Thus, before they will renew Beano's stipend, they insist upon seeing what he has produced thanks to their largesse. This creates something of a dilemma for our protagonist because, as it turns out, he has nothing to show them.

The problem is that Beano cannot draw. He makes a hash of everything he does. Rather than admit defeat, Beano decides that the problem rests not with him but with the anatomy books from which he has been working. "I've found out what's wrong with these anatomy books, and therefore all modern sculpture," Beano proclaims. It seems that "the anatomy books are wrong because they use a man only five feet ten inches tall for their charts. . . . According to Beano they should have used a man six feet tall because the perfect modern man is six feet tall. All modern sculpture is based on these books and therefore all modern sculpture is wrong." Apparently, it is not just a matter of increasing the proportions in the anatomy books by an extra two inches. "A six foot man," Beano tells us, "is not only taller but different."[1]

Beano is determined to prove his thesis, but in order to do so, he must have a corpse. He manages to procure one from the morgue, "a dead sailor who has been fished out of the Seine." (As an aesthete Beano finds this corpse especially appealing for the way "the blue was just beginning to show through the [sailor's] sunburn.") In order to save money on an ambulance, the artist wraps him up and stuffs him in the backseat of a taxicab. Instead of going home, however, Beano asks the driver to stop at a popular café so that he can show off his prize to his expatriate cronies. The body creates such a stir that soon all the bandages have been torn off in an effort to get a peek at it. Having satisfied the curiosity of Beano's cronies, the corpse is left behind in the cab. Meanwhile, Beano is toasted all around. Of course, one drink leads to two, and then several more—until the revelry is ended by a scream. It seems that a tourist, who has come to gawk at the bohemians in their native habitat, has unwittingly climbed into the cab only to find herself side-by-side with Beano's dead sailor.

The police are summoned, and Beano is thrown in jail along with his corpse. Undaunted, Beano asks for charcoal and drawing paper, and he instructs the police to call the philanthropic organization that is sponsoring his work. He hopes that when the philanthropists find him there, busy drawing his corpse, they will be impressed by his dedication. After all, Beano reasons, "A guy had to be a pretty serious artist to go to such lengths, and it would remind [them] of Van Gogh's ear."[2] The philanthropists, however, do not need any convincing. They are so pleased by the publicity Balso's arrest has secured for their foundation that they renew his stipend on the spot. When Beano's friend comes to his cell the following morning to tell him the good news, he finds Beano lying beneath his corpse raving like a lunatic. Beano is subsequently diagnosed as completely mad—apparently beyond all cure—whereupon he is committed to an insane asylum. Perhaps this is just another performance on Beano's part. Perhaps not. Not even his friends know for sure.

"The Fake," or "L'Affair Beano" as it was later called, is a marvelous comic send-up of expatriate life, which had already become something of a cliché by the time West himself got to Paris in 1926.[3] Although Beano's antics seem harmless enough, their fatuousness belies the earnestness of this critique as well as West's own investment in the outcome. While this story hints at West's anxiety about his abilities as a beginning writer— despite his bluff and bravado, Beano Walsh lacks talent—it also indicates West's preoccupation with his own belatedness. By 1926 European modernism had already become something to be copied out of books—a dead corpus. Beano's cockeyed attempt to salvage it only underscores its moribund status. West was prescient enough to realize that it would do no good either to repeat the grand experiments of his predecessors or to indulge in meaningless revisions.[4] (Such efforts result in the opéra bouffe this story chronicles.) Instead, he inaugurates his career with an investigation into the status and function of the artist, as well as the problem of representation and its existing aesthetic paradigms.

In particular, "The Fake" mocks the cultivation of "scandal," which had become something of a rite of passage for any would-be artist anxious to be admitted to the inner circle of the anointed. Beano's disdain for the law and public morality, his fascination with the gesture that is at once arbitrary and significant—all trumpeted in the bold language of the manifesto—constitute the lineaments of the classic dadaesque *geste*.[5] But the traditional *cri de guerre* of the avant-garde—"*épater le bourgeois!*"—is wholly absent here. Or, rather, it is reduced to a mere attention-getting device. A publicity stunt. "It would be more profitable for the farmer to raise rats for the granary than for the bourgeois to nourish the artist," Chekhov once defiantly observed.[6] But in "The Fake," the bourgeois nourishes the artist from his ample granary without fear of reprisal. It is an arrangement that turns out to be "profitable" for both parties. The "rebellion" of the artist is thus patronized in every sense of the word, while the "outrage" of the bourgeoisie serves as a source of entertainment, a relief from ennui. As a result, the artist is left with nothing but the pose of opposition, metonymically displaced into a variety of meaningless aesthetic debates and self-indulgent idiosyncrasies. This allows the bourgeoisie and their philanthropic organizations to indulge themselves in their most sentimental notions about the "craziness" of the artist. In return for his acquiescence, the artist is coddled like an exotic house pet. As the narrator of this short story observes, "'Artists are all crazy'. . . . Of course, these ideas and others like them were foisted on us by the nonartist, but we didn't realize it then. We came to *the business of being an artist* with the definitions of the non-artist and took libels for the truth. In order to be recognized as artists, we were everything our enemies said we were" (italics mine).[7] With the collapse of critical distance, the relationship between the artist and the bourgeoisie devolves into an endless round of simulation from which it is impossible to recover. Hence the confusion at the end of the story about whether Beano is really crazy or just feigning craziness. It is impossible to tell. And it is unlikely that Beano himself knows, so meaningless have the distinctions become.

The havoc wreaked by this state of affairs not only affects the possibility of a meaningful social criticism, it raises troubling questions about the capacities of representation as well. It is not just that Beano cannot draw because he lacks talent. He cannot draw because the old ways of "measuring man" are no longer viable. Beano's quest for the ideal, for the exact, natural proportions upon which all art might rest—the six-foot man—is reduced to pun and parody. The pun, of course, involves the concept of *nature morte,* which has provided the basis for Western theories of representation ever since the Renaissance. But in "The Fake" *nature morte* is translated literally as "dead nature"—the rotting corpse around which the story revolves. The wellspring of representation is thus muddied at its source. There is no authoritative ideal, no Rosetta Stone that can guarantee the authenticity of Beano's art.

Rather than viewing all of this as a decline and looking back with nostalgia on a tradition that once guaranteed the validity of representation, "The Fake" offers an alternative approach. Beano, as the title suggests, is not so much an artist as a con artist. In place of the six-foot man, Beano substitutes his own performance. Hence the cultivation of the eccentricity, scandal, and madness alluded to above. They are props that provide the ambience necessary to persuade Beano's audience of his "authority." And *persuasion* is what this Brave New World is all about. What matters is not the authority of a nonexistent "ideal" or "original," but rather the élan and zest with which Beano performs his part.

While this theatricalization of authority ultimately robs art of its traditional idealizing functions, it does have the unintended consequence of forcing that authority out into the light of day where its constitution is more easily scrutinized. Instead of an appeal to tradition, origin, referent, Beano is forced to adopt the strategies of the market—i.e., persuasion, publicity, commodification—which ground representation on an entirely different plane. The artist becomes a businessman who must hoodwink or con his audience into granting its approval, thereby conferring legitimacy on his representations. But if this involves a measure of subterfuge, no one seems to mind. Beano's audience does not take his project any more seriously than he does. They merely want to be entertained, and if that requires some nonsense about a six-foot man, so much the better. They are willing to pay for it. And that financial calculus—as "The Fake" so amply demonstrates—is the only "measure of man" that continues to have any meaning.

I. ON ART AND ANIMAL ACTS

"The Fake" anticipates many of the themes that West will take up in his first novella, *The Dream Life of Balso Snell* (1931), and looks forward to several others—performance, the collapse of critical distance, commodi-fication—that will preoccupy the author in the books to follow. Like that short story, *Balso Snell* is a dadaesque *geste* at the expense of art. This time around, however, West undertakes not just a disavowal of high mod-ernism and the idealism of its art-for-art's-sake aestheticism, but a cri-tique of nothing less than the grand tradition of Western culture upon which it depends. That critique results in a thorough housecleaning, an operation that will dispense with everything from Plato to Picasso. In the process, West extends his initial preoccupation with the problem of rep-resentation into a full-fledged analysis of the discursive and philosophi-cal conditions upon which authorship and authority depend.

Despite this ambitious agenda, *The Dream Life of Balso Snell* is per-haps the least widely read or appreciated of the books in the brief oeuvre of Nathanael West. Its status, even among those who champion his work, is relatively low. It has been dismissed as "schoolboyish" (Hyman), "scat-ological and pretentiously wise" (Aaron), "a not very successful exercise in [the] vein of phantasmagoria" (Wilson), "barely worth reprinting" (Cowley).[8] None of this criticism would come as a surprise to West. He has, in fact, already anticipated his critics: "Stark, clever, disillusioned stuff" (32), observes one of the characters in the novella. "Interesting psychologically, but is it art?" wonders another. Or better yet: "I'd give [him] a B minus and a good spanking" (23).

Whether one ultimately decides on applause or a good spanking, there is little doubt that the architecture of West's imagination emerges *in toto* here. In fact, *Balso Snell* constitutes a virtual breviary of images, interests, and techniques that West will go on to develop in the work to follow. Ex-amples abound. One might point to West's penchant for writing in small, carefully cropped frames or episodes, linked in a loosely threaded narra-tive, whose recurrent motifs—laughter, violence, excess—are the real subjects of his novels. Or one might point just as easily to John Raskol-nikov Gilson and his alter ego, Balso Snell. As confidence man and naif, they anticipate the recurrent struggle between "the cheaters and the cheated" that is one of West's most cherished themes.[9] Or finally, one might simply cite the dead rabbits (14), cardboard noses (14), and isosce-les triangles (35), as well as the "Ambylornis inornata" (26), "the devil's serenade from Faust" (18), and "the chauffeur within" (29), which serve as runes for a set of concerns—the status of the "real," discursivity, sub-limation, performance, hysteria, the constitution of the subject—to which West will return again and again.

Accordingly, *Balso Snell* will be treated here as something of a pre-text for and introduction to the later work. The burden of this chapter will be to articulate those distinctive qualities that will ultimately provide the foundation for West's singularly powerful and incisive social criticism. If the specific content of that criticism remains inchoate in *Balso Snell*, its peculiar mode of inquiry and apprehension is strikingly manifest: On the one hand, West pursues a metaphysics riven into mutually exclusive po-larities of "high" and "low," the "singular" and the "plural," idealism and materialism; on the other hand, he demonstrates a preoccupation with discourse *qua* discourse. However unpromising or loosely related this combination would appear to be, it has the virtue of being readily avail-able for examination in *Balso Snell* before it becomes submerged into the larger themes and interests of West's later work.[10]

Summarizing the plot of this novella is not an easy task. *Balso Snell* is, to say the least, an odd book. The story follows the adventures of the "poet" Balso Snell who happens upon the Trojan horse of the Greeks. "The mouth was beyond his reach, the navel proved a cul-de-sac" (3), leaving Balso no choice but to enter via the horse's anus. As he journeys through the intestinal labyrinth, a series of fantastic adventures befall our hero.[11] Here we may as well appeal to the dust jacket of the first edition where West's offers his own version of what transpires:

> He [Balso] hires a philosophic guide who insists on discussing the na-
> ture of art. After a violent argument, Balso eludes him only to run into
> Maloney the Areopagite who is attempting to crucify himself with
> thumb tacks. Maloney tells Balso that he is writing a life of Saint Puce.
> This saint is a flea who built a church in the armpit of our Lord, a
> church "whose walls are the flesh of Christ, whose windows are rose
> with the blood of Christ." After Maloney, he meets John Raskolnikov
> Gilson, the twelve year old murderer of an idiot, and Miss McGeeney,
> a school teacher who is writing the life of Samuel Perkins, a man who
> can smell the strength of iron or even the principles involved in an
> isosceles triangle.[12]

Samuel Perkins, we discover, wrote the "biography of the man who wrote the biography of the man who wrote the biography of the man who wrote the biography of Boswell." And so it goes, Miss McGeeney explains, "rat-tling down the halls of time, each one in his or her turn a tin can on the tail of Doctor Johnson" (33). West's novella is itself a tin can tied to the tail of Western culture, or if you prefer, a Duchampian mustachio affixed to the *Mona Lisa*'s kisser. Indeed, one might say the dynamic of *Balso Snell* con-sists of a dadaist attempt to besmirch a variety of Western culture's most cherished ideals—Christianity, progress, sentimental culture—which purport to transfigure what West sees as the essentially intractable nature of material existence. Like Alfred Jarry at the premiere of *Ubu Roi,* West shouts, "*merde!*" and thus self-consciously places himself in a tradition of disdain for the institution of art and its associated idealisms.[13] After congratulating the "smart, sophisticated, sensitive yet hardboiled, art-loving frequenters of the little theatres [on their] good taste in preferring Art to animal acts," West's Jarry *manqué*—John Raskolnikov Gilson—fantasizes a scenario in which the ceiling of the theater opens to "cover the occupants with tons of loose excrement" (30). "After the deluge," he explains, "the patrons . . . can gather in the customary charming groups and discuss the play" (31). And so with a bow to the author we will go on to do just that.

2. EUCLID'S ASSHOLE

The Dream Life of Balso Snell begins in a series of puns that function to structure the thematic concerns of the novel. The puns start early and start in earnest, prompted by the fortuitous homeomorphism that exists between two seemingly disparate entities: the perfect circle of Euclid's geometry and its less than perfect counterpart found in nature, the anus. Circles and assholes: once conceived the author pursues this unlikely pairing with a philosophical and literary élan such as one might expect to find in the graffiti on the bathroom wall of a university library. This results in a book almost exclusively constructed out of scatological puns. Bad puns. Dirty jokes. Real stinkers.

Balso's opening song—"Round as the Anus"—contains the w/hole:

> Round as the Anus
> Of a Bronze Horse
> Or the Tender Buttons
> Used by Horses for Ani

> On the Wheels of His Car
> Ringed Round with Brass
> Clamour the Seraphim
> Tongues of Our Lord

> Full Ringing Round
> As the Belly of Silenus
> Giotto Painter of Perfect Circles
> Goes . . . One Motion Round

Round and Full
Round and Full as
A Brimming Goblet
The Dew-Loaded Navel
Of Mary
Of Mary Our Mother

Round and Ringing Full
As the Mouth of a Brimming Goblet
The Rust-Laden Holes
In Our Lord's Feet
Entertain the Jew-Driven Nails. (4–5)

The subjects of West's burlesque are adumbrated in a quick succession of "perfect" circles: "A Brimming Goblet" (plenitude), "The Dew-Loaded Navel/Of Mary Our Mother" (Christianity), "Tender Buttons" (aestheticism). But, of course, we are never allowed to forget that these idealized circles find their obscene analogue in a quite different variety of tender buttons: "O the Rose Gate! O the Moist Garden! O Well!" (5). (Even the typescript of exclamation—"O"—conspires in the p (f) un).[14]

The pun itself is a clue to West's strategy. For West's symbolist predecessors the pun was one of the principal means of moving beyond denotation so that a more inclusive range of meaning might be incorporated into the text. If Mallarmé's ideal of perfection was to see the world absorbed into "The Book," the pun's capacity to multiply meaning was seen as central to those designs.[15] *Balso Snell* stands self-consciously at the end of that tradition, inheriting its resources without a corresponding faith in its project. Again and again, West exploits the moment in which the symbolist desire for all-inclusiveness instead multiplies the relations between objects to the point of absurdity.[16] Much is at stake here. *Balso Snell*'s preoccupation with the circle coyly offers itself as a dismantling of a simple, geometric figure; but as West makes all too apparent, that simple geometric figure constitutes nothing less than the central symbology of Western culture's most cherished meanings.

Perhaps the best place to start our investigation is with the book's opening reference to Anaxagoras, whose pre-Socratic philosophy was preoccupied with the theme of the One and the Many, the ideal of perfect unity and the detritus of heterogeneity. A few pages later, West formulates the problem in a mock philosophical debate between Balso Snell and his tour guide:

"After all, what is art? I agree with George Moore. Art is not nature, but rather nature digested. Art is a sublime excrement. . . ."

"Picasso says," Balso broke in, "Picasso says there are no feet in nature. . . ."

"The statement that there are no feet in nature puts you in an untenable position. . . . Picasso, by making this assertion, has placed himself on the side of monism in the eternal wrangle between the advocates of the Singular and those of the Plural. As James puts it, 'Does reality exist distributively or collectively—in the shape of *eaches, everys, anys, eithers* or only in the shape of an *all* or *whole?*' If reality is singular then there are no feet in nature, if plural, a great many. If the world is one (everything part of the same thing—called by Picasso nature) then nothing either begins or ends. Only when things take the shapes of *eaches, everys, anys, eithers* (have ends) do they have feet. Feet are attached to ends, by definition. Moreover, if everything is one, and has neither ends nor beginnings, then everything is a circle. A circle has neither a beginning nor an end. A circle has no feet. (9)

Circles with feet? This is the debate that, to a large extent, shapes the various encounters of Balso Snell throughout the rest of the novella. Again and again, the plural or "podiatric" nature of experience is set against the monistic idealisms that would try to appropriate and ultimately redeem it. However, this debate does little more than beg the question. After all, West's choice of setting—the bowels of a horse—provides the "ideal" vantage point from which to observe the fate of the plural as it is unified into a singular and most unmetaphysical substance.[17]

Indeed, George Moore's unfortunate characterization of art as "nature digested" is taken literally by West. Hence, the plethora of artists who perforce dwell in the bowels of the Trojan horse. Like them, Moore is really one of several "Phoenix Excrementi" who "eat themselves, digest themselves, and give birth to themselves by evacuating their bowels" (5). They are, in short, a grotesque parody of the monistic aspiration for Unity or the Ideal. The oxymoron in their name suggests their dilemma. They cannot surmount their own materiality. Hence, they serve as an alter ego of sorts for George Moore, Balso Snell, and so many others in West's fiction, who confuse generation and evacuation, Euclid's geometry and Euclid's asshole.

Returning, then, to Picasso's claim that there are no feet in nature, we might adopt the opposite position and argue that in West's fiction there are nothing but feet: stumbling feet (30), sore feet (13, 19, 37), "splay feet" (37), crucified feet (5), and even an assortment of stinking, soiled

shoes (17, 29), all of which serve to conjure a reality that exists distributively "in the shape of eaches, everys, anys, eithers."

If West was interested in feet, he was also especially interested in noses.
In fact, one might say that *Balso Snell* constructs its own private "nosolo-
gie," not unrelated to that of *Tristram Shandy,* or for that matter,
Freudian psychology. For Sigmund Freud, the moment when the human
race stood erect forever altered the priorities of the senses, with eyesight
and its corresponding rationality triumphing over smell and its emphasis
on more intimate bodily functions. Balso readily condenses this phy-
logeny into his own simpleminded injunction: "Take your head from
under your armpit. Stop sniffing mortality" (13).

Samuel Perkins follows this advice with a vengeance. Perkins, we recall, is the biographer of the biographer of the biographer of Johnson's
Boswell. But as Miss McGeeney, his own would-be biographer, assures
us, Perkins is interesting in his own right. Apparently, Perkins' sensibility
has more than equipped him to become a dandy in the grand tradition of
Huysmans' Des Esseintes. But fate has dealt him a cruel hand. Deaf and
blind, cursed with a "dull insensitive tongue" (34), Perkins is forced to
rely on his nose to acquaint himself with the richness and variety of creation. In a version of Emersonian compensation, an ever benign Nature
"compensates for the loss of one attribute by lavishing her bounty on another. . . . Concentrated in his sense of smell [were] all the abilities usually distributed among the five senses" (34).

Thus equipped, Perkins is free to indulge in the delights of synesthe-
sia, the dream of his symbolist contemporaries: "He could smell a chord
in D minor, or distinguish between the tone-smell of a violin and that of
a viola. He could smell the caress of velvet and the strength of iron" (35).
Although nature has provided Perkins with an exquisite means of apprehending experience, it cannot readily be said that "she" was so forth-
coming in the variety of stimuli she made available for his perusal.
Perkins complains that the world is something of a treadmill. The image
used by way of illustration is a circle. Not the circle of plenitude, but of
redundancy: "A step forward along the circumference of a circle is a step
nearer the starting place." As Miss McGeeney explains, one might indeed move "from the smell of new-mown hay to that of musk and vervain [from the primitive to the romantic], and from vervain to sweat and
excrement [from the romantic to the realistic]" (35), but one must necessarily return to the new-mown hay again. Perkins, brave thinker that
he is, confronts this circularity squarely. He knows that the man of true
sensibility will be able to distinguish a gradation between smells so sub-

tle that the circumference of the circle becomes infinite in size—in effect, a straight line.

Perkins' triumph, however, like all such obsessions with the absolute here and throughout West's fiction, is betrayed by the material conditions upon which it is predicated. By tilting his nose at the ideal, Perkins attempts to evade the more intimate bodily functions with which his nose was originally acquainted. The inauthenticity of the situation finds its abject emblem in the contortion of the body into an obscene parody of the idealist's aspiration:

> When I met Perkins for the first time, his face reminded me of the
> body of a man I had known at college. According to gossip current
> in the girls' dormitory this man abused himself. The source of these
> rumors lay in the peculiar shape of his body: all the veins, muscles and
> sinews flowed toward and converged at one point. In a like manner the
> wrinkles on Perkins' face, the contours of his head, the lines of his
> brow and chin, seemed to have melted and run into his nose. (34)

West has truly outdone himself. Suffice it to note that here as elsewhere monism is revealed to be a species of onanism.

What are we to make of all this? Perhaps the best way to explore the implications of West's absurd metaphysics is by comparing his approach with that of French surrealist Georges Bataille with whom he has a great deal in common (as well as some important differences). Beyond a general conviction regarding the "essential contradiction of the high and the low," Bataille shares with West a particular interest in the "burlesque value" of the foot—especially with regard to its social and ontological status.[18] In a brief essay entitled "The Big Toe" (1929), Bataille meditates on "Man's secret horror of his foot," "the imbecilic way it is doomed to corns, calluses, and bunions . . . to the most nauseating filthiness." The reason behind the foot's "secret horror" is not far to seek. As Bataille explains, "the function of the human foot consists in giving a firm foundation to the erection of which man is so proud. . . . But whatever the role played in the erection by his foot, man, who has . . . a head raised to the heavens and heavenly things, sees it as spit, on the pretext that he has his foot in the mud." Despite the fact that "blood flows in equal quantities from high to low and from low to high," Bataille explains, "there is a bias in favor of that which elevates itself, and human life is erroneously seen as an elevation."[19]

This disdain for idealism leads Bataille to formulate a radically new conception of matter for which the foot is only one example in a repertoire very much like that of Nathanael West—a repertoire that includes among other things, excrement, Siamese twins, severed fingers, and, yes, assholes. For Bataille, matter's heterogeneity, its thoroughly "base" nature, serves as an affront to and negation of the idealizing aspirations of human consciousness, which seek to redeem it through various abstract systems of thought. This no doubt explains the source of friction between Bataille and surrealists like Breton whom he disparages as "fucking idealists."[20] Even Marxism—specifically Hegelian Marxism—is dismissed by Bataille, despite his sympathies with its political objectives, because of its inclination to recuperate negation into an abstract dialectic. As Allan Stoekl explains, "unlike pragmatic or functionalist theories of materialism," Bataille's conception of materialism "does not pass beyond matter in the construction a 'scientific' conceptual edifice. . . . Instead, base materialism posits a matter that cannot be reduced to systems of scientific or political mastery."[21]

In place of the idealizing tendencies of these various approaches, Bataille invests matter with a monstrous power of its own, a power drawn from the Manichean universe of Gnosticism. In "Base Materialism and Gnosticism" (1930), he explains,

> In practice, it is possible to see as a *leitmotiv* of Gnosticism the conception of matter as an *active* principle having its own eternal autonomous existence as darkness (which would not be simply the absence of light, but the monstrous *archontes* revealed by this absence), and as evil (which would not be the absence of good, but a creative action). This conception was perfectly incompatible with the very principle of the profoundly monistic Hellenistic spirit, whose dominant tendency saw matter and evil as degradations of superior principles.[22]

Perhaps the best example of this "monstrous *archontes*" in action can be found in the "immense travail of recklessness, discharge, and upheaval" to which Bataille gives the name *potlatch* (a term borrowed from the anthropologist Marcel Mauss to describe the periodic destruction of property during the festivals of the North American Indians).

We will return to Bataille's notion of *potlatch* later (especially as it pertains to the final pages of *The Day of the Locust*). For now it is enough to compare Bataille's Gnostic conception of matter with West's. West has often been called an "apocalyptic" writer. But, as with the description of West as a surrealist, the qualities that explicate that moniker are rarely articulated. What most critics seem to have in mind, however, is something akin to Bataille's conception of matter as an "active principle." There is some justification for that reading. Like Bataille, the status of matter is a delicate issue for West. Indeed, it constitutes what may be the central drama of his work. One might argue that in *Balso Snell* West has set out to write a manifesto of sorts for a materialist aesthetics. But he cannot quite bring himself to embrace Bataille's Gnostic sensibility.[23] In West's fiction, the low is almost always figured as absence. Dead matter. Excrement. Nevertheless it is clear that like Bataille West wants to move beyond a privative conception of matter (as the "degradation of superior principles") to a more powerful formulation that invests matter with its own monstrous power or "*archontes.*" And there are moments in his fiction when he seems on the verge of doing just that. Nowhere is this more evident than in the letters of suffering written by Broad Shoulders, Sickof-it-all, Disillusioned-with-tubercular-husband, or in the final (apocalyptic?) riot on Hollywood Boulevard with which *The Day of the Locust* concludes. We will have to examine these instances carefully for what they tell us about the possibilities of liberation in an otherwise totalizing universe of mass culture.

The prospects, however, are not good. Whatever dark and genuine power these events might possess is overwhelmed (or nearly so) by the reified language of cultural abstraction, i.e., the clichés of therapeutic culture (in the case of *Miss Lonelyhearts*) and commodity fetishism (in *The Day of the Locust*). In West's fiction the low rarely if ever exists in its pure form; rather, it is the result of a disfiguring operation always already carried out by the high language of official culture. In many cases, the repression of the low is so totalizing and severe (for reasons that will be discussed later) that it ceases to exist even by way of opposition.

West, for example, would never have agreed with Bataille's claim that "any member of the bourgeoisie [must] become conscious that his most vigorous and vital instincts, if he does not repress them, [will] necessarily make him an enemy of his own class."[24] In West's fiction, anything resembling an "instinct" is so thoroughly disfigured that it is no longer recognizable as such. This is equally true for other areas of human experience that might also be construed as "low": the body, the unconscious, and even the proletariat. The low remains elusive, beyond the reach even of the lowly themselves. The rage this produces is expressed through a sadistic appropriation of the low as a means of denigration—mocking a condition they are powerless to change. Thus the "liberation" of the instincts—or for that matter, the unconscious and the proletariat—is almost always carried out under the sign of fascism in West's fiction. (This goes a long way toward explaining why "the radical press . . .

doesn't like [West's particular kind of joking], and think [it] even fascist sometimes.")[25]

If the low is subject to a radical disfiguring operation that virtually eliminates its redemptive possibilities, it exacts its own revenge. The pathology of that revenge can be aptly described in terms of hysteria. In the hysteric, terrors associated with the lower body are converted into the symptoms of a damaged psyche—a condition that is ubiquitous throughout West's fiction. John Raskolnikov Gilson ("the twelve year old murderer") offers this conceit by way of explanation:

> People say that it is terrible to hear a man cry. I think it is even worse to hear a man laugh. Yet the ancients considered hysteria a woman's disease. They believed that hysteria was caused by the womb breaking loose and floating freely through the body. The cure they practiced was to place sweet-smelling herbs to the vulva in order to attract the womb back to its original position, and foul-smelling things to the nose in order to keep the womb away from the head. (18)

The hysteric's laughter is "terrible" precisely because the hierarchy established in the body between high and low, head and womb, is confused. The confusion is compounded by the womb's capacity to multiply that skewed relation and the laughter it elicits promiscuously. This is, to be sure, not the sort of Rabelaisian "belly laugh" that would restore us to the ground of Being. Rather, the laughter one finds here and throughout West's fiction is cerebral and, hence, maddening. It derealizes the seemingly ordered "nature" of things. (One is reminded of Baudelaire's "Satanic laughter," or for that matter, Goya's "Nightmare of Reason"—one of West's favorite drawings.) Moreover, the fertility of the womb ensures that one laugh will quite literally engender another, until the fate of West's hysterics comes to resemble that of the "basso from the Chicago Opera," who started laughing and was unable to stop. (The basso was singing, appropriately enough, the "devil's serenade from Faust" [18].)

As the foregoing indicates, West knows all too well the price that is exacted for the exclusion of the low. Human life, Bataille explains, demands a back and forth movement from refuse to the ideal, and from the ideal to refuse. But that shuttle is radically problematized in West's fiction: High and low, ideal and materiality, nose and foot, circle and anus, are irrevocably sundered.[26] This is because the civilizing hand, particularly the civilizing hand of bourgeois society, has a stake in disrupting that shuttle. The bourgeoisie abhors the low for what it tells them about the repression necessary to sustain the precarious status of their own high and, hence, privileged position. But as Peter Stallybrass and Allon White explain, an identity that attempts "to block out somatic and social heterodoxy is fated to rediscover it everywhere as chaos, darkness and 'mess.'"[27] This accounts for John Raskolnikov Gilson's murderous desires and Balso's fatuous evasions in *Balso Snell*. But for Miss Lonelyhearts and Tod Hackett—the two figures in West's fiction who feel this situation most keenly—the attempt "to block out somatic and social heterodoxy" precipitates a crisis that ultimately costs the life of one and the sanity of the other.

Ultimately, West would come to see the filiation between high and low as semiotic rather than cosmic, social rather than mystical in nature. But despite this shift in terms, noses and feet, circles and assholes, remained central to his imagination. Located as they are at opposite ends of the body, they constitute a somatic compass by which West would map not only the metaphysics adumbrated above, but eventually an entire psychic and social topography. In particular, West was interested in the complex cultural process whereby the human body, psychic forms, and social organization are all constructed within interrelating and dependent hierarchies of high and low. Unlike Bataille, however, West refused to fix these shifting symbolic domains within essentialized hierarchies. Rather, he saw the assignation of those hierarchies as a function of power, and he meditated on the rhetorical and social configurations in which that power is articulated, legitimated, and eventually naturalized.[28] This makes West a good deal more complicated (and more interesting) than his reputation as a Gnostic "poet of darkness" would seem to suggest—a reputation for which Leslie Fiedler and, more recently, Harold Bloom are largely responsible.[29] If West was finally unable or unwilling to embrace Bataille's quasi-mystical formulations, his brand of materialism allows for a more intricate understanding of society—making him not a "poet of darkness" so much as one of modernity's most astute social critics.

The power of that social criticism lies in West's recognition that "dead matter" has a power of its own—not the power of *archontes*, but a power that stems from sheer recalcitrance and inertia. In subsequent novels, for example, excrement as a figure for negation goes "underground," structuring an increasingly incisive social critique that manifests itself in the detritus of unredeemed cultural artifacts: the letters of suffering written by Miss Lonelyheart's readers, whose bathetic appeals West knows to be unanswerable (*Miss Lonelyhearts*); the eyes, teeth, fingers, and legs—*disjecta membra*—of an all-American Humpty Dumpty who cannot be put back together again (*A Cool Million*); the "Sargasso Sea" of the Hollywood backlot, where dreams are first "made photographic by plaster, canvas, lath and paint" and then left to rot in the California sun (*The Day of the Locust*).[30] The scandalous presence of these unredeemed artifacts mocks the claims that are made on their behalf. In each case West exposes the cultural strategies through which experience is betrayed by a sham idealism—an idealism that seeks to transform a "distributive" reality "of *eaches, everys, anys, eithers*" into a specious "w/hole." Here as elsewhere, the integrity of West's "excremental vision" (and the peculiar insightfulness of his social criticism) lies in precisely this stubborn refusal of the metamorphoses upon which ideology depends.

3. A DISCOURSE ON DISCOURSE

The title of West's novella—*The Dream Life of Balso Snell*—is something of a misnomer. There is no "dream life" to speak of, if by dream life we mean the sort of privileged entrée into the mysteries of the unconscious that preoccupied "certain of the surrealists." In fact, the unconscious here reveals itself to be derivative, a secondary elaboration of conscious life—specifically, a conscious life informed by too much reading. "You once said to me that I talk like a man in a book," observes Beagle Darwin (another inhabitant of the Trojan horse): "I not only talk, but think and feel like one. I have spent my life in books; literature has deeply dyed my brain its own color. This literary coloring is a protective one—like the brown of the rabbit or the checks of the quail—making it impossible for me to tell where literature ends and I begin" (47). This passage recalls Shakespeare's line from Sonnet 111, "my nature is subdued/To what it works in, like the dyer's hand." And it accurately reflects the dilemma not only of Beagle Darwin but of everyone Balso Snell encounters in the Trojan horse. What is true for them is likewise true of West himself. Indeed, one might justifiably say of West what Mikhail Bakhtin has said of Dostoevski: his writing constitutes "a discourse upon discourse . . . addressed to [discourse]."[31]

West described *Balso Snell*—composed as it is of a mock philosophical treatise, symbolist manifestos, crime journals, an excerpt from an epistolary novel, etc.—as a series of "elephantine close-ups of various literary positions."[32] Following Bakhtin we might say that each of these "literary positions" constitutes its own hermeneutic circle—values, assumptions, expectations—a "worldview" that arbitrarily excludes portions of experience in order to create a self-validating system of meaning. Under these terms, language appears to yield wholly and without mediation to the speaker's intention. The relation between word and object is naturalized so that it is taken as given. Of course, this would posit language as ideal, beyond ideology, a universal grammar.

West was aware, as many of his characters are not, that once one steps outside the circle of a particular discourse—in effect, objectifying it—the limitations of its claims become readily apparent. What heretofore appeared as transparent and unitary, now reveals itself as opaque and radically variegated. Words are not neutral or final; nor are words adequate to their objects. As Bakhtin explains, they are "shot through with intentions and accents. For any individual consciousness living in it, language is not an abstract system of normative forms but rather a concrete heteroglot conception of the world. All words have the 'taste' of a profession, a genre, a tendency, a party, a particular work, a particular person, a generation, an age group, the day and hour."[33] All words, in short, are saturated with ideology.

The subject, then, is faced with the dilemma of having to choose a language that both *precedes* it and *constitutes* it. Pure intention as such does not exist; rather one must speak "indirectly, conditionally and in a refracted way."[34] For many, this situation is threatening precisely because it reveals the embattled social ground of discourse, the "interested" nature of one's own speech. And while the exclusion of heterogeneity in a unitary language may be essential to the maximization of mutual understanding, the obfuscation of its origins within this larger context is, more often than not, politically motivated.

For those inhabitants of the Trojan horse who remain *within* a closed sociolinguistic system, the messy world of competing languages would seem to pose no real conflict. If the price of their "safety" becomes the inanities of their own simpleminded assertions, they seem wholly unaware of it. "Play games. Don't read so many books. Take cold showers. Eat more meat" (13), Balso puritanically asserts in defiance of the linguistic and social heterodoxy pressing in all around him. In contrast to Balso, John Raskolnikov Gilson knows that "Order is vanity" (15) because intention is always filtered through a succession of incommensurate discursive structures. As Gilson himself observes, no one "is fooled by the fact that I write in the first person. . . . I am an honest man and feel badly about masks, cardboard noses, diaries, memoirs, letters from a Sabine farm, the theatre. . . . I feel badly, yet I can do nothing" (13).

One might say that all discourse in West's fiction wears a cardboard nose. And if, like Samuel Perkins' own storied nose, all such discourse aspires to the perfection of the circle, that discourse nevertheless betrays its

own status as a cardboard construction. This is as true of the highly stylized pastoral mode of the "letter from a Sabine farm" as it is of those ostensibly "spontaneous" and "intimate" genres, such as the diary. Hence,
statement devolves into stance; conviction gives way to convention. The
result is a kind of *mise en abîme* in which the subject continually discovers itself as a function of discourse.[35] This explains Gilson's recourse to
extremes of sex and violence (a recurrent albeit useless strategy adopted
by many in West's fiction) where the myth of pure presence would seem
to offer itself intact. But even sex and violence have their own distinctly
literary turn. Gilson discovers to his chagrin that the Marquis de Sade
and Dostoevski have been there before him. Hence, Gilson's observation,

> I find certain precomposed judgments, awaiting my method of consid-
> eration . . . render it absurd. No matter how I form my comment, I at-
> tach to it the criticisms sentimental, satirical, formal. With these judg-
> ments there goes a series of literary associations which remove me still
> further from genuine feeling. The very act of recognizing Death, Love,
> Beauty—all the major subjects—has become, from literature and exer-
> cise, impossible. (24)

The pun here, of course, is on "precompose." Pose, position, composition, decomposition: These terms are ubiquitous throughout *Balso
Snell*. Each is dependent upon the other; each, in turn, undermines the
other. One might say that West's decomposing aesthetic ex-poses the pose
in every position, the position (location or site of authority) in every composition. Composition in effect becomes de-composition—nothing more
than the dead matter of precomposed convention. Indeed, the entire conceit of this novel—set as it is in the bowels of the Trojan horse—is predicated on decomposition. (The writer "come [s] to the paper with a con-
stipation of ideas," Gilson observes. "The white paper acts as a laxative.
A diarrhoea of words is the result" [14].) Excrement thus becomes a figure for the heteroglossia of the text. The excremental bowels of the Trojan horse are at once the comic means by which the official languages of
Western culture are degraded, just as they represent the stench of their
putrefaction. Moreover, excrement becomes an emblem for the refusal of
language to submit to the codified boundaries of a unitary discourse, the
tendency of all such discourse to decompose into the impurities of what
Bakhtin refers to as the "logosphere"—the messy world of competing
languages.

West does not shrink from the decomposition of the great discourses
of Western culture; instead, he hails the ignominious results. Thus, upon

approaching the "mystic portal," Balso Snell exclaims, "O Anus Mirabilis" (3). The allusion is to Dryden's "Annus Mirabilis"—1666, the "year of wonders"—in which Charles II endured war, plague, and the great fire of London. West's own conflagration (of style rather than event) offers no authority such as Dryden's Charles II who will arise phoenix-like out of the ashes to restore order. Instead, Balso notes a quite different refrain "along the lips of the mystic portal": "Ah! Qualis ... Artifex ... Pereo!" (All Things Must Pass, 4). This was reputed to be Nero's dying lament as he witnessed the fall of Rome; it has been the nostalgic watchword of the decadent imagination ever since. But West gives the phrase a sardonic turn; for what passes through the intestines and beyond the "mystic portal"—the great discourses of Western civilization—is hardly worthy of nostalgia, at least in its present form. Nihilistic derision is more appropriate. Accordingly, Balso offers this prayer: "O Beer! O Meyerbeer! O Bach! O Offenbach! Stand me now as ever in good stead" (4). This burlesque of Stephen Dedalus' heartfelt appeal to his "Old father" exactly situates the dilemma of the subject who finds herself lost among the detritus of a broken past and a quotidian present composed of cheap beer and bad puns. West makes it quite clear that there is no father or artificer who will step in to create order out of this cultural sargasso.

Under these conditions the legitimation of authority becomes extremely problematic. In a messy world of competing languages—a world that lacks a center, a strict hierarchy, or a privileged mode of expression—how and under what terms is authority legitimated? This is a question to which West will return frequently. Thus, it should come as no surprise to find that the pages of his fiction are littered with a succession of failed or would-be "authors" who foreground this very problem. We are told, for example, that the Trojan horse through which Balso journeys is "inhabited solely by writers in search of an audience" (37). Among them: Maloney the Areopagite (hagiographer), John Raskolnikov Gilson (diarist and artist of the perfect homicide), Samuel Perkins (aesthete), Miss McGeeney (biographer), and of course, the poet Balso Snell himself, whose name bears a distinct resemblance to that of yet another would-be artist whom we have already met—Beano Walsh. But they are only the first and by no means the most notorious, authors that West's readers will encounter. In West's subsequent fiction, the denizens of the Trojan horse are joined by a number of editors, writers, actors, painters, and connoisseurs. They include Shrike, Miss Lonelyhearts and his reader/writers, Sylvanus Snodgrasse (poet laureate and pickpocket), Asa Goldstein (antique dealer and interior decorator), Faye Greener (Hollywood bit player), Harry Greener (vaudevillian), Claude Estee (screenwriter), and Tod Hackett (painter and set designer).

These various figures run the gamut from the naif who retains an "innocent" faith in the sui generis nature of his or her own authority (Balso, Perkins, McGeeney, Broad Shoulders, Faye Greener, idealists all) to the confidence man (Beano, Gilson, Shrike, Snodgrasse, Goldstein, Harry Greener, Estee) who is convinced that all authority is a matter of manipulation and falsehood. The naif's ignorance with regard to his own absurdly limited authority allows him to reside in a fool's paradise that is dangerous to himself and still more dangerous to others. On the other hand, the confidence man's amoral worldliness allows him, like John Raskolnikov Gilson, to exploit a "sequence of theatrical poses" (26), each of which is adopted without conviction, each of which contributes to the erosion of conviction altogether. Between these extremes of belief and disbelief lies the problem of authority: speaking with conviction in a fallen world.

It would be a mistake to think that West was immune from the crisis of authority he surgically explores. Like the denizens of the Trojan horse, West found himself wandering through a cultural sargasso during the thirties that lacked a center, a strict hierarchy, or a privileged mode of expression. But instead of bemoaning this state of affairs, West made a virtue of necessity, fashioning an aesthetic, or rather an anti-aesthetic, capable of negotiating the detritus of contemporary culture without appeal to the false idealizations that characterize Western culture's Trojan horse.

We have already seen how West's carnivalization of high and low participates in what Bakhtin described as a "continual shifting from top to bottom, from front to rear," resulting in a series of "comic crownings and uncrownings." West's adaptation of that strategy—albeit without Bakhtin's faith in a "pathos of change and renewal"—is fairly straightforward. Less obvious is West's adaptation of another Bakhtinian strategy, that of "inversion," in which "prevailing truths and authorities" are subjected to "the peculiar logic of the 'inside out' (à l'envers)."[36]

Instead of contaminating "truth" and "authority" with the language of the low, West simply turns the discourse of truth and authority "inside out." This strategy has several advantages. To begin with, it exposes the "precomposed" or "readymade" status of all official discourse, thereby depriving it of the "organicism" and "depth" that otherwise function to naturalize it. Moreover, by turning discourse inside out, this strategy exposes the structure and conventions of discourse. The power of this strategy is immense. It allows West to subject the structure of that discourse to an intensive scrutiny that, as we shall see, exposes the ideological "grid" through which our experience is mediated, ad infinitum, ad nauseam. If West does not explore the implications of this promising technique in *Balso Snell,* he will put that technique to good use in his subsequent fiction, where he extends his critique to take in the complex nexus of social conditions, cultural institutions, and rhetorical strategies that functioned to legitimize discourse in Depression-era America.

Part II

Chapter Three

"Lousy with Pure / Reeking with Stark"
Contact

let's start a magazine
to hell with literature
we want something redblooded

lousy with pure
reeking with stark
and fearlessly obscene
but really clean
get what I mean
let's not spoil it
let's make it serious

something authentic and delirious
you know something genuine like a mark
in a toilet

graced with g-ts and g-tted
with grace

squeeze your n-ts and open your face
                    —E. E. Cummings

In the fall of 1931, William Carlos Williams wrote to E. E. Cummings, requesting poetry for a little magazine he was editing with Nathanael West. It was called *Contact*. (Actually, the magazine was a revival of a previous publication that Williams had put out in the early twenties with Robert McAlmon.) The response Williams received from Cummings accurately, albeit somewhat parodically, characterized the magazine's ambitions.[1] If *Contact* was to be more than merely another magazine devoted to "good writing," the editors felt—in a decidedly less ironic vein—that it had to be "redblooded," "stark," "fearlessly obscene."

The editors envisioned much more than that, of course. Crucial to their vision was the idea of "contact." Just what that meant, however, is difficult to say with any exactitude. The title was first proposed to Williams back in the twenties by McAlmon, who had heard the word used by pilots as jargon for touchdown after flight. It proved to be very suggestive. For one thing, "contact" had a certain Precisionist crackle to it that was unmistakably modern; moreover, "it was consonant with the editors' desire . . . 'above all things to speak for the present.'"[2] Most important, it implied a literature written out of a direct engagement with "reality" (the experience of one's own immediate social circumstances) in contradistinction to literature written under the shadow of European culture, past and present.[3]

While acknowledging that "contact with experience" does not in itself constitute literature, Williams claimed that it is "the essential quality in literature."[4] But "contact" is possible only when the writer grounds him or herself in local circumstance. For Williams and McAlmon, the local often meant nothing more than one's day-to-day experience. But that experience was almost always interpreted within a national context. The linkage was seen as inevitable: "We will be American, because we are of America," Williams insisted.[5] As a result, the editors consistently promoted a subject matter and style of writing that was "in the American grain"—their highest accolade. (This was somewhat muted in the early issues, but taken more seriously upon *Contact*'s revival in the thirties.) At the very least, it was hoped that the magazine would allow, in Williams words, "our serious writers" a chance to develop "a sense of mutual contact."[6] At best, *Contact* promised much more: "We believe . . . that contact is the beginning not only of the concept of art among us, but the key to the technique also," Williams observed.[7] "Contact" thus became the title, key word, and animating ethos of the magazine, defining both the concept and the technique of what Williams, McAlmon, and later West hoped would become an entirely new American aesthetic.

The first four numbers of *Contact,* released sporadically between 1920 and 1921, boasted a curious melange of letters from a young California painter, Rex Slinkard; "aperitifs" from Marsden Hartley; pronouncements from Ezra Pound and Kenneth Burke; poetry from H. D., Marianne Moore, Wallace Stevens; together with a running commentary (as well as more poems and pronouncements) from Williams and McAlmon themselves. Despite the obvious virtues of their contributions, the animating idea of "contact" was lost amidst the magazine's eclecticism, making it little more than a gathering of American writing—which was, after all, one of the original goals of the magazine, albeit a modest one. Moreover, the attempt to fashion an aesthetic rooted in national experience was swamped by the din of approval that greeted T. S. Eliot's publication of "The Waste Land" along with the wave of experimental writing—expatriate and otherwise—that both preceded and followed it. *Contact*'s chest-thumping nativism seemed peevish and willfully out of touch with the breathtaking pace of artistic experiment taking place across the Atlantic. Thus, it came as no surprise when the editors of *Contact* decided to end its initial run with a fifth and final number, published in 1923.[8]

With the onset of the Depression, however, the time seemed ripe for a revival of a magazine devoted to an engagement with local experience. And in 1931 *Contact*'s original publishers, David Moss and Martin Kamin, urged Williams to resuscitate the magazine. Williams agreed, but McAlmon had become dubious about the value of experimental little magazines. Although he allowed his name to be used on the masthead as an associate editor and continued to publish his work in the journal, he was no longer interested in editing it. This prompted Williams to search for a successor. Impressed with *The Dream Life of Balso Snell* (which he had recommended to Moss and Kamin for publication), Williams approached Nathanael West. The choice proved to be fortuitous. West shared Williams' conviction about the importance of the little magazine as a venue for experimental writing; he also shared a conviction about the need for that writing to reestablish "contact" with American materials.[9] Indeed, after a brief dalliance with French Dada in *The Dream Life of Balso Snell,* West was in the midst of charting something of his own "exile's return." This association with Williams and *Contact* thus enabled West to formulate his own distinctive aesthetic at a crucial moment in his development as a writer. The result, as we shall see, was a richer and more complicated engagement with social reality, an engagement that was crucial to the gestation of *Miss Lonelyhearts* (published for the first time in the pages of *Contact*) and his subsequent fiction.[10]

I. TEXTUALIZING THE REAL

In October of 1931, while *Contact* was still in its planning stage, West sent Williams a letter in which he defined "the boundaries of our task." Limited "on the East by the Atlantic Ocean, on the South by the Gulf of Mexico," the subject of *Contact* was to be nothing less than America itself. "I suppose we should be grateful for boundaries, no matter how far flung," West concluded.[11] Defining those boundaries in less grandiose terms, however, was to prove something of a challenge. In a follow-up letter written a month or two later, West proposed to solicit manuscripts from a variety of writers whose work, he felt, was "in the American grain." The list reads like a who's who of American writers during the era (many of whom would gather under the banner of the Popular Front a few years hence, where the same problems of definition would prevail). Among others, West named the following as potential contributors: "Archibald MacLeish, John Dos Passos, Murray Godwin (what I meant by American Super-realism), Erskine Caldwell, Edward Dahlberg (Did you read *Bottom Dogs*—its pretty good and right up our alley), Josephine Herbst, Malcolm Cowley (not the Frenchified symbolist stuff), Hart Crane (Like the river part in "The Bridge" . . . Not Frenchy), Harold Rosenberg, Ernest Hemingway, William Faulkner, James T. Farrell, Edmund Wilson, Kenneth Burke, Robert Coates."[12] It is easy enough to grasp from West's parenthetical commentary what was not wanted—"Frenchified symbolist stuff." It is harder to figure out exactly what was wanted in its place.

This lack of clarity did not mean that any sort of sham substitute would automatically prove acceptable. For example, in a letter to Williams discussing plans for the upcoming cover design of the journal, West complained, "Kamin [the publisher] showed me the two drawing [*sic*] he had made for the cover and I rejected them both. They were the stinkingist fake moderne I have ever seen, completely meaningless and obviously drawn by a man who thought that a new thing could be done by a few crooked lines."[13] In Kamin's stead, West asked Williams to see if Charles Sheeler could be prevailed upon to do the cover. While it is true that Sheeler's Precisionism had served as a source of inspiration for *Contact* in the twenties, West's choice is somewhat surprising. The austere formalism of Sheeler's approach seems woefully inadequate as an interpretive frame for Depression-era America.[14] Sheeler, in any case, was unavailable, and West was forced to fashion the cover himself. It was based, curiously enough, on Eliot's *Criterion*—"but not quite so conservative"—a model the editors of *Contact* had already vociferously rejected.[15] Once again, this scenario proves how much easier it was to discern what was not wanted than what was.[16]

The difficulty, it seems, stemmed from the tenor of the times. Starting a little magazine was somewhat more problematic in 1932 than it had been ten years before. In the early twenties, the problem had been simply to distinguish *Contact*'s aims and aspirations from those of high modernism. That dialogue continued unabated with the revival of the magazine. But significantly enough, it took second place to an entirely different set of concerns that now preoccupied the editors.[17] In Williams' introduction to the first number (February 1932), it is clear that, for him at least, the moral and political challenges posed by the Depression held the key to *Contact*'s survival and legitimacy. This required him to position the revived *Contact* on very different grounds than before: "Who has the effrontery today to inaugurate a new magazine or to revive an old must justify himself for so doing in some way above the ordinary. With the confusion there is about us and the despairing minds there are, what in the world is writing good for anyway? . . . Why not take the money there is for a magazine like this and give it away—as food—to [those] living in packing cases over near the East River these winter nights?"

This is the question that was asked, in one form or another, again and again throughout the thirties, causing many socially committed writers either to reformulate the assumptions and goals of the literary enterprise or to doubt its value altogether. For Williams, the justification for a new magazine like *Contact* was not so much a matter of choosing between food for the poor and art for the elite. (After all, he pointed out, "there is food enough rotting now in the world . . . to feed them [the poor] every day of the year.") Instead, he attempted to skirt the reductiveness of this either/or proposition by insisting that it is not food or the lack thereof that is the problem but rather "bad writing." The "same sort of stupidity" that countenances "bad writing," he implied, also allows for the perpetuation of social inequality. Fix one and you will fix the other.[18]

If this strikes us as somewhat naive (and Williams could be startlingly naive about such matters), it must be understood as an attempt to carve a place for literature at some remove from the more vulgar Marxist injunctions of the day. That orthodoxy is best typified by Mike Gold's manifesto entitled "Proletarian Realism" (published in the September 1930 issue of the *New Masses*). Eschewing the "precious silly little agonies" of the bourgeois writer, Gold called for an explicitly proletarian literature that "deals with the *real conflicts* of men and women who work for a liv-

.. "Every poem, every novel and drama, must have a social theme or it is merely confectionery," he insisted. In addition, that theme was to be depicted in language that was clear, concise, and readily accessible. The worker's life need not be filled with "horror and drabness." Instead, Gold demanded a literature that at once acknowledged the difficult circumstances under which the proletariat labors and provided hope for the future. For as he explained, "we know that not pessimism, but revolutionary élan will sweep this mess out of the world forever."[19]

Needless to say, the idea of proletarian literature raised many paradoxes and still more questions. What, after all, did it mean for a middle-class writer to portray the quite alien experience of the proletariat for an audience composed largely of middle-class readers like himself? For those less sympathetic to Gold's position (the Southern Agrarians and, later, the *Partisan Review*), proletarian literature represented a dangerous exercise of will over the imagination that "encouraged a preoccupation with 'types' rather than people, slogans rather than life."[20] Finally, and perhaps most damning of all, proletarian literature instrumentalized language by forcing it to serve extraneous, even propagandistic ends.[21]

At first glance, the pages of *Contact* would seem to be surprisingly innocent of this debate. The stories, poems, and essays published here are free of the ideological cant associated with proletarian literature's most characteristic forms of expression. But for writers on the American left, the prestige and pervasiveness of this aesthetic in the early thirties were such that it provided a horizon of expectations that fixed both subject matter and approach, even as it legitimated and excluded varying forms of "contact." Those on the left who chose to write in other ways about other things were forced to do so out of a self-conscious violation of its tenets and taboos. Hence, Williams' shrill rejection of the attempt to define art as propaganda: "To plead a social cause, to split a theory, to cry out at the evil which we all partake of—gladly; that's not writing. . . . A writer has no use for theories or propaganda, he has use for one thing, the word that is possessing him at the moment he writes."[22] Williams puts the matter rather definitively here. But once asked, questions about the relationship between art and politics would not go away. The press of the times—the sense of real misery and suffering—pushed the issue of "contact" to the forefront in a way that made the declarations and results that had characterized the magazine's earlier run seem evasive and insufficient.

For the most part, the magazine's contributors tended to negotiate the difficult questions adumbrated above by opting for a vaguely defined "middle course" that combined "political commitment" of the literary left with the "aesthetic experiment" of high modernism—"contact" with an emphasis on "writing itself." There was, no doubt, some merit in this approach. The acrimonious literary wars of the early thirties tended toward crude distinctions in which politics and aesthetics were often seen as antithetical to one another. In practice, however, this middle course often lacked the moral and theoretical rigor of one side and the technical rigor of the other. This ultimately left *Contact* open to certain vagaries of its own.

The first number reflects this problem in several ways. It is distinguished more by West and Williams' intentions for the magazine than by its rather thin literary output. Moreover, what is there seems to go its own way. Where McAlmon's nostalgic sketch of expatriate life and manners in the twenties—"It's All Very Complicated"—runs directly counter to the editors' designs, Cummings' playful jibe (quoted above and printed in the opening pages of the magazine) raises doubts about the legitimacy of the enterprise as a whole.[23] One is hard-pressed (beyond Charles Reznikoff's "My Country 'Tis of Thee") to find much that resembles the animating ideals of *Contact*. Only Williams' "The Colored Girls of Passenack" and an excerpt from West's *Miss Lonelyhearts* give any indication of what was to come—although, as we shall see, each approaches the problem of "contact" from a very different point of view.

With the second and third numbers, the hodgepodge of the first issue gives way to something of a consensus.[24] But if *Contact*'s contributors rejected Mike Gold's attempt to define art as propaganda, as well as the aestheticism of high modernism, they ultimately replaced those propositions with a paradigm of dubious merit: neonaturalism. Neonaturalism was in many ways the predominant literary genre of the decade, serving as the basis for novels such as *Studs Lonigan, Bottom Dogs,* and *The Grapes of Wrath.* It was also the subject of intense debate in the latter part of the thirties and well into the forties, particularly among those critics associated with *Partisan Review.* In his "Notes on the Decline of Naturalism," for example, Philip Rahv gave naturalism "historical credit" for revolutionizing nineteenth-century American writing by "liquidating the last assets of 'romance' in fiction and . . . purging it once and for all . . . of the long-standing inhibitions against dealing with the underside of life . . . regarded as too 'sordid' and 'ugly' for inclusion within an aesthetic framework." But Rahv went on to argue that despite "its past accomplishments," naturalism's preoccupation with the sordid and ugly had since hardened into a "mere convention of truthfulness." He concluded, "It is no longer possible to use this method *without taking reality for granted.*"[25]

For neonaturalist writers in the thirties, taking reality for granted meant that the "real" was seen as a stable and immediately accessible entity. "There exists . . . a thing called *reality*," Lionel Trilling explained; "it is one and immutable . . . always reliable, always the same, always easily known." In addition to its uniformity and obviousness, Trilling went on to complain of a material reality that is "always . . . hard, resistant, unformed, impenetrable, unpleasant."[26] While neonaturalist writers were less guilty of the stylistic sins associated with this *lumpen* construction of reality than their naturalist predecessors, they too succumbed to a representation of the real that was excessively reductive. As far as Trilling and Rahv were concerned, "the dissolution of the familiar world" under modernity required a more complicated understanding of social reality than neonaturalism (or, for that matter, proletarian literature) allowed. As Rahv explained, "Naturalism, which exhausted itself taking an inventory of this world while it was still relatively stable, cannot possibly do justice to the phenomena of its disruption."[27] Consequently, they sought a literature that would problematize the status of reality itself.

This is not the place to discuss in detail the specific agenda under which this reassessment of naturalism took place.[28] Whatever the merits of that agenda, the critique of Rahv and Trilling is useful for what it reveals about the inadequacies of neonaturalism's approach to the construction of reality and its resulting social analysis—the very achievements for which it was so highly prized. These inadequacies are evident in the pages of *Contact,* where the engagement with the "real" is mired for the most part in the all too predictable obsessions and blindness of neonaturalism. (That is particularly ironic given West's vocal rejection of "the Bucks [and] Dreisers" as a model for the literature of his era.)[29] Insofar as the pages of *Contact* were devoted to patronizing stories about drunks, prostitutes, and criminals, they reveal a fascination with sordidness and strength, inarticulate speech and sexual potency. These qualities are not merely the result of an investigation into an isolated social milieu; rather, they come to signify reality itself. And a quite limited reality at that. Consequently, the writing in *Contact* aspired to an ideal of "contact" it never achieved.

The magazine's failures in this regard stem from a certain naiveté about just what it means to make significant "contact" with the "real." For most of the magazine's contributors, neonaturalism functioned—to borrow Frank Norris' infamous description—as an "instrument with which [one] may go straight through the clothes and tissues and wrappings of flesh down into the red, living heart of things."[30] The equation of insight with sexual conquest or rape betrays the crude, masculinist bias of an approach in which, again and again, the trappings of idealism—identified as female—were stripped away to reveal a putative "real." Hence, E. E. Cummings' sardonic challenge in which he mocked the magazine's contributors for confusing "contact" with squeezing their "n-ts" and opening their face.

Erskine Caldwell, for example, squeezed his "n-ts" and contributed a story about a botched abortion ("Mamma's Little Girl"), as well as a tall tale about a "sly" farmer from "Varmont" who humiliates his bride in order to outwit his creditors ("Over the Green Hills"). Julian Shapiro (later, John Sanford) followed suit. He contributed two stories ("The Fire at the Catholic Church," "Once in a Sedan, Twice Standing Up") in the tradition of Hamlin Garland, which take the seduction and betrayal of a woman as the occasion for a meditation on the parochialism and viciousness of rural, Protestant America.

Two more stories—one from Nathan Asch, the other from James T. Farrell—sum up the whole. In "Mary," Asch finds an emblem for the suffering of the Depression-wracked state of Texas in the figure of a young woman seated in a movie theater:

> She was dressed in a faded, very long, pink gingham dress, maybe clean, but washed and ironed, and many faded ribbons, and a tremendous, crazy, broken straw hat; and her shoes were old, and her hands were large and red; and she was asymmetrical, with a bent face, and frightened eyes, and rouge looking sick upon her faded skin. She was the most revolting thing I had ever seen.[31]

In "Jo-Jo," Farrell finds an analogous emblem for the debauched state of the urban working classes in the figure of a drunken Irishman:

> Jo-Jo blundered, stumbled, staggered, tripped, fell, crawled, sprawled his way through the weedy vacant lot which extended away from and in back of the Standard Oil Filling Station at Thirty Fifth and Morgan, a crossing in Chicago's Central Manufacturing District.[32]

This portrait of the blundering, stumbling, faded, and bent-faced poor is problematic at best. The poor are defined almost wholly in terms of their oppression. If the contributors to *Contact* eschewed "slogans" of proletarian literature as too explicit, they were undeniably preoccupied "with 'types' rather than people"—types, that is, of human suffering. Indeed, these characters have no life outside that suffering; at least so it would seem to those who view their lives from above. Moreover, in the case of both "Jo-Jo" and "Mary," the neonaturalist narrative enacts the same ironclad logic: The "real" becomes identified with a certain "unpleasantness" or grotesquerie in which conventional ideals are inevitably reduced to the "brute facts" of existence: i.e., birth, death, lust, isolation, betrayal.[33]

Other contributors to *Contact* (notably Williams and McAlmon) opted for a subtler metaphysics. That metaphysics was grounded in an unacknowledged but omnipresent universal law of compensation. Accordingly, whatever deprivation the poor may suffer is more than made up for by an innate "vitality" rooted in the life of the body. That vitality ultimately serves the proletariat as a touchstone, or rather as a redemptive "ground of Being." The bourgeoisie, on the other hand, lacks Being for the very reason that its existence is founded not on the life of the body but on the dead abstraction of money. Despite the power of that money, the poor retain a capacity to "endure" (to borrow the favorite phrase of Steinbeck and Faulkner, both neonaturalists in their own right). They endure precisely because they are closer to "nature" and hence closer to "life." And because they are closer to life, they possess an authenticity the bourgeoisie can only envy, an authenticity or truth that guarantees their eventual triumph.

William Carlos Williams' own contributions to *Contact* demonstrate the rather severe limitations inherent in this approach. If his poetry (with the dramatic, later exception of *Paterson*) too often succumbs to a nostalgic romance with the "real" ("in your common cup / all beauty lies—"), his prose exoticizes "contact" in a still more suspect manner.[34] For Williams, the "real" is neither a victim of the Dust Bowl nor a drunken Irishman (although it very well could be either one). Rather, it is typified by the "Colored Girls of Passenack."[35]

The memoir is composed of a series of vignettes in which Williams recounts his encounter with a variety of black women. Each vignette follows a similar narrative strategy wherein this encounter is ineluctably reduced to a confrontation with the potency and mystery of the "real." In "Colored Girls," Williams grounds the "real" in biology, or more particularly, in the "sheer vitality and animal attractiveness" of the black woman's body. Her sexualized body is associated with an exhilarating "actuality," an actuality that ultimately reduces the narrator—lacking a corresponding authenticity of his own—to mere spectatorship. Thus, for example, one vignette concludes with the young Williams as a voyeur watching his maid standing naked over her wash basin:

I remember my own turn at the peep hole as if it were this
morning. . . . She had nothing but a china basin to wash herself in.
This she had placed on the floor. She was standing in it, facing me
fully naked and washing herself with a sponge. My view was not too
good, I was half lying on the floor with the others pulling at me to
take their turn also, but it was a thrilling picture.[36]

For Williams, as for so many of the contributors to *Contact,* reality always
remained just that: something of a "thrilling picture" for the eager voyeur.

In its purest form, however, Williams' engagement with reality possesses neither nostalgia nor exoticism; nor for that matter does it rely on
the metaphysics of neonaturalism. Rather, it is almost always defined as
"experience" to which one presumably has direct and immediate access.
Williams is not naive about this. He recognizes that reality is recalcitrant,
that it requires all the poet's talents and abilities to find a language adequate to the reality she seeks to express.[37] But—and this is the important
point—for those whose senses and linguistic resources are particularly
keen, the object stands wholly revealed. "Language," Williams asserts in
one of *Contact's* editorials, "must adapt itself to the truth of our senses.
Clichés must disappear. . . ."[38]

Meanwhile, West was busy concocting a literature composed almost
entirely of clichés. This, precisely because he understood the power of
those dead metaphors to mediate experience. Instead of joining Williams
in praising "the truth of our senses," West offered his own parodic,
cliché-ridden paean to them in an early draft of a chapter from *Miss
Lonelyhearts* (published in *Contact*). "Life, for most of us," Miss Lonelyhearts counsels his readers, "seems a terrible struggle full of pain and
heartbreak, without hope or joy":

But, oh, my dear readers, it only seems so. Everyman, no matter how
poor or humble, can teach himself to use his senses. See the cloud-
flecked sky, the foam-decked sea . . . Smell the sweet pine and heady
privet . . . Feel of velvet and of satin . . . As the popular song goes,
"The best things in life are free." (Ellipses not mine)[39]

West makes it abundantly clear in the foregoing passage that Williams'
expansive claims on behalf of the senses are mere wishful thinking. The
senses lack any truth of their own. Rather, they are constituted by the discourse of aestheticism as it is mediated through therapeutic culture, codified in the advice column, and disseminated through the commercial institution of a metropolitan daily newspaper. In contradistinction to
Williams' famous insistence on "wiping soiled words . . . clean . . . or tak-

ing them bodily from greasy contexts," this passage shows that for West words are inevitably soiled by the contexts that produce them.[40] For unlike Williams, West harbors no illusions about the accessibility of the "real." It is always already structured by ideology.

Curiously, this fundamental difference between West and Williams was never articulated, or perhaps even appreciated, by either of them while they were involved with *Contact*. That is surprising, especially since in *The Dream Life of Balso Snell*, West had problematized any idealized presumption of "contact" with reality ("the low") from the beginning. In that novel, John Raskolnikov Gilson remarks,

> Reality! Reality! If I could only discover the Real. A Real that I could know with my senses. A Real that would wait for me to inspect it as a dog inspects a dead rabbit. But, alas! when searching for the Real I throw a stone into a pool whose ripples become of advancing less importance until they are too large for connection with, or even memory of, the stone agent.
> *Written while smelling the moistened forefinger of my left hand.*[41]

Here, reality does not wait for inspection like a dead rabbit. Moreover, the attempt to articulate the relationship between the advancing ripple and the stone that caused it exceeds the observer's capacities. This does not mean that reality as such ceases to exist simply because it cannot be explained. Quite the contrary. As the speaker notes with perverse glee, it manifests itself in the smell of a "moistened forefinger," which assaults the putative dignity of official interpretations with its own unmistakable, furtive presence.

In *Balso Snell*, this assault on any and all "official interpretations" of reality left West free from any sense of responsibility to the "real," resulting in the nihilistic play of the volume. There, the excremental status of reality rendered it beneath contempt, an object of derision, valued only insofar as it could be used to puncture the pretensions of various idealisms. But that stance became harder to sustain after the year West devoted to *Contact*. The letters of despair that he was then struggling to incorporate into *Miss Lonelyhearts* testify to a reality whose claims were more difficult to shake off. The early versions of chapters from *Miss Lonelyhearts*, published in *Contact*, make it clear that West was in the midst of formulating a complicated engagement with the "real" in which he acknowledged its material conditions even as he explored its textuality, its vertiginous loss of any stabilizing "ground" or constellating master narratives. In West's hands, the "real" becomes a multifarious entity of shifting planes and duplicitous surfaces, "a nest of Chinese boxes" to borrow one of his own phrases.[42]

Thus, in contrast to the neonaturalist inclination to "go straight through the clothes and tissues and wrappings of flesh down into the red, living heart of things," West was almost entirely preoccupied with the "clothes and tissues and wrappings" by which those "things" are constituted and positioned within a complex social world. Thanks in part to this construction of reality, West did not succumb to the dubious metaphysics of neonaturalism, which invariably dissolved a highly structured and thoroughly mediated social realm into an indistinguishable soup of vitalism.

2. IN THE AMERICAN GRAIN

We will have occasion to examine the results of West's approach in the following chapters. For now it is enough to explore West's evolving response to the problem of "contact" in his role as editor and contributor to the magazine. For the most part, West's letters to Williams are filled with the matter-of-fact details involved in editing a literary journal, details of the sort we have already seen: i.e., which writers to include, cover designs, editorial policy, and so on. Secreted within those details, however, is a chronicle of West's own growing engagement with the ethos and aesthetics of "contact." Complaining in one letter that much of the material he received "wasn't anything except lyric, lyric crap,"[43] West goes on in another to list his reasons for rejecting certain submissions:

> "Being Exclusive": . . . not idiomatic, no grain, rather dull.
> "You Know How": . . . lacks punch, romantic escape—labor is picturesque like the South Seas.
> "19 is: 20 is": A smart idea but faked. Half the lines meaningless, full of false awareness, too much trembling on the brink. TOO FAKEY.
> "Familiar Objects": an adolescent poem of revolt against poetry— no more stars sez you—too literary—very week [sic].
> "One": The wrong kind of visions, too subjunctive and personal— what we want is torture, not sickness, and no visions except in the form of warnings, sermons, moral and didactic. . . .[44]

These notes read like a checklist of the aesthetic values that would ultimately animate, if not *Contact,* then certainly West's own fiction. Thus, we might translate West's peculiar shorthand in the following manner: "idiomatic" (in the American vernacular), "grain" (the circumstances and contradictions of our national experience), "trembling on the brink" (rejection of a narcissistic subjectivity), "no more stars" (a weariness with otherworldly aestheticism and its literary subject matter), "torture, not sickness" (disdain for the evasions of "healthy-mindedness"), "no visions" (a social criticism rooted in the visible world rather than in idealized projections). This language is no doubt borrowed from Williams himself. What is important is not so much who these words belong to, but the uses that are ultimately made of them. And in this instance, West is seen working out an aesthetics and politics of "contact" that would soon be proclaimed in his own literary manifesto "Some Notes on Violence."

The title of the manifesto suggests a focus on violence itself. But it is more than that. As the last word in the last number of *Contact* (October 1932), "Some Notes on Violence" constitutes a summary of West's ambitions for the magazine as well as for his fiction. Together with a related manifesto, "Some Notes on Miss L" (published in *Contempo* a year later), "Some Notes on Violence" articulates just what it means to write "in the American grain," to make significant "contact" with reality.

The catalyst, which forced West to formulate these ad hoc insights into a coherent manifesto, was a rather jaundiced review of the first issue of *Contact* that appeared in the pages of T. S. Eliot's *Criterion*. The reviewer, Hugh Sykes Davies, raised doubts about the magazine's raison d'être—specifically, its attempt to "cut a trail through the American jungle without the use of a European compass."[45] But for Davies, the most troublesome feature of the journal seemed to be its reliance on violence, and he singled out West's fiction as a prime example:

> The use of an American compass has involved most of the contributors in violence, some of them in unnecessary violence. Mr. West's story, for example, of the clumsy sacrificial slaughter of a lamb by drunken students has the typical faults of the latest realistic manner; the thing is incredible, as an event, in spite of its careful detail, simply because such things cannot happen without arousing the strongest emotions in the spectator. Accordingly, only an emotional description of the scene will be credible, and this attitude of impersonal observation, of scientific and photographic reproduction defeats its own object; robs the account of all realism, and leaves the reader not impressed, but reflective: if it really happened, then it must be regretted that Mr. West feels like that about it, if, on the other hand, it is imaginary, as it seems to be, then it is almost pathological.

While the review did concede that "For this number at least, violence and energy make *Contact* good reading," it doubted whether the magazine's contributors could "keep themselves goaded up to this pitch for long."[46]

In "Some Notes on Violence," West responds to this criticism with a pointed question of his own: "Is there any meaning in the fact that almost every manuscript we receive has violence for its core?" If the "sweetness and light" of the genteel tradition filled the literary "magazines before the war, and Art those immediately after it," West argues that violence may be the *métier* of the thirties. "We did not start with the idea of printing tales of violence. We now believe that we would be doing violence by suppressing them."[47]

West's perverse celebration of violence calls attention to certain historical developments that gave violence a special prominence in the thirties. Indeed, there is a sense in which Americans might be said to have "rediscovered" violence during these years, albeit in unexpected ways. No longer located on the frontier where it had once been so easy to mythologize, violence began to take on a myriad of urban forms that called into question the foundation of American society itself. Excoriated by the guardians of "civilization," sensationalized by the media, exploited by various members of the "underworld" in the pursuit of wealth, violence was the key trope for a variety of constituencies during the thirties. The gangster in particular became a lightning rod for much of this debate. While he was being romanticized in the films of the early thirties, the gangster was also being reviled elsewhere as an object lesson in the perfidious qualities of an inassimilable immigrant population. As with his Indian predecessor, the gangster's status as an "outsider" allowed Americans to indulge in the luxury of seeing violence as extrinsic to American society.

For those on the left, however, there was a growing recognition that violence was not limited to the gangster alone; violence was, to their way of thinking, intrinsic to American society itself. In defiance of a heretofore sacrosanct democratic rhetoric, American radicals in the thirties reluctantly came to recognize that the legitimation of authority was derived not so much from the consent of the governed as from the threat of violence. For many, this conclusion was based on the inescapable logic of Marxist analysis; for others the link between authority and violence began with the execution of Sacco and Vanzetti in 1927, only to be dramatized again and again in the ugly labor disputes that took place in Gastonia, Harlan County, and elsewhere during the Depression. But if violence was seen as a source of repression, it could also be recuperated and "ennobled" as a potential source of liberation. An authority constituted by violence might just as easily be overthrown by violence. Emboldened by the example of the Russian Revolution, some on the American left (notably the I.W.W.)

construed violence as the "midwife of history," a legitimate means by which long-delayed social aspirations might be realized.[48]

Although he was sympathetic to the views of the left, West never succumbed to the tendency to massage away the dangerous side effects of this proposition in a hazy romanticism. If anything, West might be criticized—as indeed he was—for his utter lack of faith in "regeneration through violence." For West, violence is far more likely to be wielded under the sign of fascism. Whatever its status, there is little doubt that violence is everywhere in his fiction, serving as index and nightmarish analogue to one of the primary preoccupations of the decade. Thus, we find Balso Snell administering "a terrific blow in the gut" to Miss McGeeney;[49] Miss Lonelyhearts twisting the arm of "all the sick and miserable, broken and betrayed, inarticulate and impotent" who will murder him in the end,[50] Lemuel Pitkin losing an eye, his teeth, a leg, through beatings and other mishaps too numerous to mention—all of which culminates, so it would seem, in the figure of Tod Hackett caught amid the final, apocalyptic riot on Hollywood Boulevard. This violence is so ubiquitous, in fact, that it is hard to think of a scene or chapter that does not end with some sort of "bang."

The aforementioned litany of beatings, rapes, riots, and homicides is not the product of a "sordid" imagination, as one early reviewer put it. ("Sordid? Good God!" William Carlos Williams snorted in West's defense.)[51] Nor is it a glorification of antisocial criminality in the manner of the more fashionable "hard-boiled" novelists of West's generation. West makes no attempt to explain or justify the presence of violence in his fiction. Rather, it is treated as a thoroughly banal, matter-of-fact phenomenon, utterly lacking in the grandeur of tragedy. And herein lies its horror for critics like Davies. Taking Miss Lonelyhearts' slaughter of the lamb as a case in point, Davies observes, "such things cannot happen without arousing the strongest emotions in the spectator. [To which West responds, 'Does not H.S.D. mean, in the *breast* of the spectator?'] Accordingly, only an emotional description of the scene will be credible." West's refusal to describe this violent scene in an "emotional" manner—that is to say, his refusal to infuse it with his own horror and revulsion—constitutes a lapse that violates genteel standards of appropriateness and decorum. But more is at stake than matters of appropriateness and decorum. What Davies finds so appalling is the absence of an interpretive frame by which the "incredible" can be made "credible," susceptible to explanation and, hence, exorcism. For Davies, West's failure to provide this frame means that the author ultimately "defeats [his] own object."

What exactly is West's object? He is certainly not interested in the sort of "realism" Davies advocates—by which Davies means a "psychological realism" whose highest standard is "credibility." As West explains in "Some Notes on Miss L," "Psychology has nothing to do with reality, nor should it be used as motivation. The novelist is no longer a psychologist. Psychology can be something much more important. The great body of case histories can be used in the way the ancient writers used their myths. Freud is your Bulfinch; you cannot learn from him."[52] Nowhere does West separate himself more definitively from the tradition of European high modernism—which Davies (writing for the *Criterion*) so obviously admires—than in this rejection of psychological realism. "For a European writer to make violence real," West complains in "Some Notes on Violence," "he often needs three hundred pages to motivate one little murder. But not so the American writer." When the latter's readers get their hands on a "a little book with eight or ten murders in it, [they do] not necessarily condemn the book as melodramatic. [The American writer] is far from the ancient Greeks, and still further from those people who need the naturalism of Zola or the realism of Flaubert to make writing seem 'artistically true.'" That is because "In America violence is daily." It is fantastic, inescapable. As such, it cannot be made intelligible by the traditional modes of explanation. That does not mean that violence is meaningless. But it does imply a recognition that, in America at least, violence possesses an "idiom" all its own:

> Read our newspapers. To make the front page a murderer has to use his imagination, he also has to use a particularly hideous instrument. Take this morning's paper: FATHER CUTS SON'S THROAT IN BASEBALL ARGUMENT. It appears on an inside page. To make the first page, he should have killed three sons and with a baseball bat instead of a knife. Only liberality and symmetry could have made this daily occurrence interesting.[53]

Three sons. Three strikes. Three outs. This is a "fearful symmetry" indeed. And like William Blake's cosmic query about the creation of the "Tyger," West's secularized version raises questions about an America imbued with sublime terrors of its own. Here, violence is the idiom in which America expresses at once its deepest social contradictions and its idealized vision of itself.[54] The stylized violence of this front-page newspaper account serves as a rune in which Americans discover how inseparable their national identity is from its violent underpinnings, how closely their guilt and innocence are related.

West matches this culture of violence with a peculiarly potent and highly idiosyncratic "idiomatic violence" of his own. As West himself describes it, "Violent images are used to illustrate commonplace events," while "violent acts are left almost bald."[55] The use of violent images to illustrate commonplace events functions to denaturalize those events by ripping them loose from their otherwise seamless, "commonplace" contexts. Moreover, by leaving violent acts almost bald—that is to say, by choosing *not* to contain them, or explain them away within a traditionally accepted framework—West acknowledges the volatile implications of violence, its thoroughgoing rejection of constituted standards and practices. Under the percussive force of West's idiom, the "real" is shattered, not—as neonaturalism would have it—in order to get at its heretofore undisclosed essence, but in order to perform an autopsy on its mangled parts. In the process, violence becomes not just a specialized mode of "contact" but mode of social analysis as well—perhaps the only efficacious mode of social analysis available in a society that has, as West put it, "violence for its core."

West never gave up on "the violently disassociated, the dehumanized marvelous, the deliberately criminal and imbecilic" of his self-described "French phase."[56] Indeed, his association with *Contact* gave him the opportunity to find a more appropriate home for the techniques and strategies of the French avant-garde that he had first explored in *Balso Snell*. The ostensible rejection of "imported thought" noted above ultimately proved to be a tactical retreat designed to clear the ground for an American content. In fact, the peculiar accomplishment of Nathanael West was to discover a way of adapting an avant-garde style of writing to a native social criticism. During his tenure as editor of *Contact*, West—almost alone among his fellow contributors—managed to convert "contact" into an *active*, even *critical*, mode of apprehending an otherwise elusive social reality. In doing so, he redefined the relatively neutral and poorly conceived notion of "contact" that had plagued the magazine since its inception.

EPILOGUE

This vision, alas, went largely unheeded—at least in the pages of *Contact*. Or rather, it would be more accurate to say that the injunctions enumerated above never coalesced into a distinct mode of writing beyond a generalized insistence on the necessity for engagement with social reality. That, however, was not enough—particularly during the thirties. It was inevitable that *Contact* would succumb to the tenor of its times just as its predecessor had in the twenties. On this occasion, it was politics rather than literary experimentalism that was the deciding issue. Neither era was particularly receptive to a magazine that tried to straddle both sides of the question. The difficulty or challenge for the magazine in the thirties was to establish some degree of "contact" without politicizing the material to such an extent that it devolved, as Williams put it, into a literature about events rather than becoming an event in itself. But that sort of restraint always seemed a bit irresponsible in such desperate times. If Cummings could chide the editors of *Contact* for confusing the "authentic and delirious" with bathroom graffiti, their gambit was equally vulnerable from the left.

In this case, the pressure came from *Contact*'s publisher, Martin Kamin. Like his contributors, Kamin also took his cue from the magazine's title—this time, pushing *Contact* in an unaccustomed, politicized direction. "Contact III," Kamin wrote to West, "must be a huge issue and it must have contributions from Gorky and Rolland down to Mike Gold. . . . I have lists of authors who contribute regularly to the USSR magazine of the Social Revolution and we'll write to them." West and Williams were originally receptive to the idea. But as Kamin's plans crystallized, they became increasingly apprehensive. Kamin responded by challenging their political commitment in a tone that leaves little doubt as to where their respective prejudices lay: He wondered aloud "whether [his editors] are interested in essays and critical dissertations . . . (to satisfy the theoretician), or do you want merely good prose and good poetry . . .? Do you want scientific application and interpretation of Karl Marx, or merely material on the proletarian awakening, unscientific, devoid of conscious formulae . . .?" Kamin's obvious preference for "conscious formulae" reveals an unstinting loyalty to the kind of scientism that in the hands of Andrei Zhdanov imposed notorious limitations on art. This aroused Williams' concern; he wrote back immediately, insisting that *Contact* must be "a forum of good writing. All we'll get by a communist issue is a reputation for radicalism and not for good writing— which is our real aim."[57] Ironically, such dissension points to the very debates over literature and politics that *Contact* had sought to avoid.

It was the magazine's failure to establish a rich and nuanced "contact" with the "real" that led to its embattled status and eventual demise. Having failed to convince the left of its value, West and Williams could only fall back on the importance of "good writing." But there was precious little of that—not enough, at any rate, to please those who prize good writing as such. Moreover, there was little to distinguish that stance from the literary experimentalism of the twenties—the very position from which they presumed to take their departure. More than anything else, *Contact* foundered on its own inability to realize the task it had set for itself. *Contact*—genuine contact—remained as elusive as ever. Only West would take that elusiveness as his subject.

The third and last issue of the magazine, which appeared in October of 1932, was not the communist number Kamin had envisioned. In fact, it was much like the numbers that had come before it. For a while it seemed as though the magazine might survive regardless of the dispute. West and Williams discussed a fourth number. But nothing was to come of it. At last, in December of 1932, West quarreled irreconcilably with Kamin. "If it's all the same to you," West wrote to Williams, "I'd just as soon call the third issue our last. I've lost too many friends over this thing already."58

Williams reluctantly agreed. His own, earlier notice on behalf of West—which appeared on the literary page of *Il Mare,* edited by Ezra Pound—provides a fitting epitaph:

> When another of the little reviews that appeared in the United States . . . died, I thought it was a shame. But now I think differently. Now I understand that all those little reviews ought by necessity to have a short life, the shorter the better. When they live too long they begin to dry up. But they have had at least one excuse for their existence—they have given birth to at least one excellent writer who would not otherwise have had the means to develop. *Contact* has produced N. West. Now it can die.59

Chapter Four

The People Talk
Miss Lonelyhearts

PROLOGUE

During the thirties there was an unparalleled attempt to record, transcribe, or otherwise gain access to the voice and image of the people. "The people" (as they were affectionately, and sometimes proprietarily, known) talked and talked and talked. In return, they were recorded, photographed, and even tagged as specimens. Their wan, haggard, but always heroic physiognomy was captured in thousands of memorable photographs—most notably, those taken under the auspices of the Farm Security Administration—that have come to symbolize the very essence of the Depression. Likewise, their words were tirelessly collected through countless interviews, resulting in such books as *These Are Our Lives* (the Federal Writers' Project), *The People Talk* (Benjamin Appel), *Let Us Now Praise Famous Men* (James Agee and Walker Evans), *The Inman Diaries* (Arthur Inman).[1]

From the first, this rediscovery of the people was bathed in mythology. For many, the people were the repository of truth. Somehow, out of their suffering, out of the very ordinariness of their lives, it was hoped that America might salvage an exemplary set of first principles. The whole decade, it seemed, was devoted to a prolonged pastoral interlude in which the people were constructed as poor but virtuous shepherds whose patience, endurance, and probity might extricate their wayward brethren from the collapse of the industrial machine.[2] Indeed, the increasingly incomprehensible nature of American capitalism and the still more befuddling experience of its apparent demise made for a nostalgic swerve toward a myth of pure presence. It was as if the rhythms of speech, the lineaments of the human face, faithfully transcribed or photographed, could somehow restore value by providing a bracing antidote to the abstractions out of which the crisis seemed to emanate.

Such constructions of the people served a variety of explicitly political ends as well. The work sponsored by the FSA and the WPA, for example, laid the groundwork for the social programs of the New Deal by depicting an American populace that was neither angry (potentially violent) nor downtrodden (beyond help). Instead, their faces and voices conveyed stoic patience under suffering and the capacity for resilience. This portrait made it clear to anxious taxpayers that whatever help was extended would be accepted reluctantly and only temporarily. On the political right, particularly in rural, Protestant America, the image of the people was drawn from the organic, stable world of a long-lost antebellum era. For many, like the Southern Agrarians, the traditions and practical arts of these *volk* stood as a standard against which to measure the failings of a non-Protestant, ethnic population located in the cities. On the left, the people were subjected to yet another set of politically motivated stereotypes.[3] Populists, romantic socialists, and communists—among them, Carl Sandburg, Waldo Frank, and Mike Gold—found in the people an impossibly extravagant, heroic ideal.[4] Meanwhile, their more sophisticated academic counterparts—most notably, the Frankfurt School—lost their faith in the people altogether. Traumatized by their experience in Nazi Germany, the Frankfurt School depicted the American populace as so thoroughly maimed by life under capitalism that they ceased to function as the agents of history; instead, the Frankfurt critics emphasized their susceptibility to fascism.

Whatever their political persuasion, almost everyone agreed that the people as they were defined and represented by the "culture industry" were beneath contempt, disfigured beyond recognition. Indeed, for many on the left, the culture industry was the preserve of "mass man"—a thoroughly mediated and media-created entity.[5] In contradistinction to "the masses," who presumably developed the consciousness necessary to alter the course of history, mass man did not know his own mind, and if he altered the course of history, it was likely to be in the direction of fascism. Mass man was inert, undifferentiated, standardized, passive. I use the term "man," but actually "he" was a "she." Mass man, especially in the eye of his critics, is gendered as female: prone to consumption, lacking in reason, a creature of desire.[6] Whether active or passive, male or female, mass man's very existence was seen by many on the left and the right as a "symptom or cause of social decay."[7]

There were, however, those during the thirties who viewed mass man more positively—"populists" like Vachel Lindsay and Gilbert Seldes. But in the case of Lindsay and other advocates like him, their praise tended to fall prey to the worst aspects of a windy, prairie tradition that accepted uncritically whatever won the allegiance of broad numbers of people. As for Seldes, his tastes were too eclectic to serve as a model for others to emulate.[8] For the most part, the people who tended to take mass man most seriously were those who profited most from him—those on Madison Avenue, Broadway, and in Hollywood.

Of all the primary sources available to those wishing to "document" the people, the advice column surely provided a record of ordinary suffering that seemed to epitomize the dislocation caused by the Depression. And yet, though it was available every morning at the breakfast table, the advice column was largely overlooked, if not disdained outright, by those one would expect to be most interested in it. In part this was because the voices that were heard there failed to project the heroic image of the people that many so desperately sought as a foundation for the political programs they were advancing. Instead, the advice column seemed to offer the pitiful record of mass man's debauchery and servitude.

It was left to Nathanael West to make the disfiguring operation of the advice column explicit without concluding in disdain for the people themselves. Instead of writing about mythical figures like Ma Joad (in whom he did not believe), West writes sympathetically about "people who want to add inches to the[ir] biceps and to develop [a] bust," people "who want to live the life of an artist . . . and develop a grip that would impress the boss."[9] Moreover, in contrast to much of what was later published through the WPA, the FSA, and other documentary sources, West does not use the advice column as a repository for "local color." (That is to say, he makes no attempt to mine its discourse for a folksy vernacular that would stand as an emblem for the innate "honesty" and "resourcefulness" of the people.)[10] Nor does he present the advice column as the agent for an emerging fascist order (as Theodor Adorno was to do later with horoscopes). Rather, in West's hands the people are portrayed as neither heroic nor demoralized, but as a much richer and more complicated entity that is harder to define. Indeed, one might say that in *Miss Lonelyhearts* "the people talk," but they do so in a manner that forgoes the myth of pure presence; instead, West focuses on the site or location in which that talk is mediated. Perhaps it would be more accurate to say, he focuses on the function of mediation itself.

I. THE PEOPLE TALK

Few periods in American history have been more obsessed with the possibilities and limitations of public dialogue than the 1930s. The national prominence of Dorothy Dix, Roosevelt's fireside chats, the interview with the man in the street, the "true confession" featured in the pulps, all reflected a desire to participate in a national conversation over the trials and tribulations caused by the Depression. Even the *New Masses* got into the act: Under a headline that read "WE WANT TO PRINT," Mike Gold asked the readers to submit

> Confessions—diaries—documents—
> The concrete—
> Letters from hoboes, peddlers, small town atheists,
> unfrocked clergymen and schoolteachers—
> Revelations by rebel chambermaids and night club waiters—
> The sobs of driven stenographers—
> The poetry of steel workers—
> The wrath of miners—the laughter of sailors—
> Strike stories, prison stories, work stories—
> Stories by Communist, I.W.W. and other revolutionary workers.[11]

The new media that made this national conversation possible tended to inspire extremes of optimism and pessimism. Beginning "with the daily press opening to its readers space for 'letters to the editors,'" Walter Benjamin observed, "an increasing number of readers became writers."[12] Bertolt Brecht shared a similar optimism about "refunctionalizing" an emerging technology of communications. In a series of notes about radio written the same year that *Miss Lonelyhearts* was conceived, Brecht spelled out one set of possibilities for the new medium: "Radio is one-sided when it should be two. It is purely an apparatus for distribution. . . . So here is a positive suggestion: change this apparatus over from distribution to communication. The radio would be the finest possible communication apparatus in public life. . . . That is to say, it would be if it knew how to receive as well as to transmit, how to let the listener speak as well as hear, how to bring him into a relationship instead of isolating him."[13] (In the Age of Talk Radio, it is difficult to appreciate the intoxication that once inspired such roseate visions.)

If, on the other hand, one were to ask mass media's harshest critics about its viability as a forum for public debate, they would probably subscribe to a version of Jean Baudrillard's observation that "what characterizes the mass media is that they are opposed to mediation, intransitive, that they fabricate noncommunication—if one accepts the definition of communication as an exchange, as the reciprocal space of speech and response, and thus of *responsibility*." Baudrillard continues,

> Now the whole present architecture of the media is founded on this last definition: they are what finally forbids response, what renders impossible any process of exchange (except in the shape of a simulation of a response, which is itself integrated into the process of emission, and this changes nothing in the unilaterality of communication). That is their true abstraction. And it is in this abstraction that is founded the system of social control and power.[14]

Baudrillard's commentary offers a peculiarly apt description of the advice column. Although it presents itself as a free and open forum for public debate, it could be said that the advice column merely simulates a response that is integrated into the process of emission. The reader who would become a writer—to use Benjamin's phrase—is faced with the dilemma of speaking in a language that both precedes and constitutes her, in this case the therapeutic language of Mind Cure or Positive Thinking. Among other things, Mind Cure begins by transforming social problems into individual ones and then insists that there is no personal problem that the mind cannot cure given the appropriate maxim and sufficient resolve. The reader/writer must accept this fundamental premise before she can even begin to formulate her question. In this way a dialogue becomes a monologue, a sham exchange between two parties who have already agreed upon the answers.

There is much in *Miss Lonelyhearts* that supports this account of the advice column's hegemonic strategy. The polite locutions that characterize the letters written to Miss Lonelyhearts, their ludicrously stilted language, their ubiquitous healthy-minded maxims, their frequent bows to the superior authority of the column's editor: all this attests to what Mikhail Bakhtin might describe as the "double-voicedness" of language, writing that anticipates the response of an Other. Indeed, these letters are structured *in advance* with an ideology of healthy-mindedness that both formulates suffering and burlesques it in ways that exceed the sufferers' understanding. Despite its incurable nature, suffering is construed as a definable lack that can somehow be filled by an expert who presumably "no's." ("I figured maybe you no something about it because you have read a lot of books and I never finished high," one supplicant declares [47].) This presumption functions to limit the range of possible responses, leaving Miss Lonelyhearts' readers powerless and utterly dependent upon him. Thus, after telling Miss Lonelyhearts "no boy will take me [out] because I was born without a nose," Desperate wonders, "Ought I commit suicide?" (3). That a question of such enormity could be cast in this polite, interrogative voice reveals the extent of this reader's betrayal.

If the questions posed in the advice column are terrible, the answers are worse: "Do not let life overwhelm you," Shrike urges Miss Lonelyhearts to write to his readers. "When the old paths are choked with the debris of failure, look for newer and fresher paths. Art is just such a path . . ." (4). Even worse than the advice itself is the lack of feeling with which it is conveyed. Shrike, who might be said to embody the "spirit" of the advice column (against which Miss Lonelyhearts rebels), parries the most heartfelt queries by responding in the blank parody of "deadpan": "Although his [Shrike's] gestures were elaborate, his face was blank. He practiced a trick used much by moving-picture comedians—the dead pan. No matter how fantastic or excited his speech, he never changed his expression" (6). The pun here is, of course, on a dead Pan, the Greek god of nature. (To be sure, the thoroughgoing assault on nature in this anti-pastoral novel is such that there is almost nothing left that even remotely resembles nature.)[15] But the deadpan is also a means by which the comedian denatures his or her own speech. He does so by refusing to imbue the speech act with its proper affect, ground, or context. In the absence of any naturalizing gestures, the "presence" that is presumed to inhere in the spoken word is problematized, even negated. Sundered from its supposed origins in the body, language quite literally becomes disembodied. As such it devolves into "mere" rhetoric or afflatus that floats above and seemingly beyond the subject until it resembles the balloons of dialogue that hover over cartoon characters in a comic strip. Whatever critical potential this demystification of language might possess for Shrike, it is completely lost on Miss Lonelyhearts' readers. For them, the loss of aura is experienced as reification: dead words in a dead world. Shrike acknowledges as much by engaging in a deadpan parody of the Lord's Prayer. "Give us this day our daily stone," he intones.

It is no accident that West chose the deadpan and the comic strip as key figures in the construction of *Miss Lonelyhearts*. Both are drawn from the mass media in a deliberate attempt to implicate their apparatus in the alteration of the speech act's status. The capacity of mechanical reproduction—the essence of mass media—to reproduce speech endlessly, without regard either to the original site of its articulation or to the multiple sites of its eventual reception, radically problematizes the act of communication. In effect, mass media reproduce the same bifurcation of the speaker and language that we have already seen in the deadpan—only they do so on a much grander scale. This renders the "message" ubiquitous, autonomous, and virtually impervious to criticism. More than anything else, it is this loss of ground or context that makes the mass media a one-sided mechanism for distribution rather than communication, or as Baudrillard puts it, unmediated, intransitive, irresponsible—deadpan.

2. ADVISE AND DISSENT

Rather than dismiss the advice column as hopelessly contaminated because of this and other forms of betrayal, West chose to take it as a *model* of public discourse during the thirties. By that I do not mean that West held up the advice column as an ideal form of communication, but rather that he used it *à l'envers* to investigate the codes, conventions, and subject positions—the possibilities and limitations of public dialogue—within the constrictions of mass culture's totalizing designs. While many of his contemporaries sought to circumvent those designs by going "directly" to the people themselves, West's decision to use the advice column as the organizing structure for his own "documentary" was meant to be taken as a not so gentle reminder that all such contact is necessarily mediated by a variety of discursive and ideological structures.

That does not mean that communication is rendered impossible. Quite the contrary. In West's hands, the advice column reveals itself to be a far more volatile and highly charged discursive space than Baudrillard's description would allow. For West knew that there is a certain "static" that cannot be shut out of even the most hegemonic discourse. In *Miss Lonelyhearts* the production and reception of such discourse are shot through with hesitations, confusions, ambiguities, and evasions of every sort, and hence, open to contestation. One might say that for West the advice column becomes the scene of a rhetorical struggle in which the ideology of therapeutic culture contends with the symbolic resistance of the column's readers, thereby problematizing the colonization of the subject at every turn.

Nowhere is this more amply demonstrated than in the spelling, grammar, and punctuation of the letters themselves, which reveal the grotesque penetration of official ideology even as they demarcate its limits. The letters are ridden with misspellings ("operatored" [2], "naturally" [40], "hystirical" [41]); adjectives used as adverbs ("I was married honorable" [2], "asking to see you personal" [25]); awkward locutions

("I need some good advice bad" [25]); malapropisms ("patriotic stunt"
for patriotic stint [40]); clichés ("a baby boy was added to our union"
[40], "spick and span" [41], "lo and behold" [41], "living off the fat of
the land" [46]); mixed metaphors ("What I want to no is what in hell is
the use day after day with a foot like mine when you have to go around
pulling and scrambling for a lousy three squares with a toothache in it
that comes from using the foot so much" [46]); run-on sentences ("I am
kind of ashamed to write to you because a man like me dont take stock
in things like that but my wife told me you were a man and not some
dopey woman so I thought I would write to you after reading your answer to Disillusioned"); repetition ("I am sixteen years old now and I
dont know what to do and would appreciate it if you could tell me what
to do" [2]). The cumulative effect of all this is to register the texture of
pain and suffering—the orthographic equivalent of onomatopoeia—even
as that pain and suffering are themselves textualized.

It is important to understand the precise nature of the pain and suffering delineated here. Though I have used the two terms interchangeably,
they are not synonymous; the former is physical while the latter is primarily social in nature. The *pain* in these letters emanates from a genetic
defect, physical violence, and so on. But the *suffering* that makes these letters almost unbearable to read emerges out of the gap between that pain
and the impoverished social explanations that are tendered by way of response. These explanations, largely derived from the healthy-mindedness
of a liberal Protestant theology, literally create the suffering they are supposed to answer. For example, Miss Lonelyhearts' readers are so debauched by the sentimental clichés of American culture—home, marriage,
and true love—that they cannot imagine any other response to their pain.
"Every woman is intitled to a home isnt she?" Broad Shoulders asks in
the face of mounting evidence to the contrary (43). Such maxims are invoked like mantras in a bid to exorcise pain, but in the end they serve only
to compound suffering by creating expectations that cannot be realized.

Likewise, explanation founders on the maxims of patriotism, which are
deployed as a means of circumscribing the class conflict that is implicit
throughout these letters. These letter writers are members of a semi-illiterate
"working class," although they would never identify themselves as such.
They are pinched by the economic effects of the Depression, atomized
and isolated by their participation in mass culture. But it is only in rare
moments that any sense of class consciousness ever breaches the surface,
and then only to be submerged quickly again: "What I want to no is why
I go around pulling my leg up and down stairs reading meters for the gas

company for a stinking $22.50 per while the bosses ride around in swell cars living off the fat of the land" (46). Peter Doyle immediately backs off from the radical implications of his question: "Dont think I am a greasy red. I read where they shoot cripples in Russia because they cant work but I can work better than any park bum and support a wife and child to" (46). Having said that, Doyle thereby deprives himself of the self-understanding necessary to redress the most egregious aspects of his situation. His predicament is shared by the other letter writers as well, who, like Doyle, lack the resources to explore the social dimensions of their situation adequately. They unwittingly accept the categories assigned to them and hence labor under monikers like "retard," "whore," and "cripple" that they are powerless to change.

If suffering is gratuitous, pain is not. A girl is born without a nose; an emotionally disturbed child is raped on the roof of a tenement; a woman is terrorized by her husband. "What I want to no," one man asks, "is what is it all for . . ." (46). There is no cure for the pain related in these letters. These are cries that cannot be answered. And that is precisely the point. If pain cannot be alleviated, neither can it be betrayed. Indeed, pain functions in *Miss Lonelyhearts* much the way excrement does in *The Dream Life of Balso Snell*. That is to say, it resists metamorphosis almost entirely. Its stubborn presence undermines the polite locutions, the stilted language and healthy-minded maxims that characterize these letters and exposés the discourse of healthy-mindedness for just that: a discourse rather than a cure. The very process of putting pain into words forces us to recognize its power, its capacity to erupt into the decorous order of language and *spoil* it. And as such it inaugurates a potent form of symbolic resistance.

Strange as it may sound, pain serves Miss Lonelyhearts' correspondents both as a source of insight and as a source of truth.[16] Among other things, pain holds out the utopian promise of release from a suffocating social structure that interpellates a rich and varied humanity within a series of radically impoverished subject positions: i.e., Desperate, Sick-of-it-all, Disillusioned-with-tubercular-husband. As such, it represents a longing for presence in the midst of absence, or as Miss Lonelyhearts' correspondents would have it, a longing for the Living Word instead of the dead words of a reified social milieu. In *A Cool Million* and *The Day of the Locust* the attempt to overcome the absence, mediation, and contingency of modernity through the restoration of a pastoral world of presence, immediacy, and wholeness results in a reactionary turn toward fascism. But in *Miss Lonelyhearts* West displays a genuine empathy for this aspiration. (It is this empathy more than anything else that distinguishes *Miss Lonely-*

hearts from the other novels and gives it its peculiar power.) In *Miss Lone-lyhearts* at any rate, pain preserves the meaning of presence, immediacy, and wholeness, even as it testifies, paradoxically enough, to their absence.

To return to the problem of communication with which we began, one might argue that the pain that permeates these letters is the very essence of the response that Baudrillard insists is lacking in the mass media. "To understand properly the term *response*," Baudrillard argues, "one must appreciate it in a meaning at once strong, symbolic, and primitive."[17] Is that not precisely what we find in the letters written to Miss Lonely-hearts: a set of utterances that are "at once strong, symbolic, and primitive"? They are so strong, in fact, that the simulated conversation within the advice column breaks down—at least for the reader who is prepared to read it against the grain. If the advice column does not offer a legitimately Baudrillardian "reciprocal space of speech and response" (such was never its intention), neither can it smother the eruption of pain "with a thick glove of words" (33). As a result, this "exchange" is fissured, leaving two incommensurate discursive structures side-by-side—open for further scrutiny. In *Miss Lonelyhearts,* then, the letters of Desperate, Sick-of-it-all, Disillusioned-with-tubercular-husband, et al.—riddled as they are with clichés, structured by the discourse of the Other—nevertheless possess a monstrous power, or to borrow Bataille's term, an *archontes* of their own. For perhaps the first and last time in his fiction, West found access to a "discourse of the low" that retained a degree of integrity, a discourse that was not already thoroughly appropriated by the official *doxa* of American culture.

EPILOGUE

1. Miss L in Hollywood

> Miss LONELYHEARTS, what will I do?
> I am a LONELYHEART, writing to you,
> Hoping that through your column you'll drop me a line,
> Saying you know a LONELYHEART as lonely as mine.
> —Irving Berlin

In May of 1933, Darryl F. Zanuck bought the rights to Nathanael West's *Miss Lonelyhearts* for Twentieth Century Pictures. By Hollywood standards at least, *Miss Lonelyhearts* did not appear to be a very promising acquisition. And with good reason. For one thing, the first printing sold less than two hundred copies. Moreover, the initial reader's report, submitted to Twentieth Century on 26 April 1933, summed up this "saddist" (*sic*) novel in the following fashion: "This is a book which could not possibly be translated to the screen. Great stress is laid on fornications and perversions, and on disgustingly intimate details which seek to define the psychopathic character but which do little to further the slight plot. The convention [*sic*] reader of fiction would class this novel as vile and without apparent purpose save to shock."[18]

It is difficult to know just what Zanuck's interest in *Miss Lonelyhearts* could have been. He may have wanted merely to acquire the rights to the novel's title. Or perhaps he was hoping to cash in on its slightly scandalous reputation. But if that was the case, then the strategy would eventually backfire on him (as we shall see). It is more likely that Zanuck simply wanted to capitalize on the success of movies like *The Front Page* (1931) and *Hi Nelly* (1932), which initiated a cycle of newspaper movies that culminated in *His Girl Friday* (1940), *Citizen Kane* (1941), and *Meet John Doe* (1941).

Whatever Zanuck's reasons may have been for buying the rights to *Miss Lonelyhearts*, the adaptation of the novel shows quite clearly how little interest there was in pursuing the novel's "vile" themes or "slight plot." Leonard Praskins, the man charged with adapting *Miss Lonelyhearts* to the screen, was fairly successful in eliminating most of its (sad and sadist) "fornications and perversions." In his hands *Miss Lonelyhearts* became a story about "doing the right thing," of "one man's redemption," of "True Love lost and found." (That is to say, West's novel was turned back into the comic strip from which it originally took its point of departure and inspiration.) But if this sounds hackneyed, it is too easy to dismiss his adaptation as a mere "hack job."

The adaptation of a novel or any other material into a screenplay is always a complicated affair involving a web of determinants. It is, in the truest sense, a collaborative effort in which writers, producers, and studio executives struggle, sometimes in sync, sometimes at cross-purposes, to give shape to a screenplay as it undergoes a succession of story conferences, rough drafts, more conferences, and still more drafts before receiving the studio's final imprimatur. What emerges is the result of local pressures (budgetary restrictions, exhibition practices, available talent, etc.), generic expectations (prescribed *mise-en-scène*, plot devices, beginnings and endings, etc.), as well as cracker-barrel theorizing on everything from character motivation to projections of "what America wants"—which are in turn shaped by still larger ideological constraints that quite literally make certain possibilities unimaginable.

This process is often mystified under the sign of "entertainment," but it is not at all innocent. The disassembly and reconfiguration of certain privileged cultural codes in a persuasive manner is an essential part of any society's ability to respond to shifting historical circumstances and their resulting social pressures. During the difficult years of the Depression, Hollywood assumed unprecedented power in this regard. The movies it produced were instrumental in providing the ideological groundwork necessary to reimagine the country during a time of crisis. Thus the process of honing and refining a screenplay—especially material as recalcitrant as *Miss Lonelyhearts*—provides an unparalleled opportunity to watch that ideology "at work." And Praskins' adaptation in particular provides us with a guide to the remarkably parochial *Weltanschauung* of middle-class America in 1933, or rather Hollywood's version of it.

What follows, then, is a study of the process by which West's darkly critical text was censored—through a series of demurrals and evasions, displacements and substitutions, even outright repression—in order to make it acceptable for the screen. But this puts the matter much too negatively, for it assumes that adaptation must always result in betrayal. As we shall see, Praskins' revision of *Miss Lonelyhearts* was also *enabling*. If Praskins obscured West's troublesome reading of America, he did so in order to open up a whole new spectrum of ebullient possibilities. The result is illuminating for what it reveals about not only the "culture industry" that West dedicated himself to exploring throughout his career, but also the momentous cultural struggles under way in 1930s America—in particular, the ongoing tension between a residual Protestant middle-class culture and the newly emergent mass media together with their ethnic immigrant audience.

Praskins wasted little time in emptying out most of what was genuinely subversive in West's novel. But he did so in order to tell a quite different story—a story that, unlike its predecessor, is finally affirmative of America's most cherished values. While West's *Miss Lonelyhearts* ultimately tells the story of Protestant America's loss of faith in its own once powerful vision, Praskins' treatment and subsequent drafts construct an antithetical fable about the recovery of faith within a newly emergent immigrant culture. Thus, instead of West's wan and effete Miss Lonelyhearts in which "no one could fail to recognize the New England puritan" (3), Praskins cast his "star reporter" after the fashion of the virile Irishman Spencer Tracy. Of course, Spencer Tracy himself was decidedly beyond the reach of this B movie. But the explicit comparison of the protagonist to "a man's man" like Tracy says everything about Hollywood's rejection of the ennui and loss of confidence that animates *Miss Lonelyhearts*. And the choice of an actor with a recognizably ethnic identity indicates an ambition to shift the ideological ground of this novel from descent (and its cognate dissent) to ascent (and its cognate, assent) in what was by then a familiar rite of assimilation.

Moreover, that rite of passage was facilitated by a potent new "culture industry" that functioned to articulate a shared set of newly minted symbols essential to the assimilation of an uprooted population.[19] The construction of that symbology, however, did not take place unchallenged. It was hampered, on the one hand, by older ethnic loyalties and on the other, by a native (and nativist) strain of Anglo-Saxon Protestantism. There was, then, something of a pact between mass culture and its urbanized ethnic audience in which these obstructions were shunned in an effort to create some third term: a recognizably American identity rooted in the ethos of consumption, the raison d'être of mass culture. Praskins' adaptation of Nathanael West's novel is especially interesting for the way it dramatizes the tactics, strategies, and the inevitable compromises associated with this transformation.

2. The Politics/Poetics of Censorship

How then was "a book which could not possibly be translated to the screen" translated to the screen? The plot and themes of West's *Miss Lonelyhearts* were largely abandoned under Praskins' new configuration, although some superficial resemblances remained. Most of the important changes took place in the initial "treatment."[20] There, Lee Tracy—this is the name Miss Lonelyhearts is now given and the name of the actor who eventually starred in the movie—is depicted as a hard-boiled tough guy fashionable in the popular literature of the thirties.[21] It seems that Tracy is in love with "a pretty little eighteen year old girl from upstate who is . . . working as a cashier in her Aunt's millinery store" (Treatment, 12). Praskins' depiction of Tracy's "love interest" (Hollywood jargon for female lead) unwittingly recalls Betty in *Miss Lonelyhearts,* and hence it is one of the few ways in which the adaptation remains faithful to the novel. But that is probably because West's Betty is herself a parody drawn from the stock characters of movies like this one. (The ironies multiply as the borrowings compound one another.) At any rate, Tracy's "girl"—she is not given a name in the treatment—has little respect for his profession. She wants him to quit and come to work for her brother as an auto mechanic. But Tracy is addicted to the "newspaper game" and its "devil-may-care" lifestyle. He eats peppermints when he is with her to cover his drinking and explains away the rouge on his collar as red ink from the funny papers. Praskins observes, "This unusual type of romance between a hard-boiled, hard-drinking New York newspaperman and a sweet, conventional prudish young girl, can develop into a swell romance as well as tremendous comedy . . ." (Treatment, 13).

The relationship between Miss Lonelyhearts and his editor, Shrike—in which the Tortured Soul confronts his Grand Inquisitor—is radically altered under this new version. Tracy is actually Shrike in disguise.[22] That is to say, Tracy assumes Shrike's irreverent demeanor, albeit without the latter's corrosive gall. Since there is no longer any difference between them, West's exploration of their respective philosophical outlooks is trivialized into a "long-existing rivalry between the Managing Editor and the Star Reporter" (Treatment, 1). This rivalry results in a series of "weak-sister assignments" (Treatment, 1) that Tracy always manages to turn to his own advantage.

Frustrated by his inability to keep a good man down, the editor concocts an inspired means of revenge. "For some funny reason or other," it seems that the person who dispenses advice to the lovelorn has had "a nervous breakdown and wants a three month vacation." The editor grants this request, calls Tracy into his office, and slyly offers him his own column and byline. Tracy is thrilled until he realizes that he has been made the editor of "a column on the Woman's page of the paper called 'Miss Lonelyhearts'" (Treatment, 3). But there is nothing he can do. He reluctantly takes his place in an office bedecked with a variety of "love symbols": "bleeding hearts, whole hearts—hearts of every kind all over the place . . . sofa pillows with mottoes embroidered on them," and a plaster of Paris Cupid that has been "chipped . . . in an important place" (First Draft, 25).[23]

This is a sentimental paradise with a vengeance. And like West's Miss Lonelyhearts, Tracy discovers that it is inundated with letters asking for help. But these letters bear no resemblance to the missives of suffering that ultimately overwhelm West's empathic Christ. There is little of what Shrike derisively describes in *Miss Lonelyhearts* as "Pain, pain, pain, the dull, sordid, gnawing, chronic pain of heart and brain" (53). Recognizing that such grotesquerie would only alienate an audience that wants to leave the theater "feeling good," Praskins deliberately lightened the load. In effect, he shifted the ground of their complaint from unredeemable despair to "lust-ridden" (First Draft, 18) appeals from a frustrated female readership. This results in what Praskins described patronizingly as "very funny letters" filled with "funny questions" (Treatment, 5) that revolve exclusively around issues of sex—both premarital and adulterous. Given the nature of these letters, it is not surprising that the depth of Miss Lonelyhearts' crisis would be utterly lost on Tracy. Tracy's curse is not ennui, but a lack of will born of indifference—a question of his own halfheartedness versus his capacity for wholeheartedness. While Miss Lonelyhearts' breakdown is precipitated by a subjectivity whose boundaries are agonizingly vulnerable to the world without, Tracy remains blithely indifferent to any such threat. Like the tough guy that he is, Tracy makes the self a citadel and he remains entrenched there.

In *Miss Lonelyhearts,* the "humiliation" of having to adopt a female pseudonym is a concession to a putative "feminization of American culture" that produces rage and even fantasies of violence. In Praskins' treatment, however, the humiliation of the male takes an entirely different form. Cupid's castration notwithstanding, Tracy's dilemma is not experienced as an anxiety about cultural authority, or even one's place in the larger world. Rather, the humiliation Tracy experiences is personal: the consequence of professional rivalry, his own perpetual inebriation, and bad timing. The forced assumption of a female identity and duties is merely the occasion of his humiliation; it is not foisted upon him by deep-seated social pressures.[24]

The anxiety this situation elicits—"No man is a man," Tracy observes, "who writes a woman's column" (Treatment, 13)—is never allowed to become threatening. Tracy is in no danger of becoming infected by the advice column's sentimental ethos. He remains thoroughly hard-boiled from first to last. Nor, for that matter, is there any danger of this "woman's column" contaminating the hard news of the city desk. The two worlds remain firmly separated. Instead, Tracy's predicament is portrayed as a source of titillation and humor—something on the order of a fraternity hazing that has gotten out of hand. He good-naturedly endures the "ribbing" of his colleagues and goes on to turn the situation around to his own advantage. In fact, Tracy's situation, much as he may hate it, actually empowers him at the expense of his female readership. He successfully exploits his position in such a way that he manages to succeed with women on a scale to which West's Miss Lonelyhearts can only aspire. If nothing else, Praskins' adaptation of *Miss Lonelyhearts* rejects West's thesis regarding the "feminization of American culture"—at least insofar as it is seen as the ubiquitous and threatening phenomenon West portrays. Here as elsewhere, certain themes simply do not translate from high culture to low.

If anything, Tracy is inclined to dismiss the feminized world of the advice column as hopelessly out of date: "Say, can you imagine a paper still carrying an obsolete, antiquated column like this advice to the lust-ridden? It's silly! It's ridiculous!—It ain't modern!" He goes on to read from the day's advice column words that West's Miss Lonelyhearts could have written (and did):

> Hey, listen to this . . . "Do not let life overwhelm you. When the old
> paths are choked with the debris of failure, look for newer and fresher
> paths. Love is just such a path. Those who love are the elite of the
> world. Love is the road toward happiness and understanding." (First
> Draft, 18)

What "ain't modern"—and West would agree—is the hopelessly genteel language of this kind of advice. But secreted within that language is an ethos that, if it isn't itself modern, is the essential prerequisite for modernity. The insistence that love in *this* world "is the road toward happiness" marks an important departure from an older Puritan conception in which gratification is perpetually deferred in anticipation of the next. That sea change makes a newer, modern ethos of consumption possible. If this relationship between sentimental culture and modernity is understood by the partisans of the former, it is rarely acknowledged. Sentimental culture, in an act of bad faith that verges on schizophrenia, finds itself in the untenable position of castigating an ethos it has covertly sanctioned already.

Miss Lonelyhearts can do little but mourn this state of affairs and hanker after a now bygone Puritan "Age of Faith." Unlike other partisans of sentimental culture, he recognizes the inadequacy of his answers to the heartfelt questions of his readers—hence, his crisis. For Tracy, on the other hand, there is no crisis at all. The advice column is perceived by him to be somewhat prudish. Tracy is unable to address the needs of its constituency not because he doesn't have the answers they seek, but because those answers will violate a peculiarly genteel decorum. The advice column is simply in need of an update: a certain "broad-mindedness . . . [a] modern viewpoint . . . [an] understanding of the needs of youth today" (First Draft, 55), as the newspaper's advertising manager puts it. And that is precisely what Tracy provides.

Thus, in response to a question from "Anxious" who is in love with a young man who cannot afford to get married, Tracy writes,

My dear Anxious—What does it matter that you and your young man haven't enough money to get married? What is marriage?—Only a meaningless, empty convention. . . . Love transcends all. Do not wait until old age has claimed you both and the fires of passion have become embers. Laugh at convention! Act now! (First Draft, 38)

"This is the kind of note," Praskins tells us in his treatment, "that Miss Lonelyhearts *should* answer on the standpoint of morals, etc." (Treatment, 5; italics mine). But Tracy revels in this transgression of decorum and responds to the subsequent letters in the same spirit of carpe diem. His plan is to "put so much dynamite" (First Draft, 24) in this column that he will force the editor to either give him his old job back or fire him outright. He doesn't care which. But Tracy has gravely miscalculated the effects of his strategy. His column does create the uproar he anticipates, but it also gives a huge boost to the newspaper's circulation. For the first time, the paper has secured the advertising dollars of nationally marketed merchandise—companies who know that nothing sells like scandal. The editor wants to fire Tracy, but he can't. Instead, the column is moved to the front page and given to him as a permanent assignment. Tracy thus becomes something of a celebrity. He writes monthly "Hints to Wives" for *True Confession* magazine, lends his name to the Amalgamated Brassiere Corporation for his own line of bras and girdles. (The latter, so the slogan goes, "clings to you like an Ardent Lover" [First Draft, 62].) There seems to be no end to the merchandising possibilities.

Thus, where Miss Lonelyhearts fails to provide his readers with the sustenance they need, Tracy succeeds all too well and as a result becomes more deeply mired in his predicament than ever. Praskins makes a travesty of Miss Lonelyhearts' melancholia by depicting Tracy as "so sick and disgusted" with his *success* "that it drives him 'nuts'—letters, letters, letters—interviews, lousy, sex-crazed people—he is going to turn into a eunuch to get away from it" (Treatment, 10). While Miss Lonelyhearts longs for a sexual potency that will revitalize the wasteland he inhabits, Tracy—exhausted by the erotic energy he has unleashed—fantasizes a return to equanimity through the absence of desire.

This success is not solely attributable to the fact that his readers find sexual promiscuity titillating. Sexual energy is emblematic of a more generalized release of energy that accords with the deepest injunction of a modern consumer society. By discarding the restrictive injunctions of the advice column, Tracy has inadvertently incited a riot of seething passion upon which mass culture depends. The real tension in the screenplay lies here—in what is essentially a struggle between the claims of a genteel middle-class ethos of feminized healthy-mindedness and those of the mass media that find those injunctions a drag on their attempt to respond to a newly emergent, immigrant culture.

While the ideology of expenditure is, as we have seen, the logical culmination of sentimental culture, those charged with defending the genteel precepts of the latter often bridle at the less palatable manifestations of the former. As a result, mass culture has been forced since its inception in America to contend with periodic bouts of censorship from anxious authorities concerned about the impact on its most cherished values—especially those archsentimental values of Childhood, Family, True Love.[25] In the film business, at least by the 1930s, a precarious truce had been worked out in which movies were reviewed by self-created censorship boards that either banned certain content altogether or allowed a degree of expenditure—usually in the form of sex and violence—so long as it was tidied up at the end in the predictable Hollywood ending.[26] The latter strategy established something of a disingenuous ritual in which mild transgression was followed by still milder rebuke. Inevitably, the energy released by such transgressions would erode the standards of the censors until a public outcry over some particularly melodramatic incident would end in their reinstatement.

In the advice column, the fault line is more static and more obvious, running as it does between letters filled with a variety of unrequited appetites and the officially sanctioned, decorous responses they receive. Praskins' screenplay reveals the fundamental antagonism this "partnership" obscures: a secret desire within the ideology of expenditure for the liberation of mass culture from all constraint. For this screenplay constitutes nothing less than a brief on behalf of mass culture. As such, it inscribes the very cultural conflict in which it is also a partisan. Tracy is, as it were, the genie in the bottle; once released he chants the transformative possibilities of expenditure. And that sells papers—lots of them. And presumably, movies too. At least, that is what Darryl Zanuck was counting on.

3. Expurgating the Expurgations

Story notes provided by the project's producers indicate a general satisfaction with the Praskins' treatment and first draft. The alterations requested amount to little more than excising "flat" scenes, punching up gags, and clearing up discrepancies in the plot that might confuse the au-

dience. There was some concern, however, about the content of the letters and the responses they elicited in the advice column. Although Praskins had gone a great distance in expurgating West's "saddist" novel, that
apparently was not enough. The exchanges between Tracy and his readers, the story notes complain, "are a little too rough," and Praskins was
advised to "soften" them.[27]

The problem, of course, is that the humor of the story depends wholly
on the violation of convention implicit in Tracy's advice. "Softening" that
advice would clearly rob the story of whatever interest it might still possess. More important, this would impose the same form of "censorship"
on the script that Tracy railed against in the story—an irony that was lost
on the project's producers. Praskins must have been successful in arguing
for the retention of the letters in the titillating fashion he had written
them, because in two subsequent drafts they remain relatively unchanged
except for the elimination of a description of marriage as "only a meaningless, empty convention" (First Draft, 38). But the release of *Harrison's
Reports*—"A Motion Picture Reviewing Service Devoted Chiefly to the
Interests of the Exhibitors"—stepped up the pressure to censor Praskins'
screenplay still further.

In a 26 August 1933 notice entitled "A Sample of Darryl Zanuck's Genius" Harrison wrote this devastating diatribe:

> During the three years of my publishing . . . I have read more than five
> hundred books, plays, or magazine stories. Among these there have
> been some very dirty ones: William Faulkner's 'Sanctuary' . . . is one
> of them. . . . But I have never read anything to compare in vileness and
> vulgarity with Nathanael West's 'Miss Lonelyhearts,' announced by
> Twentieth Century Pictures. I am surprised that its publication should
> have been permitted, particularly because of its implications of degen-
> eracy. It cannot be defended on the grounds of art; it has none: it is just
> low and vulgar, put out undoubtedly to appeal to moronic natures.[28]

Harrison went on to warn that the screening of this picture would anger
newspaper editors and bring both the studios and the exhibitors bad publicity. He even sent letters to the leading newspapers throughout the
country asking them to protest the production of the film. Clearly, Harrison saw himself as protecting jittery exhibitors from their "irresponsible" suppliers. But his charges against *Miss Lonelyhearts* were also part
of a larger campaign against the movie industry that had come to a head
in 1933. The American Catholic Church, for example, had recently created a nationwide organization, called the League of Decency, to cam-

paign against and eventually boycott movies it considered indecent. With the Depression taking its toll on the box office—attendance was at a five-year low—the exhibitors could not afford to alienate such a significant portion of their audience.

Harrison need not have worried. As we have seen, much of the sanitation of West's novel had already been accomplished with the original June treatment. But now, apparently, even this was not enough for a studio that was as fearful of incipient Comstockian wrath as it was anxious to protect its good relations with exhibitors and the media. In order to escape association with West's "low and vulgar" book, the title of the film was changed from *Miss Lonelyhearts* to *Advice to the Lovelorn*. In addition, the studio hired a reporter as a technical adviser and promised that the movie would reflect the journalistic profession's "high image of itself." Meanwhile, the letters were toned down still further until they became a parody of Praskins' original version—itself a travesty of West's novel. Indeed, by the time this latest round of revision was over, the exchange between Tracy and his readers no longer even possessed the integrity of a run-of-the-mill advice column in the daily newspaper—to say nothing of West's own investigation of that dynamic discursive space.

One example will suffice. Recall that in an earlier, "unexpurgated" draft, Tracy received a letter from two young lovers who desire each other passionately but cannot get married, and he advised them to "Laugh at convention! *Act now!*" In the revisions of September 26, this was changed to read,

> My dear Anxious—What does it matter that you and your young man haven't enough money to get married on? . . . Get married—and worry about paying for it later. . . . Love transcends all. Do not wait until old age has claimed you both and the fires of love have become cold.[29]

What was once a question of passion and restraint is now a matter of dollars and cents. And instead of urging the prospective newlyweds to "*Act now!*" Tracy proposes love on the installment plan: "Get married—and worry about paying for it later." Not all the letters were revised this dramatically. Where he could, Praskins simply eliminated any explicit sexual content and left everything as ambiguous as possible. All that remains of the original exchange is a vague sense of the need for activity rather than passivity, energy rather than stasis. It is ironic, to say the least, that a script that had begun by celebrating its liberation from the "antiquated" values of a genteel culture found itself with little recourse but to submit to them in the end.

On 13 December 1933, *Advice to the Lovelorn* opened in New York's Rivoli Theatre on the same bill as "that delightful Disney prismatic cartoon, 'Santa's Workshop.'" *Variety* criticized the movie as "an unauthentic newspaper story," while the *New York Times* observed, "It is obviously a story which would have been infinitely more satisfactory had the lighter vein been sustained."[30] Thus, instead of a script filled with scandal, Zanuck ended up with a movie that was scandalously tame. Needless to say, it sold few tickets at the box office.

Chapter Five

The Folklore of Capitalism
A Cool Million

PROLOGUE

In 1934, Nathanael West went to work on a Broadway musical revue he called "American Chauve Souris." The revue marked a revival of interest in American folk materials during the Depression that resulted in, among other things, Howard Hanson's opera *Merry Mount,* Carl Carmer's collection of Southern folklore, *Stars Fell on Alabama,* and George Gershwin's *Porgy and Bess.* In an outline sent to his agent, West describes the sources he planned to draw upon for "American Chauve Souris" (which was, alas, never staged):

> Nantucket during the great days of the whaling industry including a ballet of a whale hunt. . . . Natchez-Under-the-River . . . full of horse thieves, gamblers with lace cuffs . . . river men . . . creoles and planters. The songs would be the whore house ballads of the period, boastful and extremely sad. . . . [A celebration of the Resurrection in the] ancient Moravian church at Bethlehem, Pennsylvania, a folk event, older than the American Revolution. . . . The Erie Canal at the time of its construction in a canteen on one of the company barges pay-day afternoon. . . . A gathering of mountaineers ending in a coon hunt and the "Hound-Call Song". . . . A Harlem rent party, using real scat music.

"I could keep this sort of thing up forever," West observed. Indeed, the outline goes on to enumerate several more suggestions, including songs from a barbershop quartet, the Salvation Army, Cajun Louisiana, as well as an "Oregon Trail scene." West proposed to constellate these choreographed musical numbers around one-act interludes in each half of the show, written by playwrights like Paul Green or Eugene O'Neill. The continuity of the revue would be provided by a "master of ceremonies" whose speeches would be drawn from "the wonderful comic monologues that Nye, Artemus Ward and Mark Twain used to recite on their tours." Although this outline was clearly written with an eye toward eliciting the interest of financial backers, West's interest in these materials appears to be sincere. "I feel," he wrote to his agent, "that the material should be as authentic as possible . . . in no case should it be permitted to deteriorate into the 'folksy' or 'arty' in a Cape Cod Tea Shop sense."[1]

It is interesting, to say the least, that West should have been involved in a project that was so thoroughly at odds with one he had just completed, *A Cool Million* (also published in 1934). Where the folk materials in that novella (i.e., Pennsylvania Dutch, Old South, Log Cabin Pioneer, Victorian New York, Western Cattle Days, California Monterey, to name just a few) "deteriorate" into the *faux* history of the "Cape Cod Tea Shop," that process is reversed in "American Chauve Souris," thereby allowing those same materials to be presented as authentically as possible. Indeed, one might say that "American Chauve Souris" attempts to reconstruct what *A Cool Million* has so assiduously torn asunder.

How is one to explain this rather curious situation? It is possible that West was simply hoping to capitalize in purely mercenary fashion on a contemporary interest in American folk revivals. Or, more likely, it may be that West himself was not immune to the general anxiety over the dismantling of American life that he chronicles with such glee in *A Cool Million*. Whatever the case, there is little doubt that "American Chauve Souris" betrays the author's desire to put Humpty Dumpty back together again.[2]

In this he was not alone. The rediscovery of culture—specifically, the folkways of America's collective past—was so widespread during the thirties that cultural historian Warren Susman has singled it out as *the* defining feature of the decade. Indeed, Susman argues, "No fact is more significant [to the thirties] than the general and even popular 'discovery' of the concept of culture." In contradistinction to Matthew Arnold's notion of culture as "the best that has been thought and said," culture in the thirties was increasingly defined as "all the things that a group of people inhabiting a common geographical area do, the ways they do things and the ways they think and feel about things, their material tools and their values and symbols." This shift in thinking is found in a number of important books written during the period: from sentimental depictions of Native American, Mexican, and Southern culture (e.g., Oliver La Farge's *Laughing Boy* [1929]), Stuart Chase's *Mexico: A Study of Two Americas*

[1931], and Margaret Mitchell's *Gone with the Wind* [1936]) to more serious attempts to define various aspects of mainstream American culture
(like Constance Rourke's *American Humor* (1931) and Van Wyck Brooks'
The Flowering of New England [1936]). Indeed, Susman argues, "It is not
too extreme to propose that it was during the thirties that the idea of culture was domesticated."[3]

To be sure, this "rediscovery of culture" did not begin with the Depression. Rather, it was part of an ongoing response to the corrosive
process of modernization that has shadowed—or to be more accurate,
constituted—American life since its very beginnings. That process has
eroded the traditional folkways that once provided texture and body to
everyday life. The loss of these folkways has resulted in a vague but
chronic dissatisfaction, and on more extreme occasions it has contributed
to a variety of antimodernisms that seek to recreate a world that has been
irretrievably lost.[4] For much of American history, prosperity (or more important, the promise of prosperity) has managed to hold that dissatisfaction at an "acceptable" level. But with the arrival of the Depression,
Americans were forced to come to terms with the lack of *communitas* or,
indeed, any meaningful sense of "wholeness" that might offer both a foundation and a vision for an otherwise fragmented society.[5]

This search for a sense of "wholeness" or unity took on different in-
flections in accordance with the shifting historical circumstances of the
decade. Thus, during the darkest years of the Depression in the early thirties, the revival of American folkways served as a touchstone for a nation
buffeted by a catastrophe that appeared to be without explanation. Later,
with the initiation of the Popular Front in 1935, American culture served
to define a democratic way of life against the specter of fascism. And finally, as war in Europe grew increasingly likely, those same cultural interests were quite literally drafted into service once again, as a means of
motivating American energies for the herculean task of war. Throughout
the decade there was a widespread feeling that the ability to confront
these various crises effectively was contingent upon defining a "usable
past" in which history, myth, and culture combined to provide Americans
with a sense of national purpose.[6]

The problem was that this interest in the past could easily devolve into
what Howard Mumford Jones (a vocal proponent of the need for a usable past) described as "the chauvinism, economic self-interest, or racial
snobbery of the totalitarian states."[7] As a result of mounting pressure
from dangerous developments abroad and the dislocation caused by the
Depression at home, the "American way of life" (a term coined during the

period) readily became the credo for an isolationist and exclusionary popular response. Under this scenario a usable past became, in effect, a reified past congenial to fascism. It was precisely this likelihood that Nathanael West explored in *A Cool Million*. All but ignored at the time it was published, *A Cool Million* stood as a potent warning about the potentially dangerous uses to which this headlong "rediscovery" of Americana could be put.

Again and again, throughout *A Cool Million,* West is attuned to the strategies by which the past is constituted, appropriated, and exhibited. However, this results in not so much a Broadway revue as an off-Broadway burlesque. Thus, for example, we find Lemuel Pitkin's Vermont farmhouse—"built about the time of General Stark's campaign against the British"—"lovingly" reassembled down to the last detail in a New York antique store owned by Asa Goldstein.[8] Interest in this piece of Americana is so keen that "there is some talk of his selling it to the Metropolitan Museum" (96), the mother of all Cape Cod tea shops. "Wowed" by this spectacle of authenticity in their midst, one of Goldstein's sales representatives even invites Pitkin to serve as a "consultant" on the construction of the house in which he once lived and the disposition of its colonial contents:

> "I wonder if you would be so kind as to furnish me with a little information?" asked the clerk, pointing to a patched old chest of drawers. "Where would your mother have put such a piece of furniture when she owned it?" . . . After a little thought, he [Lem] pointed to a space next to the fireplace and said, "I think she would have set it there."
>
> "What did I tell you!" exclaimed the delighted clerk to his colleagues, who had gathered around to hear Lem's answer. "That's just the spot I picked for it." (102)

As Goldstein's role in both the foreclosure of the Pitkin home and its subsequent display makes clear, the same deracinating process of capital underlies both. The rediscovery of America's folkways is indistinguishable from their exploitation. Under the guise of paying homage to the colonial past, Goldstein turns it into an antique, a relic—thereby depriving it of all significance. Goldstein's instructive example recalls that of Henry Ford, who likewise went around the American countryside collecting mementos of a way of life that his automobile had destroyed.[9] Ford's dalliance was more than bad faith masquerading as nostalgia. It was symptomatic of a larger cultural strategy during the thirties in which a variety of folk materials were dredged up in a bid to establish a specious continuity with a past that capitalism had already helped to undermine.

The complications arising from this phenomenon are clearly drawn in Wu Fong's "House of All Nations." Like his counterpart and business associate, Asa Goldstein, Wu Fong deals in what might be euphemistically described as "cultural treasures." But instead of an antique store, Wu Fong runs a brothel, featuring women from around the world. With the onset of the Depression, however, Fong realizes "that the trend was in the direction of home industry and home talent, and when the Hearst papers began their 'Buy American' campaign, he decided to get rid of all the foreigners in his employ and turn his establishment into an hundred per centum American place":

> He engaged Mr. Asa Goldstein to redecorate the house and that worthy designed a Pennsylvania Dutch, Old South, Log Cabin Pioneer, Victorian New York, Western Cattle Days, California Monterey, Indian and Modern Girl series of interiors. In general the results were as follows: Lena Haubengrauber from Perkiomen Creek, Bucks County, Pennsylvania. Her rooms were filled with painted pine furniture and decorated with slip ware, spatter ware, chalk ware and "Gaudy Dutch." Her simple farm dress was fashioned of bright gingham. . . . Patricia Van Riis from Gramercy Park, Manhattan, New York City. Her suite was done in the style known as Biedermeier. The windows were draped with thirty yards of white velvet apiece and the chandelier in her sitting room had over eight hundred crystal pendants attached to it. She was dressed like an early "Gibson Girl."

And so on through,

> Dolores O'Rielly from Alta Vista, California. In order to save money, Wu Fong had moved her into the suite that had been occupied by Conchita, the Spanish girl. He merely substituted a Mission chair for the horsehide one with the steer-horn arms and called it "Monterey." Asa Goldstein was very angry when he found out, but Wu Fong refused to do anything more about it, because he felt that she was bound to be a losing proposition. The style . . . was not obviously enough American even in its most authentic forms. (125–26)

This is the stuff of potboilers and exposés on the white slave trade, written with all the loving attention to accoutrement that one might expect to find in the society pages of a Hearst paper. The obvious relish with which West recounts these details (not once, but twice [93–95, 125–29]) makes this scene a set piece within the novella. As such, Wu Fong's brothel constitutes a rune—a rune to which West will return again in *The Day of the Locust* (when the brothel will become the back lot of a Hollywood movie studio). In meantime, West has transformed Wu Fong into something of a Chinese Florenz Ziegfeld—making Fong's brothel the perverse realization of Ziegfeld's claim to "glorify the American girl."

Wu Fong's "Buy American campaign" is an elaborate send-up of Depression America's rediscovery, or rather—to West's way of thinking— prostitution, of its own culture. West's lengthy rendition of the props of sexual fantasy purports to offer us the spectacle of plenitude—historical plentitude, the ambience of history itself. After all, it was "Mr. Goldstein's boast that even Governor Windsor [should he chance to find himself in Betty Prail's New England boudoir] could not have found anything wrong with the design or furnishings" (94). In Fong's brothel, history— that is to say, American history—is intended to serve as an aphrodisiac for Fong's ethnic, immigrant clientele, the "orientals, Slavs, Latins, Celts and Semites" (125) who would otherwise remain excluded from "an hundred per centum" American past. Prostitution presumably offers them a substitute form of possession, the means by which they might quite literally "Buy American." But like the "pockmarked Armenian rug merchant from Malta" (95), they in turn become reduced to a gallery of ethnic stereotypes and grotesques constructed by the very history that elicits their desire.

Moreover, despite appearances these Daughters of the American Republic do not offer an invitation to erotic pleasure. Quite the opposite. One might recall, by way of explanation, Roland Barthes's own description of the striptease artist here: "the furs, the fans, the gloves, the feathers, the fishnet stockings, in short the whole spectrum of adornment constantly makes the living body return to the category of luxurious objects which surround man with a magical decor."[10] (This submersion of the "living body" into the objects that surround it is a process we will chronicle throughout *A Cool Million* where, at least in Lemuel Pitkin's case, the body becomes no more than a collection of detachable parts.) The accoutrement that surrounds Barthes's striptease artist and Fong's prostitutes everywhere betrays the secret truth of fetishization. Fetishization is a strategy by which the unconscious attempts to allay the fear of castration implied by the absence or lack of the phallus in the female. The fetishized object is almost always metonymically related to the knowledge the subject cannot bear to confront. In the case of Wu Fong's brothel, what the subject (or "john") cannot bear to confront is the absence of history itself. Castration comes from being "cut off" from the very past these articles represent. The "miscellaneous articles" with which Wu Fong surrounds, for example, "Powder River Rose from Carson's Store, Wyoming"—

"spurs, saddle blankets, straw, guitars, quirts, pearl-handled revolvers, hayforks and playing cards" (127)—do not symbolize a past so much as they "create" one. Or at least, they create a cartoon of the past by displacing whatever "real" history might have existed. And in the process, a once genuine American folklore, which defined a fabulous historical and regional diversity (so amply demonstrated in West's "American Chauve Souris"), is transformed into little more than sham culture for profit.

Unfortunately, some—like the Maharajah of Kanurani—are compelled to find this out the hard way. Instead of an erotic interlude in the "ship's cabin" with a "pithy thailer boy" surrounded by "sextants, compasses and other such gear," the maharajah watches mortified as Lem's false teeth and glass eye fall from his head and are "smashed to smithereens on the floor" (131), thereby revealing the gaping "wounds"—the *horror vaccui*—that were implicit from the very beginning. Confronted by the object of his desire lying in pieces before his very eyes, the maharajah is moved to wonder, "What kind of a pretty boy was this that came apart so horribly?" (132). The maharajah's question bears repeating for it goes to the heart of West's novella (and ultimately to the heart of the Depression itself): What kind of pretty boy (or for that matter, what kind of country) is this that comes apart so horribly? The answer to that question lies in an examination of the folklore that created them both and that eventually contributes to their dismantling as well: the folklore of capitalism.

I. THE FOLKLORE OF CAPITALISM

The folklore of capitalism goes by many names: the American Dream, the American Way, the Gospel of Success. It has evolved (or rather devolved) from its own Puritan beginnings (in the secular "calling" of the merchant); to the era of the Jacksonian "man on the make" (which saw the expansion of political liberty into economic laissez-faire); to the era of the robber baron and large-scale combinations (which effectively eliminated autonomy within a Brave New World of complex interdependency); to a philosophy of Mind Cure (which sought to surmount the experience of a fractured existence through "the power of positive thinking").[11] Despite these various permutations, no one would doubt that the "Horatio Alger story" is one of its principal texts. As West himself explained, "Only fools laugh at Horatio Alger and his poor boys who make good. The wiser man who thinks twice about that sterling author will realize that Alger is to America what Homer was to the Greeks."[12] (If that is so, then *A Cool Million* constitutes something of an anti-Iliad—which is not altogether surprising given that West began his career by examining the entrails of the Trojan horse.)

For nearly a century Alger's name has been synonymous with the Gospel of success. Yet despite Alger's status as a mythmaker (or perhaps because of it), his precise articulation of the Gospel of Success is often misunderstood. Alger has acquired an erroneous reputation as a spokesman for the gross materialism of the Gilded Age during which he wrote his novels. In fact, his fiction constitutes a nostalgic look backward toward an idealized antebellum world of mercantile capitalism that is imagined as organic, ordered, stable—and most of all, *whole*. As such it is deeply imbued with the values of a rural and relatively homogenous, Protestant worldview. In fact, Alger's rags-to-riches mythology is the supreme expression of the Populist mind, a last gasp attempt to hold the Gilded Age accountable to the ideals of individual achievement derived from an earlier era.[13]

Alger's protagonists are invariably young Anglo-Saxon males who have reluctantly left the rural circumstances of their youth owing to a "change in circumstances." The modern city is conceived as both a biblical Sodom and a source of "fortune." There, Alger's heroes encounter a succession of confidence men adept at manipulating a world of shifting signs. The protagonists must learn to read those signs and, to a certain extent, manipulate them themselves without violating an inner code of honor. Success is contingent upon a combination of "luck" and "pluck," which is essentially a secularization of the old Puritan metaphysics of grace and good works. That is to say, a young man must display all the Puritan virtues of diligence, frugality, and hard work—pluck. But at the same time he remains dependent upon God's grace, here constituted as luck, in order to *transform* that pluck into a means of salvation. If the source of that luck—e.g., the drowning son of a rich merchant—reads like a parody of its theological sources, it is no less efficacious for all of that. It is Alger's peculiar genius to have taken a conventional plot device of popular melodrama—the coincidence—and imbued it with metaphysical significance.

Success, when it finally arrives, is a good deal *less* than one might expect. Alger's heroes are not embryonic Rockefellers. (It is true that Rockefeller often depicted himself in Algeresque terms. But as Matthew Josephson observes, there was in Rockefeller "a feverish calculation, a sleepy strength, cruel, intense, terribly alert" that far exceeded anything an Alger farm boy could imagine, much less emulate.)[14] Rather, Alger's modest ideal of the successful man is closer to the antebellum farmer, artisan, or merchant than to the robber baron. The appeal of these figures lies in their relative autonomy from the thoroughly mediated world of finance capitalism that characterized the Gilded Age. Moreover, the degree of their wealth is nowhere near the extravagant standards set during that era. (An intrepid scholar "in a mathematical mood" once figured out that the average fortune of an Alger hero is not much more than $10,000.)[15] For Alger, wealth is hardly the point. Upward mobility is what matters. It is for this reason that we always leave Alger's hero *in medias res*. Having seen him to the point where he has managed to secure a junior position under the watchful eye of a wealthy benefactor, the reader can close the volume secure in the knowledge that Alger's hero will continue to "work and win" according to his merits. This at any rate is the folklore of capitalism—or at least Alger's version of it.

A Cool Million incorporates (or plagiarizes without apology) many of Alger's most famous motifs and conventions: e.g., the humble, rural origins of the protagonist; the arrival of the naif in the city; the necessity for and danger of "confidence" in strangers; the careful tally of accumulating assets; the frequent tests of character that prove the worthiness of the protagonist when (never "if") success arrives; the life-threatening situation that puts the man of wealth in debt to our young hero and hence sets him on the road to success. West casts all of this in Alger's banal, paratactical style, punctuated by frequent interruptions, which allow the author the opportunity to draw a "suitable" moral exemplum. Indeed, the "gentle reader" is treated to a bellyful of maxims, adages, and truisms to live by. There are admonitions against loitering (68), morbidity (90), despair (98), as well as against the use of alcohol or tobacco (95). And finally, there is Alger's irrepressible faith in the American Dream itself, or at least West's parodic version of it: "Don't believe the fools who tell you that the poor man hasn't got a chance to get rich any more," Shagpoke Whipple counsels our young hero. "Office boys still marry their employers' daughters. Shipping clerks are still becoming presidents of railroads. . . . Despite the Communists and their vile propaganda against individualism, this is still the golden land of opportunity. Oil wells are still found in people's back yards. There are still gold mines hidden away in our mountain fastnesses. America is . . ." (98).

Unlike Whipple, Goldstein, and Wu Fong (who manipulate this folklore for their own selfish ends), Lemuel Pitkin accepts it all without a murmur of skepticism. This faith in the American Dream makes him the unwitting victim of a series of misadventures. When, for example, Lem observes a runaway carriage bearing down on a wealthy old gentleman and his beautiful daughter, he acts promptly to save them in true Alger fashion. Like Sylvanus Snodgrasse, poet and pickpocket, we cannot help but be struck by "the classicality—if I may be permitted a neologism— of [the] performance. Poor Boy, Flying Team, Banker's Daughter . . . it's in the real American tradition." (107). Whatever the "classicality" of the performance, the results are more aptly described as low comedy. It seems that the wealthy old gentleman "misunderstood the nature of our hero's efforts and thought that the poor boy was a careless groom who had let his charges get out of hand" (104). Thus, instead of rewarding Lem with the hand of his daughter and a position in the bank, the gentleman wants him arrested. Lem just barely escapes arrest, but not before he is kicked in the groin and pickpocketed by the very poet who sang his praises. As if that is not enough, his eye is surgically removed owing to the injuries he sustained in performing his heroic deed.

This scene sets the pattern for a succession of Algeresque encounters where West undercuts the expectations usually associated with Alger's novels. In each case, Lem acts according to the guidelines set out in the Gospel of Success only to find an obscene disparity between its dictates and social reality. Instead of domesticating the world to Lem's purposes, these guidelines obscure its reality, leaving him grotesquely vulnerable. The reader watches in horror as Lem's vow to "go and do as Rockefeller and Ford had done" (75) leads to his gradual "dismantling"—the loss of teeth, eye, thumb, leg, and scalp. Eventually Lem ends up living in a piano crate beside a lake in Central Park (171)—the very image of the "forgotten man" during the Depression.

West refuses to patronize the "forgotten man" after the fashion of the thirties. Instead, the novelist depicts him as a "stooge," a sideshow freak in a vaudeville routine called "Fifteen Minutes of Furious Fun with Belly Laffs Galore." After examining the "gray bone of [Pitkin's] skull [which] showed plainly where he had been scalped," as well as his wooden leg, which "had been carved with initials twined hearts and other innocent insignia by mischievous boys," the comics declare themselves quite pleased with their find: "'You're a wow!' . . . Boy, oh boy, wait till the puspockets and fleapits get a load of you" (172). Pitkin's role as a "stooge" requires him to stand between Riley and Robins, affecting a "sober dignity" while they run through their vaudeville routine. They engage in a "breezy crossfire of smart cracks." But whenever a joke fails to get a laugh the vaudevillians turn on our hero and beat him mercilessly on the head with rolled up newspapers:

Their object was to knock off his toupee or to knock out his teeth and
eye. . . . Then Lem . . . bent over and with sober dignity took from the
box at his feet, which contained a large assortment of false hair, teeth,
and eyes, whatever he needed to replace the things that had been
knocked off or out. . . . For a final curtain, they brought out an enormous wooden mallet labeled "The Works" and with it completely
demolished our hero. (173–174)

This is success of a sort, although not the sort our hero imagined for himself when he first set off from Ottsville. Despite a rather severe headache,
Lem is not displeased with the results. "After all," West observes dryly,
"with millions out of work, he had no cause to complain" (174).

The dismantling of this all-American Humpty Dumpty is accompanied
by a concomitant fragmentation of discourse. Just as Pitkin's mangled
body lacks the integrity it once possessed, so too the American Dream fails
to retain the powerful integrity and scope it once possessed. Like Balso
Snell in West's first novella, Lem must make his way through a tangled
labyrinth of discourse, only now that labyrinth is the "American Scene"
itself: a grotesque fantasy world of mythology, folktales, half-baked truisms, and clichés—the *disjecta membra,* one might say, of the American
Dream. This breakdown of narrative unity results in a carnival that might
in other contexts prove *enabling.* But for Lem it is quite literally *disabling.*
Instead of demystifying the American Dream and thereby liberating Lem
from its narrative compulsions, the carnivalization of the American Scene
results in a stunning loss of coherence. Severed from the animating vision
of America's central mythology, these narrative fragments produce only a
series of blind alleys in which Lem, half blind himself, wanders haplessly.

For those Americans who stumbled along behind Lemuel Pitkin during the thirties this situation was almost too much to bear—producing
what the Native American revolutionary Chief Satinpenny aptly describes as a "soul-corroding doubt" (156). Many responded to that doubt
by attempting to reassert the original claims of the American Dream with
a vehemence that bordered on hysteria. The reasons for this are not far to
seek. As we have seen, the rags-to-riches mythology has served as the animating ethos of America almost since its inception. To doubt its efficacy
is to raise doubts about the raison d'être of America itself. It is precisely
because the Gospel of Success is about more than merely making money,
because it is about an entire worldview—a cosmology of manners,
morals, and ideals—that so much is at stake. That is the reason why
Americans won't—can't—let it go without a wholesale psychic trauma,
the pathology of which bears a distinct resemblance to fascism.

2. LEMUEL PITKIN'S EXQUISITE CORPSE

The foregoing goes a long way toward explaining why Lemuel Pitkin "comes apart so horribly." But if *A Cool Million* were solely a critique of Horatio Alger, then it would not be much different from a host of other, similar complaints that have been lodged against "that worthy" almost from the moment he began writing. Ultimately, *A Cool Million* offers much more than a critique of the Gospel of Success; among other things, it analyzes the problem of representation in a society that could no longer depend on its own founding mythology. The key to that analysis lies in the subtitle of the novella, "The Dismantling of Lemuel Pitkin." Like the notion of decomposition in *Balso Snell*, dismantling is the bad joke around which the novella revolves. In fact, one might say that *A Cool Million* is composed of little else but a series of comic dismantlings to which West returns again and again like an old vaudeville routine. But more is at stake here than bad jokes and old vaudeville routines. Once again the body serves as a somatic compass, much the way it did in *Balso Snell*. This time, however, it is not noses and feet (high and low), but arms, legs, teeth, and fingers (part and whole) that are at the center of the novella's concerns. This perverse dismantling of the social "body"— Lemuel Pitkin is after all an All-American hero—suggests a loss of wholeness and with it the loss of the capacity to represent the social totality.

Needless to say, this radical dismantling of the social whole posed a challenge for America in general and the novel in particular—especially if the latter was to fulfill its traditional cognitive function of mapping social reality the way, say, the classic nineteenth-century realist tradition had done for its readers. West, however, refused to accept that challenge, or at least one might say he refused to accept the necessity for reconstructing social reality by indulging in idealized pastoral fantasies of organicism, wholeness, immediacy, presence, and innocence. Instead, *A Cool Million* remains mired in their material opposites: a sargasso of artifice, contingency, mediation, absence, and complicity.

Perhaps the best explanation for West's refusal to overcome this dissolution of social reality is to be found not in *A Cool Million*, but in the dream sequence from *Miss Lonelyhearts*. There Miss Lonelyhearts finds himself standing in front of a pawnshop window "full of fur coats, diamond rings, watches, shotguns, fishing tackle, [and] mandolins." These disparate, forfeited items—which Miss Lonelyhearts aptly describes as the "paraphernalia of suffering"—serve as an abject emblem for the pain and loss of the Depression itself. Burdened by a keen sense of responsibility to minister to that loss, Miss Lonelyhearts indulges himself in a fantasy in which he attempts to transform this Depression-era sargasso into a grandiose series of redemptive designs: "A trumpet, marked to sell for $2.49 gave the call to battle and Miss Lonelyhearts plunged into the fray. First he formed a phallus of old watches and rubber boots, then a heart of umbrellas and trout flies, then a diamond of musical instruments and derby hats, after these a circle, triangle, square, swastika. . . ."[16]

Nothing could sum up West's social vision more succinctly than this. Miss Lonelyhearts' assemblage of parts—old watches, umbrellas, and trout flies—is an attempt to create some ideal of order or wholeness, whether it be in the form of a phallus (sex), a heart (love), a diamond (wealth), or even, as we have seen in *The Dream Life of Balso Snell,* a perfect circle. But Miss Lonelyhearts knows—as Lemuel Pitkin does not—that such aspirations are doomed to failure. Indeed, the progression from circle to square to swastika betrays an abiding suspicion of all these idealizing tendencies. If the circle recalls the failed geometry of Western culture's most basic principles, the swastika anticipates the rage for order that threatened to overwhelm America itself in the absence or failure of these other organizing schemes.

For West, then, the "paraphernalia of suffering" and the "dismantling of Lemuel Pitkin" are both a sign of capitalism's corrosive power *as well as proof against its own pretenses and evasions.* By that I mean, its very corrosiveness prevents its recuperation. It is important to emphasize that because, as I mentioned at the outset of this book, West has been accused of submitting to the very processes of reification he chronicles so intently. In *A Cool Million,* however, West offers one of the most subtle analyses of reification and its deleterious effects available in American literature. And here again, the key to that analysis lies in the subtitle of the book.

One might have expected West to speak of the "Dismembering of Lemuel Pitkin" rather than his dismantling. The substitution of a mechanistic discourse for the expected, organic one alerts us to the tension that invigorates the narrative. Indeed, throughout *A Cool Million,* West courts a deliberate and fundamental confusion between the organic and the inorganic, or rather, to use the terminology of the novella, the "animate" and the "inanimate." Hence, the grotesque dismemberment of Lem's teeth, eyes, legs, and scalp, each of which is replaced with inanimate parts—false teeth, a glass eye, a wooden leg, a toupee—until he is neither, as it were, fish nor fowl, neither human nor machine. This results in an ontological confusion of the first order.

It may be illuminating to recall that the substitution of the inanimate for the animate was a common ploy used by West's Dada predecessors in their efforts to deflate a variety of idealist and humanist pretensions (art, subjectivity, true love). One finds these body-machines everywhere: from Duchamp's bachelor who "grinds his own chocolate" to Picabia's "portraits" of Stieglitz, De Zayas, and *une jeune fille américaine* (the latter portrayed as a spark plug). The surrealists were similarly fascinated with what they liked to call "exquisite corpses"—primarily in the form of mannequins and automatons. The reasons are not far to seek. As Hal Foster has observed, "the mannequin evokes the remaking of the body . . . as a commodity, just as the automaton, its complement in the surrealist image repertoire, evokes the reconfiguring of the body . . . as a machine."[17] For Dada and surrealism, as well as for West himself, these body-machines offer a potent meditation on the dangers of reification. One might say that the dismantling of Lemuel Pitkin is directly attributable to a society in which the animate consistently becomes inanimate and vice versa. In the process, each becomes subject to the laws of the other.

Although the "Horatio Alger story" presents itself as the living embodiment of the American Dream, it is a machine like any other—a "narrative machine" that offers something of a do-it-yourself kit for the self-*made* man. The driving force or engine of this narrative machine—the farm boy or bootblack who "works and wins"—is not the organic entity he appears to be. Rather, the Alger hero is a type, and as such he/it is generic, standardized, infinitely reproducible. West makes no attempt to breathe life into this ideological construction. Instead, he foregrounds its status as such. Since Lemuel Pitkin is a machine, his dismantling inspires neither pity nor indignation, thereby making West's hero unsuitable as a cause célèbre or an object of nostalgia. This may explain much of the discomfort with which this novella was received during the thirties. By casting his protagonist as a machine, West deliberately sets out to prevent his readers from retreating to a sentimental humanism that functioned to recuperate liberal capitalism under the guise of criticizing it.

If West fails to provide his readers with the comforts they have come to expect, he does so in order to enlarge the possibilities of his own criticism. Nowhere is this more aptly demonstrated than in the "Animate and Inanimate Hideosities" on display in the "Chamber of American Horrors" (160)—a scene that serves as an emblem for the novella as a whole. As its title suggests, the show is divided into two parts. The "animate" part of the show reads like a parody of West's ambitions for "American Chauve Souris." Instead of a ballet of a whale hunt or a Moravian Easter celebration, this "Pageant of America" (subtitled "A Curse on Columbus") consists of "a series of short sketches in which Quakers were shown being branded, Indians brutalized and cheated, Negroes sold, children sweated to death" (163). The "pageant" culminates in a "small playlet" that presents the melodramatic story of a poor widow cheated out of her life savings by a "sleek salesman" from the "Indefatigable Investment Company." In the final scene the "sleek salesman," now a millionaire, gingerly sidesteps the dead bodies of the widow and her family while worthless South American bonds swirl in the wind. The "master of ceremonies" for this particular exhibition, Sylvanus Snodgrasse, "tried to make obvious the relationship between these sketches and the 'inanimate' exhibit by a little speech in which he claimed that the former had resulted in the latter" (164). Following Snodgrasse's lead, we might expect that a history of lies is likely to produce objects that are themselves lies, and vice versa. And that is just what we find.

Thus, side-by-side with this troubled history, the unsuspecting patriot finds a room filled with a rather curious array of "inanimate" objects, or rather, "hideosities." The chief characteristic of these objects, we are told, lies "in the great skill with which their materials had been disguised." Thus, "paper had been made to look like wood, wood like rubber, rubber like steel, steel like cheese, cheese like glass, and, finally, glass like paper." The narrator continues, "Other tables carried instruments whose purposes were dual and sometimes triple or even sextuple. Among the most ingenious were pencil sharpeners that could also be used as earpicks, can openers as hair brushes. Then, too, there was a large variety of objects whose real uses had been cleverly camouflaged. The visitor saw flower pots that were really victrolas, revolvers that held candy, candy that held collar buttons and so forth" (163).

With this exhibit, the confusion that we have been chronicling above becomes complete. To the promiscuous mingling of the animate and the inanimate that resulted in the obscene detachment of parts and wholes, we must now add the confusion of form and function, signifier and referent. Thus, rubber is made to look like steel, steel like cheese, cheese like glass, and so on, in an endless daisy chain in which nothing is what it appears to be. Here as elsewhere *A Cool Million,* or rather America itself, threatens to dissolve into a world that is disconnected, multiple, substanceless.

One would hope that a world so thoroughly dismantled might offer manifold possibilities for reconstruction. At first glance, the flowerpots that turn out to be victrolas and the can openers that also function as hairbrushes recall the *objets trouvés* that so delighted the surrealists. Indeed, the playful manipulation of the signifier would seem to offer a certain liberation from the tyranny of its referent. But the Chamber of American Horror offers no entrée into a privileged realm of wit and playfulness. Instead, play serves as a form of obfuscation and denial. Just as guns are turned into candy holders, Indians, Negroes, and children are turned into chattel. These misleading forms and signifiers thus hide a more complicated indebtedness to a social history rife with betrayal and violence.

The reason for this state of affairs is not far to seek. For mixed in with the exhibits mentioned above are "an equally large number of manufactured articles"—"clever cigarette lighters," "superb fountain pens," as well as a variety of other commodities (156). The presence of these commodities among the hideosities (both animate and inanimate) described above betrays the source of their disfigurement. Commodities are by definition "useless." That is to say, they have converted use value into exchange value, and in the process they have ruptured the integrity of the sign. Thus, steel might as well be cheese; there is, after all, little difference between them—at least insofar as both are sundered from their use value in order to be homogenized into commodities that can be readily exchanged.[18] These queer, inanimate hideosities are, in fact, the objective correlative for the genuine "hideosity" of the commodity—the token of a world in which everything is subject to exchange.

The answer to the maharajah's question should be clear enough by now: In a world of parts that seem to bear no necessary relation to one another, the pursuit of "wholes" (whether it be a usable past, an organic society, the commodity, or the body itself) results only in the parodic inversion of "holes." (We are back to a version of the pun that animated *Balso Snell*.) Meanwhile, the only viable "wholes" that are to be found in *A Cool Million*—such as the antique store, the brothel, and Whipple's hundred percent American past—are deceptive, coercive, and ultimately fascist.

3. THE IRON LAW OF EXCHANGE

The ubiquity of this iron law of exchange is amply and conclusively demonstrated in an article by John Spivak for the *New Masses,* on William Dudley Pelley, whose fascist organization—the Silver Shirts—served as the inspiration for *A Cool Million*.[19] The article was entitled, "Silver Shirts Among the Gold," and there is little doubt that West read it.[20] In it, Spivak interviews one of Pelley's lieutenants (although he calls himself a captain) in charge of the California chapter of the Silver Shirts, Captain Eugene R. Case. Spivak's interview reveals Case and Pelley to be mercenary demagogues without principle or agenda beyond a desire to exploit the fears of their Depression-wracked audience for what they hope will be "plenty of dough." ("'To summarize it,' I [Spivak] said, 'you are a soldier of fortune after the coconuts.' 'That's right,' he [Case] agreed amiably.")

The best example of this cynical amorality lies in Case's frank admission about the economic motives behind his use of anti-Semetic rhetoric:

> "You got to get the suckers excited about something. Christ! You can't get a gentile excited about a gentile. You got to give them something to get mad about. It's business. What the hell! The official shirtmaker for the Silver Legion is a Jew. Look—"

He pointed to an advertisement in the Silver Ranger:

MILTON'S TOGGERY
Official Shirt Maker for
Silver Legion
Complete Line of
Gent's Furnishings
904 West Second Street
Phone Madison 3223
Room 662   730 So. Grand Ave.

The irony of all this was not lost on West, who incorporated the advertisement into *A Cool Million* in the following form:

EZRA SILVERBLATT

Official Tailor
to the
National Revolutionary Party

Coonskin hats with extra long tails
deerskin shirts with or without fringes,
blue jeans, moccasins, squirrel rifles,
everything for the American Fascist
at rock bottom prices. 30% off for Cash. (113)

This appropriation not only confirms West's indebtedness to Spivak's article but offers an illuminating insight into the likely characteristics of a homegrown fascist movement. What is most striking about this advertisement is the suzerainty of the profit motive *über alles*. In America, apparently even the most virulent hatred is reducible to a commodity in which both the persecutor and the persecuted profit (almost) equally. Nothing, it seems, withstands the bathos of the commodity—not even fascism. "It's business," Case observes. "What the hell!"

EPILOGUE

1. A Cool Million: *Starring Bob Hope*

In 1934, the Joyce-Selznick Agency sold the film rights to *A Cool Million* to Columbia Studios. It is doubtful that Harry Cohn, Columbia's notoriously irascible president, bothered to read the book that his underlings had purchased on his behalf. If he had, he might have indulged himself in one of the tantrums for which he was justifiably famous.[21] And with good reason. Columbia's own story department summed up the book's theme thus: "Honesty will buy you pain and disgrace."[22] This premise is so thoroughly at odds with the healthy-mindedness of Hollywood that it is hard to imagine what Columbia's executives saw in it. West would eventually describe the story as unfilmable.[23] He was right. And yet no less than four different writers would take a crack at it, including West himself.[24] The project was eventually dropped, but not before it was considered—in a moment worthy of Kenneth Anger's *Hollywood Babylon*— as "a vehicle for Eddie Cantor or Bob Hope."[25] Imagine that (if you can):

A COOL MILLION
starring
BOB HOPE

Long before such absurdities were contemplated, however, *A Cool Million* languished in the files of Columbia's story department. It did not elicit any interest for nearly six years, until West himself returned to it in September of 1940. By that time, he had become moderately successful as a screenwriter in Hollywood. He was savvy enough to know that he could not simply cast *A Cool Million* into screenplay form without alteration. If he was to have any hope of selling it, the story would have to be reconceived almost entirely.[26] The result—a fourteen-page "adaptation" written with his partner, Boris Ingster—deviates substantially from *A Cool Million*.[27]

The adaptation does retain some recognizable elements from *A Cool Million*. As in the novella, Joey Williams (formerly Lemuel Pitkin) leaves Oatsville (formerly Ottsville) determined to make his way in the world, only to find himself down and out in New York City—the victim of a picked pocket and an arrest stemming from his attempt to halt the runaway horse of a banker's daughter. But these preliminary scenes only prepare us for more important developments that take the plot in an entirely new direction. Thanks to a letter of introduction given to him by the principal of his high school, Williams manages to land a job as a clerk in a bank. When the chief accountant takes a vacation, Williams is asked to fill in. Joey is overjoyed by this vindication of his faith. But the strain of overwork causes him to make several clerical errors. It is not long before the bank president notices a discrepancy. Joey is called into the president's office and told that a million dollars is missing. Since Joey is responsible for the bookkeeping, the president assumes that he took the money. Fearing a scandal and a run on the bank, the president does not wish to have Joey arrested. Instead he bargains with Joey over cigars and drinks.

All of a sudden, Joey Williams finds himself in the unaccustomed position of being treated with enormous respect. Once news of the theft hits the papers, Joey becomes something of a celebrity. He is extended credit all over the city—including a room at the Waldorf. This prompts Joey's rueful complaint that in contradistinction to Alger's creed, "no one cared how you got your million as long as you had it."[28] There was, of course, never any theft to begin with. As soon as the insurance company discovers that fact, Joey is unceremoniously dumped by the bank and his creditors. But before this occurs, Joey cleverly uses his credit to open up a brokerage account on Wall Street. Thanks to the advice of a tramp with an eye for good stocks, Joey manages to turn that nonexistent million dollars into a tidy sum of money.

The most likely source of inspiration for West and Ingster's adaptation was the screwball comedy, a genre that was then immensely popular with movie-going audiences.[29] At the heart of classic screwball comedies like *It Happened One Night* (1934), *My Man Godfrey* (1936), *Easy Living* (1937), and *Holiday* (1938) is an unlikely set of circumstances (often a case of mistaken identity) in which a common man is propelled into a higher social class. In each case, this occasion allows for the incursion of populist values into the heretofore sacrosanct realm of the "idle rich." In the sentimental world of this populist genre, class conflict is rewritten as a conflict between two headstrong personalities—more often than not, between a man and a woman (one wealthy and one poor) who are in love with one another but do not know it yet or cannot bring themselves to accept it. Each must demonstrate his/her essential humanity through antic or "screwball" behavior before class distinctions (like the "Walls of Jericho" in *It Happened One Night*) can come tumbling down.[30]

In some instances—notably, *Mr. Deeds Goes to Town* (1936), *Nothing Sacred* (1937), *Mr. Smith Goes to Washington* (1939), *Meet John Doe* (1941)—the screwball comedy extends its meditation on class to include an exploration of celebrity as well. Here an emissary from the American village is transformed into the center of national attention, exposing the cupidity and hollowness of the media's celebrity-making machinery. This situation ultimately leads to the redemption of the cynical urban newspaper reporter (usually female) who is responsible for creating that sensation in the first place. In this pastoral version of the screwball comedy, the resolution of class conflict is supplanted by a victory of populist, rural values over the decadent modernity of the city.[31] As concern over class conflict in the early and mid-thirties gave way to the threat of war from abroad, this version of the screwball comedy championed the American Way of Life with a patriotism that verged on chauvinism. Certainly West and Ingster's adaptation fell well short of this celebration of country or class unity. But as we shall see, West and Ingster laid the groundwork for subsequent revisions that would refine their adaptation into a full-fledged screwball comedy of its own.

2. Mr. Deeds, Mr. Smith, and Mr. Pitkin?

West and Ingster's adaptation of *A Cool Million* was assigned to Columbia's preeminent screenwriter, Sidney Buchman. Buchman had been the author of a number of successful screwball comedies during the thirties, notably *Theodora Goes Wild* (1936), *The Awful Truth* (1937), *Holiday* (1938), and, most famously, Frank Capra's *Mr. Smith Goes to Washington* (1939). The selection of Buchman, on the heels of his tremendous success with *Smith*, indicates Columbia's enthusiasm for the project. Part of the studio's enthusiasm was surely derived from the story's obvious similarities with *Smith*, which was in turn patterned after its even more successful precursor, *Mr. Deeds Goes to Town*—both Columbia pictures. Like them, West and Ingster's adaptation follows the fate of a young naif, who embodies America's most sacred ideals, as he confronts a decadent, urban milieu. Columbia revived this project with an eye toward duplicating this successful formula. But there may also have been an ulterior motive. Owing to a disagreement with Harry Cohn, Frank Capra—the most successful director in the studio's history—had recently severed his relationship with Columbia. It is possible that Cohn was hoping to lure Capra back by assigning his top writer to a project that was, in many ways, strikingly similar to the director's previous and most successful movies. In any event, what is clear is that under Sidney Buchman's hand, *A Cool Million* was well on its way to becoming a worthy successor to *Deeds* and *Smith*—whether Capra directed it or not.[32]

Buchman made no attempt to hide his efforts to craft his treatment of *A Cool Million* in the image of both *Deeds* and *Smith*. Buchman's version

of Joey Williams is the spitting image of Longfellow Deeds and Jefferson
Smith. Like them he goes to town, or rather to the metropolis, only to find
more than he bargained for. Like them, his resolute faith in the ideals of
the American system eventually triumphs (though, as we shall see, with
far less certainty). Buchman's primary contribution to the evolution of the
project, however, lies in his attempt to heighten the opposition between
rural and metropolitan values that is at the heart of both *Deeds* and *Smith,*
as well as the Horatio Alger story. That opposition serves as the basis for
a series of contrasts between honesty and falsehood, simplicity and so-
phistication, hard work and speculation, substance and appearance. In
each case the former is identified with the small town while the latter is
identified with the city. Those opposing values eventually come face-to-
face in a climactic, final confrontation.[33] In a scene that anticipates *Meet
John Doe,* Joey returns home to Oatsville (still a millionaire) in order to
receive the adulation of the townspeople. Surrounded by "American flags,
tin pans and horns" (31),[34] Joey makes a shattering declaration. Instead
of offering his success as proof of their faith in Horatio Alger's creed,
Joey insists that his success is in every sense a violation of it:

> He had left Oatsville with impeccable honesty, with industry, with fair
> dealing—and with the respect with which all these things ordinarily
> endow a man. This was his equipment and this was the equipment
> that he put to work on leaving Oatsville. And was that how he suc-
> ceeded? No! NOBODY WAS INTERESTED IN IT. HE RECEIVED
> NO RESPECT. IN FACT, NOTHING BUT CONTEMPT. HONESTY
> AND INDUSTRY WERE EVIDENTLY A DRUG ON THE MARKET.
> PEOPLE CARED ABOUT OTHER VALUES. THE RESPECT THAT
> EVERY MAN SEEKS FOR HIMSELF—THE ADMIRATION OF HIS
> QUALITIES AND APPLAUSE FOR HIS ABILITIES, THIS RESPECT
> HE SUCCEEDED IN ACQUIRING ONLY WHEN, ALL ELSE FAIL-
> ING, *HE STOLE* A MILLION DOLLARS! (34)

The citizens of Oastville are outraged by this "right uppercut to American values." Joey has, they complain, "shattered the props of the great
American legend" (35); they fear his confession will "erode the foundations of the entire civilization" (37). But of course, Joey has not betrayed
America; America has betrayed him. His "false" confession merely reveals this scandalous state of affairs. As Buchman explains, "Joey has
made his assertion for what value it may be to young people and to men
who run the world; it is his way of calling attention to the depravity the
world has sunk to and to the need to alter values" (38).

Joey's "confession" closes what should be the third and final act of the adaptation. But there is another act yet to come, this one dictated largely by the Hays Commission.[35] West and Ingster's adaptation saddled Buchman with as many problems as it solved, most notably the question of how to evaluate Joey's dubious route to success. Though Joey does not actually steal any money, he does misrepresent his assets in order to obtain credit. It does not matter that he was almost entirely passive in this regard; his actions are technically a violation of the law. As Joey himself explains, in language that might have been taken directly from the Hays Commission itself,

> "If you look in Webster's dictionary you see that 'to steal' means to have come into possession of something unlawfully, unrightfully. Whether I had that million in my possession or not, it was the belief on the part of many people that I did have it that brought me opportunity, respect, and success. Therefore, to all intents and purposes, I *had* a million dollars. And since I had no lawful right to it, I had *stolen* it!" (39)

Situations like this one were a cause of particular concern for the Hays Commission. In the "General Principles" of *The Motion Picture Production Code of 1930,* it was argued that unlike books and plays, which are "intended for only *certain classes of people,* the exhibitor's theatres are for the masses, for the cultivated and the rude, mature and immature, self-restrained and inflammatory, young and old, law-respecting and criminal" (italics not mine). Consequently, "the motion picture has special moral obligations" to refrain from presenting material that might appeal to the baser motives of what were thought to be the weaker members of this audience. In light of such obligations, it is clear that Joey Williams is, at the very least, a bad example. His "success" violates the first tenet of the code's "Working Principles": "No picture should lower the moral standards of those who see it. This is done when evil is made to appear *attractive,* and good is made to appear *unattractive.*"[36]

In addition, Joey's dramatic "confession" before the citizens of Oatsville merely compounds the problem. However well-intentioned he might be, his words are potentially inflammatory and likely to inspire emulation. (After all, Joey did not receive any respect until he had stolen a million dollars.) Indeed, his confession engenders the very contempt for "honesty and industry" he seeks to criticize, prompting the district attorney in the story (or is it perhaps the Hays Office?) to wonder whether Joey "realizes the effect of his words upon the social morale" (37). Buchman's problems with the adaptation did not end here. Even an admission of guilt and remorse might not have been enough to satisfy the Production Code. If the movie were to portray Joey's salad days on misappropriated credit with all the comic gusto Buchman could muster, it would be in danger of violating yet another tenet of the Production Code: "Even if later on the evil is condemned or punished, it must not be allowed to appear so attractive that the emotions are drawn to desire or approve so strongly that later they forget the condemnation and remember only the apparent joy of the sin."[37]

According to Jay Martin, Buchman was so frustrated with these complications that he eventually called West and Ingster into his office to ask them "for advice on how to make [a] movie from the story. He shook his head and asked over and over, 'How do you do it?' Gleefully, they told him that he simply *couldn't* film it."[38] Buchman, however, was not so easily dissuaded. In the final pages of the adaptation, he tried to answer each and every violation of the Production Code adumbrated above. Did the Production Code warn against the presentation of evil in such a way as to "inspire others with a desire for imitation"?[39] Buchman not only acknowledged the legitimacy of this concern, he incorporated it into the story as a plot development. Thus, as a result of Joey's devastating slander of Horatio Alger and his values, we learn that "there was a rash of bank robberies in the country. In two cases, the motive could be traced to the inflammatory utterance of Joey Williams. . . . demonstrat[ing] how dangerous Joey's statements were . . ." (39). Did the Production Code insist that evil not be "presented alluringly"?[40] Buchman saw to it that Joey was punished: "The only thing to do to counteract such a dangerous influence," he argued, "was to prove that theft does not pay—that patent dishonesties in society never pay. . . . the law must exact its toll" (39). Accordingly, Joey is arrested and tried for his crimes.

Having satisfied the Hays Commission, Buchman also had to satisfy his audience who would not accept Joey's conviction. This required some eleventh-hour theatrics. Following the conventions of screwball comedy, the hero's martyrdom wins the heart of the skeptical, female urbanite (Angela) who "through him [has] come to see values she didn't know existed." Joey also wins over her cynical, wealthy father (Silone), whose underworld connections enable him to find the real culprit. The man responsible for stealing the million dollars—a fellow clerk at the bank—is brought into the courtroom and exposed "at the very moment that Joey was [about to be] sentenced" (42). This vindication sets the world to rights once again by restoring harmony between the letter and the spirit of the law.

While these developments answer the needs of the plot, they do not address the primary thematic concern of the movie: the status of Horatio Alger and his Gospel of Success. Buchman takes this up in the final scene of the adaptation. Tabor (the tramp with an eye for good stocks) and Silone (a shady businessman) each attempt to persuade Joey to pursue fame and fortune with them. But Joey turns them both down. "He doesn't approve of the market nor of Silone's enterprises. He would like to find a job—any honest work—to start from the bottom—his recommendations being exceptional industry and honesty" (43). This decision, however, does not affect Angela's commitment to him. She is convinced that they can "make an excellent start on about twenty-five dollars a week." The story ends as "she and Joey retire, holding hands, to discuss a budget" (44).

With this conclusion, it appears as though we are right back where we started. And to a certain extent we are. Unable to find a place for Horatio Alger in the speculative world of the stock market or the businessman, Joey is lamely forced to reassert the values with which he began, values that have thus far failed to produce anything but pain and humiliation. "Is the boy crazy—after all he's been through?" Buchman asks. "To that last question, Joey very simply rejoins that if values are wrong in the world, you don't help things any by going the wrong way. You simply put every little bit of honesty to work—and it's like drops of water on a stone—those little drops of honesty will finally crack anything" (43). Despite the merits of these final sentiments, there is little question that they represent a retreat from the buoyant optimism of Horatio Alger. The potent faith that allowed the Alger hero to venture forth into the city, secure in the knowledge that he would "work and win," here begins to sound more like that of a martyred saint, condemned to wander alone through the desert of rural America.

Curiously, Buchman was unable or unwilling to supply the ringing endorsement of the American system he managed to contrive so convincingly in *Mr. Smith Goes to Washington.* What he offers instead is a minimal code of personal morality within a larger world of American society that is seen as indifferent, if not actively hostile, to that morality. Buchman was not alone in this conundrum. It was, one might say, the result of a crisis that had developed within the screwball comedy itself. As the genre evolved through the thirties, its "authors" gained a deeper awareness of the contradictions implicit in the genre's subject matter: the fundamental incompatibility of rural and metropolitan values they sought to bring together under the sign of the Horatio Alger story. This made it increasingly difficult to provide a resolution that was either emotionally or aesthetically compelling. We have seen how such difficulties resulted in the cumbersome plot machinations and the still more cumbersome attempts to explain them in Buchman's adaptation of *A Cool Million*. Those same difficulties would plague *Meet John Doe* as well, forcing Capra and Riskin to experiment with several different endings—none of them satisfactory.

Ten years later, Sidney Buchman would experience the darker side of the populist pastoral he tried to rehabilitate in his adaptation of *A Cool Million*. Like Mr. Smith, Mr. Buchman also went to Washington—not as wide-eyed senator, but as an "unfriendly" witness before the House Un-American Activities Committee. During the course of that hearing, Buchman testified that he had joined the Communist Party in 1938 because he felt that it was the most effective way to combat fascism. (He subsequently lost faith in the party and left it in 1945.) Despite intense pressure, Buchman refused to name names, arguing that "it is repugnant to an American to inform."[41] But his admission of involvement with the Communist Party was enough to make it impossible for him to work in Hollywood for the next ten years, effectively ruining his career.[42]

Chapter Six

The Clichés Are Having a Ball
The Day of the Locust

PROLOGUE

"What about the Barber in Purdue? He's been cutting hair all day and he's tired. . . . What the Barber wants is amour and glamour."

It is tempting to think of *The Day of the Locust* as a redaction of J. K. Huysmans' *A Rebours,* with the Barber in Purdue as demotic heir to the dandy, and the back lot of a movie studio as the absurd analogue to the dandy's boudoir. The Barber in Purdue is the slightly condescending name by which the public or "mass man" (a condescending term in itself) is known in Hollywood.[1] "What the barber wants," so we are told, "is amour and glamour." And like the dandy, he depends on artifice—or rather, an artificial paradise conjured up by Hollywood—to provide it for him. In lines that uncannily anticipate West's description of a studio back lot in *The Day of the Locust* Huysmans writes, "there is not a single one of [nature's] inventions, deemed so subtle and sublime, that human ingenuity cannot manufacture; no moonlit Forest of Fontainebleau that cannot be reproduced by stage scenery under floodlighting; no cascade that cannot be imitated to perfection by hydraulic engineering; no rock that papier-mâché cannot counterfeit."[2]

The power of artifice to overcome nature is taken by Huysmans' Des Esseintes as the supreme mark of human genius. But the dandy's heady tribute to artifice belies the cautionary tale that Huysmans has buried in *A Rebours.* The jewel-encrusted turtle that Des Esseintes imports to adorn his living room dies, an ominous harbinger of what is to come. Huysmans scrupulously follows Des Esseintes' obsession with artifice to its inexorable conclusion. We watch, hypnotized, as he perverts every natural process until even daily sustenance is taken solely in the form of enemas. Huysmans describes his protagonist's elation: "Des Esseintes could not help secretly congratulating himself . . . his taste for the artificial had now, without even the slightest effort on his part, attained its supreme fulfillment." This "slap in the face of old Mother Nature" leaves the dandy in a desperately weakened condition.[3] Moreover, the union of anality and artifice betrays their secret affinity. And it illuminates a dark parable: "Anyone who dreams of the ideal prefers illusion to reality." For Des Esseintes this dream of the ideal culminates in a romance with death.[4]

Although the Barber in Purdue is incapable of the dandy's exquisite sensibility, he nevertheless shares his obsession and his fate. The thoroughgoing manner in which the barber finds himself traduced by artifice is discoverable at every turn in *The Day of the Locust*. Indeed, the latter serves as a virtual index to the barber's pain. The source of that pain, however, goes beyond Des Esseintes' eclectic obsessions. In *The Day of the Locust* the artificial paradise of the dandy's boudoir has been supplanted by an artificial wilderness of clichés, prescribed social roles, and perhaps most dangerous of all, the commodity. These readymades not only fill up the object world of *The Day of the Locust*, they overwhelm subjectivity itself and pervert nearly every human relationship. In the process, "Being"—described by Mikhail Bakhtin as "eternal, incomplete, unfinished"—finds itself frozen within the readymade's artificial dimensions.[5] West records the resulting grotesquerie unflinchingly in *The Day of the Locust*, and in doing so he manages to transform Huysmans' little parable into a rich and subtle critique of consumer capitalism that both draws on the achievements of his preceding fiction and exceeds them.

I. "THE CLICHÉS ARE HAVING A BALL"

The readymades in *The Day of the Locust* are so manifold that one might borrow a phrase from Umberto Eco and suggest that in West's fiction the "clichés are having a ball." Eco explains, "Two clichés make us laugh. A hundred clichés move us. For we sense dimly that the clichés are talking among themselves, and celebrating a reunion. Just as the height of pain may encounter sensual pleasure, and the height of perversion border on mystical energy, so too the height of banality allows us to catch a glimpse of the sublime."[6] Hence, the sublimity of even the most clichéd plea: "Who do you follow . . . in the Search for Health, along the Road of Life?" Adore's mother asks.[7] She means it. In West's fiction *Opportu-*

nity—quite literally—*knocks;* there is a *Road* upon which *Life* may be found, and so on. These are *allegories* of experience that serve as the soul in paraphrase, heaven in ordinary, something understood. Or if you like, they are what Kenneth Burke might have called a "strategy for living," capitalized to insure their greater authority. Absurd transparencies, they are also the hieroglyphic runes of the culture. In effect, the clichés in West's fiction all say, "Campbell's Soup"—after the fashion of Andy Warhol.

Other readymades abound in a variety of forms. Homer sings "The Star Spangled Banner" to ward off his loneliness. The child actor Adore launches into a lubricious rendition of "Mama Doan Wan' No Peas." And here the sublimity of these readymades takes on an obscene dimension. Adore's performance of the song is accompanied by a series of bumps and grinds. This is more than mere precociousness. Though this eight-year-old first appears "dragging . . . a sailboat on wheels," he is tellingly "dressed like a man" (139). The confusion of toy sailboat and dance hall ditty is precisely to the point. Adore's precociousness is a figure for the oxymoronic status of his own as well as his culture's obscene innocence. It lays bare the ideological complicity of even the most innocent forms—their obscene knowingness. Nothing is immune—neither the commonsense claims of the cliché nor the most frivolous Tin Pan Alley tune. They all sing "The Star Spangled Banner" along with Homer.

By the same token, obscenity—especially the self-conscious variety—reveals itself as "innocent" and hence banal. The canned introduction delivered by the projectionist of the "blue" movie—*Le Predicament de Marie*—makes this plain enough: "It has a marvelous quality that is too exciting" (74), we are told without conviction. The erotic imagination of this well-heeled audience turns out to be puerile. Thus, it seems appropriate that when Mrs. Schwartzen calls for someone at the party to "go ahead [and] say something obscene," she elicits only "awkward silence" (70).

This conflation of innocence and obscenity allows us to understand the hidden claims of Faye's dream cards, offered to Tod as "sure-fire" movie plots. Faye's South Sea tale with its Russian counts, writhing serpents, and Cinderella theme is in fact an aggressive appropriation of experience in the name of "True Love." Like Faye herself, it encloses the world in its own "egglike self-sufficiency" (107). The resulting hermeticism is such that Tod will imagine violence as the only possible response. West understands that what makes this seemingly innocuous story so problematic is its insistence on its own innocence as constitutive lens. It neither allows nor understands a world beyond its own making. The link with the "culture industry" of Hollywood insures its ubiquity, persuasive power, and official sanction. It could be said of Faye—or indeed, of Hollywood itself—what Miss Lonelyhearts ultimately says of Betty: "Her sureness was based on the power to limit experience arbitrarily."[8]

The clichéd readymades of desire are so ubiquitous that even the architecture of the city comes to resemble the sets on the back lot. West tells us that the Hollywood hills are lined with "Samoan huts, Mediterranean villas, Egyptian and Japanese temples, Swiss chalets, Tudor cottages . . ." (61). And these temples, chalets, and cottages come decorated with an equally eclectic set of furnishings: For example, Homer's "Irish" cottage features a "very crooked stone chimney . . . and a thatched roof"; "wall fixtures in the shape of galleons with pointed amber bulbs projecting from their decks"; "a colored etching of a snowbound Connecticut farmhouse, complete with the wolf" (81).

One is tempted to think West regarded all of this as a species of postmodernist pastiche or camp. But his characters are far too dependent upon the fantasies those signs adumbrate to sustain his ironic distance. As West himself observes, "It is hard to laugh at the need for beauty and romance, no matter how tasteless, even horrible the results of that are. But it is easy to sigh. Few things are sadder than the truly monstrous" (61). Indeed, the "need for beauty and romance" quickly degenerates into travesty here. The thatched roof "was not really straw but heavy fireproof paper colored and ribbed to look like straw"; the iron hinges on Homer's front door, "although made by machine . . . had been stamped to appear hand-forged"; the "New England" style bedrooms are "exactly alike in every detail. Even the pictures were duplicates" (81). Sham materials, a cynical manipulation of signifiers, the monotony of duplication: there is no better inventory of art in the age of mechanical reproduction than this. The furniture in Homer's "New England"-style bedrooms is, alas, only a sign of their "New Englandness," placed there by design, and by unscrupulous design at that.

This manipulation of signs foregrounds an essential feature of all West's settings. No environment is left neutral; environment is always converted into atmosphere, carefully dressed with the appropriate props. And *atmosphere prescribes performance*. West's characters are all—with varying degrees of self-consciousness—actors who take their cue from the atmosphere that surrounds them and elaborate it into theater: "They took a cab to a place called El Gaucho. When they entered, the orchestra was playing a Cuban rhumba. A waiter dressed as a South-American cowboy led them to a table. Mary immediately went Spanish and her movements became languorous and full of abandon," West writes in *Miss*

Lonelyhearts.[9] He could be talking about nearly everyone in *The Day of the Locust.*

This need for "coloring," as Gilson's "pamphlet" explains in *Balso Snell,* "is a protective one—like the brown of the rabbit or the checks of the quail."[10] Like the quail and the rabbit, West's characters are hunted animals. And like the quail and the rabbit, they cling to their colors for protection. But the nudity in which nature left us is such that we cannot affect the "brown of the rabbit" except through artifice. Often that artifice takes the form of socially prescribed roles that West's characters attempt to pass off as nature. Though social roles in *The Day of the Locust* do offer a kind of protection, they do so at the cost of a derealizing relation to the world. How could it be otherwise? These roles preexist the subjects that inhabit them, and as a result those subjects must succumb to the stereotypes, caricatures, and cartoons by which their identity is mediated.

Perhaps the best example of this dilemma is to be found in a scene involving a performance by a female impersonator at the "Cinderella Bar": "What he was doing was in no sense a parody; it was too simple and too restrained. It wasn't even theatrical. This dark young man with his thin, hairless arms and soft, rounded shoulders, who rocked an imaginary cradle as he crooned, was really a woman. When he finished . . . the young man shook himself and became an actor again. He tripped on his train, as though he weren't used to it. . . . His imitation of a man was awkward and obscene" (146). West's fiction offers a virtual catalogue of signs manipulated in service to every sort of sham. But in this instance, the signifier actually creates, even triumphs over, nature—in effect creating a *second* "nature." At this point, West's understanding of the power of the signifier reaches its most insightful. Indeed, it is one of the few moments of genuine affirmation in his fiction: at the moment of its most extreme and obvious contradiction—a man impersonating a woman—West asserts that the signifier doesn't lie. The complications of subjectivity are such that the truth comes only in the most extreme form of exhibition: "What he was doing was in no sense a parody," West tells us. "It wasn't even theatrical." What is theatrical, or in fact "obscene," is the impersonator's restoration to the cartoon of his (her?) socially prescribed role: "The young man shook himself and became an *actor* again." Once that is accomplished, all the contradictions alluded to earlier come flooding back. West's burlesque of this paradox is wonderfully convoluted. One might express it this way: a man who is actually a woman feigns inadequacy to the role of a woman which he has so amply portrayed already.

For the most part, however, the potential for this sort of self-creation through the conscious manipulation of the signifier is nowhere to be found in West's fiction. The aestheticization of everyday life submerges human presence under a series of artificial gestures for which Harry Greener constitutes the reductio ad absurdum. Exhausted by a lifetime of performance, he runs through his entire repertoire of personae in a manner approaching an epileptic fit: "The last block that held him poised over the runway of self-pity had been knocked away and he was sliding down the chute, gaining momentum all the time. He jumped to his feet and began doing Harry Greener, poor Harry, honest Harry, well-meaning, humble, deserving, a good husband, a model father, a faithful Christian, a loyal friend" (91).

This little performance results in Harry's collapse. Instead of the clarity momentarily revealed in the performance by the female impersonator, Harry's performance produces only confusion, leaving him to wonder "whether he was acting or sick" (94). Moreover, performance appears to be coterminous with consciousness itself and, hence, without surcease. Harry proves as much when he wakes from his stupefaction and immediately adopts a succession of derisive cultural stereotypes—"the nasal twang . . . of a country yokel," "an exaggerated Negro shuffle" (99)—without skipping a beat. There is no rhyme or reason to this concatenation of poses; like the eclectic melange of furniture in Homer's cottage, the furniture of Harry's mind is utterly lacking in its own integrity. Both are the product of a cultural sargasso that has lost any convincing organizing principle. Harry thus stands before us as a grandiloquent martyr whose hokey death throes dramatize our own dilemma. For the most part, however, West's characters remain oblivious to this state of affairs. They repress the grotesquerie of their situation with a hysterical energy that is never quite convincing—even to themselves. The alternative is no alternative at all: Harry's laughter, Tod's sirenlike scream.

2. THE CHEATERS AND THE CHEATED

Actor and audience: there is almost no relationship in West's fiction that exists outside this rubric—Saniette and John Raskolnikov Gilson, Miss Lonelyhearts and his readers, Faye and Homer, to name a few. It is not until *The Day of the Locust,* however, that West explores the dynamic logic at the heart of this vexed and volatile relationship. There, actors and their audiences are not confined to the theater; West follows them out into the street where the explosive social dimensions of their relationship are etched more sharply.

Nowhere is this more evident than in the evening crowd Tod encounters on Vine Street moments after he leaves the studio. One of the first things Tod notices is that certain members of the crowd are in costume: "A great many of the people wore sports clothes which were not really sports clothes. Their sweaters, knickers, slacks, blue flannel jackets with brass buttons were fancy dress. The fat lady in the yachting cap was going shopping, not boating; the man in the Norfolk jacket and Tyrolean hat was returning, not from a mountain, but an insurance office; and the girl in slacks and sneaks with a bandanna around her head had just left a switchboard, not a tennis court" (60).

This spectacle would seem to offer a charmed phantasmagoria of signifiers set loose from their referents. West, however, is careful to deflate the phantasm for the reader by indicating the prosaic social function of the bearers of these signifiers: shopper, insurance man, switchboard operator. For the crowd of onlookers, however, these costumes obscure that function, creating an obfuscating texture of social reality that does not permit itself to be read. This aestheticization of everyday life effectively dematerializes social relations, leaving West's crowd to wander aimlessly through a forest of symbols that elude their understanding.

West describes this crowd in great detail: "Scattered among these masquerades were people of a different type." They are composed of a grab bag of people who have, in West's memorable phrase, "come to California to die" (60): "All their lives they had slaved at some kind of dull, heavy labor, behind desks and counters, in fields and at tedious machines of all sorts, saving their pennies and dreaming of the leisure that would be theirs when they had enough. Finally that day came. . . . Where else should they go but California, the land of sunshine and oranges?" (177). But once there they discover that sunshine isn't enough: "They don't know what to do with their time. They haven't the mental equipment for leisure, the money nor the physical equipment for pleasure. . . . Their boredom becomes more and more terrible" (178).

This reductive translation of Baudelairian "ennui" into "boredom" is to the point; "boredom" contains none of the connotations of "spirit" implicit in "ennui," with its suggestion that the "heroism of modern life" consists in the resistance of an exquisite consciousness. These people are ill-equipped for leisure and pleasure, the traditional solace of the dandy. They require the kind of titillation and gore that only the media seem able to provide: "Every day of their lives they read the newspapers and went to the movies. Both fed them on lynchings, murder, sex crimes, explosions, wrecks, love nests, fires, miracles, revolutions, war. This daily diet made sophisticates of them. The sun is a joke" (178). (It was not until Andy Warhol's *Death and Disasters* series that this concatenation of the dream life of the crowd with the media and violence would be appreciated with equal power.)

On Vine Street looking and being looked at are freighted with social meaning. The dynamics of this masquerade can be quite complicated. They seem to lead a gay life, these masqueraders, "darting into stores and cocktail bars" (60). But Tod observes that it was the stare of the "mail-order house crowd" that "drove . . . them to spin crazily and leap into the air with twisted backs like hooked trout" (62). One would have thought from the initial description of the evening crowd on Vine Street that the prerogatives belonged exclusively to the masqueraders, but not so. These exhibitionists are "hooked trout," held firmly on the line of the sullen voyeur. Though the illusion of *sangfroid* is essential to the performance, the exhibitionist is "driven" to act out fantasies that are not her own. This suggests not only that the power relations between exhibitionist and voyeur are reversible, but that they are sadomasochistic as well.[11]

One immediately thinks of Harry Greener in this regard. His vaudeville routine reconstructs the sadomasochistic dynamics of actor and audience exactly. As such it functions as a rune for the novella as a whole. In what amounts to an act of masochism itself, Harry shows Tod an old review that is demeaning in ways that the old vaudevillian is unable or unwilling to recognize. "The *commedia dell'arte* is not dead, but lives on in Brooklyn," the review intones, and Harry Greener is its "Bedraggled Harlequin." Harry is "neat and sweet" when he first comes on stage. By the time "The Flying Lings" get through with him however, he is "tattered and bloody." The review continues in an illuminating manner:

> When Mr. Greener enters . . . Mama Ling is spinning a plate on the
> end of a stick held in her mouth, Papa Ling is doing cartwheels, Sister
> Ling is juggling fans and Sonny Ling is hanging from the proscenium
> arch by his pigtail. As he inspects his strenuous colleagues, Mr.
> Greener tries to hide his confusion under some much too obvious
> worldliness. He ventures to tickle Sister and receives a powerful kick
> in the belly in return for this innocent attention. Having been kicked,
> he is on familiar ground and begins to tell a dull joke. Father Ling
> sneaks up behind him and tosses him to Brother, who looks the other
> way. Mr. Greener lands on the back of his neck. He shows his mettle
> by finishing his dull story from a recumbent position. When he stands
> up, the audience, which failed to laugh at his joke, laughs at his limp,
> so he continues lame for the rest of the act. (77)

Harry Greener first enters the stage as a spectator, a figure for the audience itself. His "inspection" of Sister Ling prompts a swift kick that effectively banishes the spectator from the contested space of the proscenium arch. After the kick, we are "on familiar ground." That is to say, Harry becomes the actor he has always been and proceeds to tell a dull joke; this frees the audience—now safely back on the other side of the proscenium arch—to see him as a clown, an *object* of derision. But Sister Ling's kick contains a deeper import, which the audience suppresses. At issue is the "innocent attention" of the spectator. Her kick does not disentangle actor and audience so much as implicate them in a perverse and knotted relation. As a consequence of his beating, Harry masochistically incorporates a limp into his act, while the audience howls its sadistic approval. The review concludes, "The pain that almost, not quite, thank God, crumples his stiff little figure would be unbearable if it were not obviously make-believe. It is gloriously funny" (77).

The violence is somehow bearable, even funny, because it is "make-believe," or so the review claims. The quite literal exoticism of the "Orientals" guarantees its make-believe status. Indeed, the proscenium arch is seen by the audience as an inviolable boundary that distances or separates actor and audience, creating in its "make-believe" space something other, something more, something worthy of the spectator's attention. Sonny Ling's "feat" of dangling from the proscenium arch by his pigtail both acknowledges and burlesques this function. In fact, all these vaudeville feats parody the aspiration for metamorphosis with a kind of crude energy that never quite surmounts its object.

Of course we know that it is not "make-believe" at all. Harry is little more than a sentient prop. What is "unbearable" is this ontological confusion that barely manages to contain potentially explosive social forces. West refuses his audience (both his readers and those attending Harry's performance) the "distance" necessary to transfigure what is taking place before them. The suspicion that the performance is real effectively destroys the fiction of distance and the concomitant "innocent attention" it allows. The interchangeability of actor and audience—Harry as spectator, the spectator as Harry—is a scandal. The vehemence of their laughter betrays them; the audience suspects that the limping vaudevillian is merely a surrogate for themselves.

The relationship between audience and actor adumbrated here is so important to the dynamics of the novel, and indeed to West's social criticism in general, that further explanation is in order. Harry's performance serves as a model for a phenomenon that is not restricted to the stage. It describes a dynamic that can be found throughout *The Day of the Locust*. West's original title for this novel was "The Cheaters and the Cheated," which suggests accurately enough, if without subtlety, the charged nature of this relation. One might say that the audience is cheated because their desire does not originate with themselves. Nor precisely does it reside in the desired object, whether that be the exotic performer on the far side of the proscenium arch or the tantalizing commodities of, say, "sunshine and oranges." Rather, unbeknownst to the crowd, their desire has already been mediated or projected by an Other, by ideology.

This morphology of desire closely resembles that limned by René Girard in *Deceit, Desire, and the Novel*. The birth of desire, Girard explains, is always attended by a third term. Moreover, the metamorphosis of the object into that which is desirable is dependent upon this triangulation. The hero of the modern novel expects his being to be radically changed by the act of possession. Desire thus places the subject in an untenable position: driven by that which it cannot satisfy precisely because that desire never belonged to the subject to begin with. As the distance between the subject and its desired object diminishes, the inadequacy of the object becomes more apparent, comprehension more acute, and self-hatred more intense, until at last the subject is abandoned to "that disappointment which is called possession." What one discovers in possession, Girard contends, is no less than "the void gnawing at [one's] self."[12]

Girard's description is not unlike Walter Benjamin's exploration of a similar phenomenon. The rage to overcome the distance by which cultural objects have heretofore remained sacralized results in a loss of "aura." For Walter Benjamin, at least the Benjamin of "Art in the Age of Mechanical Reproduction," this is a necessary prelude to the liberation of a populace cowed into submission by the "sacred" status of art. Under this scenario reality at last reveals itself as malleable, subject to human will, and, hence, available to revolutionary action. But Benjamin recounts a less optimistic version of this story in "Some Motifs in Baudelaire," which has much in common with West. There, aura is seen as a lingering repository of the meaning that objects still possess. The loss of aura precipitates a fall into a reified world of dead matter.[13] Much is at stake. As Girard explains, "The failure of desire can now have repercussions beyond the object and provoke doubts concerning the mediator [social construction] itself. At first the idol trembles on its pedestal; it may even collapse if the disillusionment is great enough."[14] Instead of the revolutionary action Benjamin envisioned in his earlier thesis, this awakening to a lifeless world provokes a rage that is closer to fascism.

3. LOVE IS A VENDING MACHINE

"Almost, not quite . . . ," to echo the reviewer of the "Bedraggled Harlequin," or rather, *not yet*. For the collapse of distance that precipitates an awakening to a lifeless world is not quite realized until the end of *The Day of the Locust*. In the meantime Tod meditates on the enigma of Harry Greener's performance: "The old man was a clown and Tod had all the painter's usual love of clowns. But what was more important, he felt that *his clownship was a clue to the people who stared* (a painter's clue, that is—a clue in the form of a symbol . . ." [76, italics mine]). Indeed, we might look for a "clue to the people who stared" elsewhere in another set of carefully orchestrated symbols surrounding Tod's invitation to visit a high-class brothel. There we discover the secret or cause behind the malaise I have been chronicling up until now.

Tod, as it turns out, is something of a reluctant "john":

"I don't like pro-sport," [he demurs].
"We won't indulge in any. We're just going to see a movie."
"I get depressed."
"Not at Jenning's you won't. She makes a vice attractive by skillful packaging. Her dive's a triumph of industrial design . . ."
"I don't care how much cellophane she wraps it in," he said—
"nautch joints are depressing, like all places for deposit, banks, mail boxes, tombs, vending machines." (72)

The conversation is revealing for the way it conflates a variety of phenomena. Prostitution, movies, banks, tombs, and vending machines are all linked as "nautch joints." In this instance, each term—*libidinal* economy/libidinal *economy*—can be taken as a metaphor for the other. Eroticism is understood in terms of financial exchange, and financial exchange is apprehended as a form of eroticism. This recalls Marx's own notion of commodity fetishism as a perverse "exchange" producing "material relations between persons and social relations between things."[15] For Marx, commodity fetishism is more than the animistic attribution of life to the world of objects; that attribution ultimately takes its toll on human participants by draining life from them. In West's language there is an asymmetry of exchange in which there would seem to be little "return" on "deposits."

Throughout *The Day of the Locust* this asymmetry of exchange makes consummation—emotional or sexual—all but impossible, resulting in a *coitus interruptus* for which the following may serve as the locus classicus: "[Homer's]" emotions surged up in an enormous wave, curving and rearing, higher and higher, until it seemed as though the wave must carry everything before it. But the crash never came. Something always happened at the very top of the crest and the wave collapsed to run back like water down a drain, leaving, at most, only the refuse of feeling" (86). Even the "blue movie," at Miss Jenning's—*Le Predicament de Marie ou La Bonne Distraite*—breaks down before its long-awaited climax. Marie, as maid to a conventional Victorian family, is the object of desire for "bearded father" and "mustachioed son" alike. She is forced to hide the one, owing to an unexpected visit from the other, and forced to hide the other as well when there is yet another knock on the door: " 'Who can it be that wishes to enter now?' read the title card. And there the machine stuck. The young man in evening dress became as frantic as Marie. When he got it running again, there was a flash of light and the film whizzed through the apparatus until it had all run out" (75).

The projector—that is to say, the vending machine—mocks the orgiastic end that the spectators are not permitted to enjoy. "Fake! . . . Cheat! . . . The old teaser routine!" (75), the audience yells (only half in jest). This wealthy audience is composed of people who are themselves masqueraders in other contexts. Here they are masquerading as a "rowdy audience [from] the days of the nickelodeon" (74), a confusion of actor and audience that recalls the example of Harry Greener. Appropriately enough, their disappointment ends in a "mock riot" (75), anticipating the violence precipitated by their déclassé counterparts at the end of the novel, when they too discover themselves to be the victims of a cheat.

As the foregoing suggests, *The Day of the Locust* constitutes a veritable textbook on aberrant sexuality, the libidinal economy gone awry: *le droit du seigneur* goes hand in hand with pedophilia in *Le Predicament de Marie,* while the infantilization of Homer is merely the flip side of Adore's sexual precociousness. Fantasies of rape abound, while exhibitionism and voyeurism (Vine Street) and bestiality (the cock fight) are everywhere. West's world is emphatically not that of the Marquis de Sade, however much it might seem to resemble it on the surface. For Sade, perversity is the inevitable result of nature left to its own devices against the more sanguine claims for nature as the ultimate repository of good. For West, on the other hand, perversity is a function of culture, specifically a culture oriented around commodities. Indeed, as W. J. T. Mitchell explains, "It is not perverse sexuality, then, that expresses itself in commodity fetishism, but commodity fetishism that renders sexuality, along with every other human relationship, perverse."[16] It is worth recalling that in the French language consumption (*consommation*) also means "consummation." But in the language of capitalism consumption can only mime consummation as vicious parody. Denied its summation or end, erotic energy must turn to more perverse means of satisfaction and debauch its participants.

"Love," Claude Estee tells Tod, "is like a vending machine. . . . You insert a coin and press home the lever. There's some mechanical activity inside the *bowels* of the device. You receive a small sweet, frown at yourself in the dirty mirror, adjust your hat, take a firm grip on your umbrella and walk away, trying to look as though nothing had happened" (72, italics mine). All of which is to say, the commodity promises more than it delivers. If the kick Harry receives from Sister Ling subverts the fiction of distance, the vending machine undermines the concomitant fiction of organicism. The commodity depends on both. In this case, the "sweet" the vending machine dispenses from its "bowels" is not something *other / more* than ourselves, but the dead matter or tomb of ourselves—the commodity as excrement. Not even the "skillful packaging" of Mrs. Jenning can hide its "industrial design," its inorganic status. The expenditure of money and erotic energy is repaid in our own offal. Instead of outrage this produces guilt and confusion. "You frown at yourself in the dirty mirror . . . and walk away, trying to look as though nothing had happened."

The embarrassed, final glance at the mirror is the perfect metaphor for what has actually transpired. Mirrors were once a standard feature on vending machines. And for good reason: they were placed there to convert the vanity of potential patrons into a sale. The commodity functions in a similar manner—in this case, as a mirror in which we read our own idealized image. Its purchase, we mistakenly believe, will have a transformative effect. But, of course, it doesn't; instead we are left with our own pathetic image in the now "dirty mirror"—yet another version of the "old teaser routine."

Excrement is the figure that inaugurated West's fictional debut in *The Dream Life of Balso Snell*. In that novella the poet crawls through the alimentary canal of "the famous wooden horse of the Greeks."[17] There, West's use of excrement is in service not so much to commodity fetishism as to a dadaist attempt to besmirch the reigning idealisms of Western culture. In subsequent work, the figure of excrement appears to drop out entirely. In fact, it merely goes underground, structuring West's deepening and ever more emphatic social criticism until it eventually emerges as a figure for commodity culture.

The link between commodity and excrement draws—metaphorically at least—on the infantile fixation with anality. In Freud's mythology, the infant's fascination with its own feces is part of a narcissistic ambition to become "father to oneself" and thus triumph over death. Excrement, in effect, becomes aliment. The narcissist produces its own food, thereby completing the hermetic circle of a self-replenishing immortal body. Norman O. Brown, among others, has shown how the consumption of commodities might participate in this same narcissistic fantasy. Commodities, as the dead objects of alienated labor, share the status of feces. But rather than being viewed as such, they are fantasized as articles of *consumption,* aliment. Of course, commodities are inedible. They do not sustain life so much as draw it off; hence the life of the body is continually flowing out into things without return.[18] The narcissistic myth of consumption recalls the "Phoenix Excrementi" in *Balso Snell.* Like the consumer, the Phoenix Excrementi "eat themselves, digest themselves, and give birth to themselves by evacuating their bowels" in an endless cycle that promises not immortality so much as redundancy. Adore's mother— a "raw foodist"—puts it more succinctly: "Death comes from eating dead things."[19]

4. THE BARBER'S SARGASSO

"What about the Barber in Purdue?" Claude Estee asks rhetorically. "He's been cutting hair all day and he's tired. He doesn't want to see some dope . . . fooling with a nickel machine. What the Barber wants is amour and glamour" (72). But instead of "amour and glamour" the barber in Purdue gets a sweet from the bowels of the vending machine, amour and glamour packaged into the "industrial design" of Faye's "hundreds and hundreds" of "sure-fire" movie plots: the commodity as excrement.

What about the Barber in Purdue? Homer Simpson is not a barber, and he is not from Purdue. "He came from a little town near Des Moines, Iowa, called Waynesville where he had worked for 20 years in a hotel" (80). That's close enough. The hotel clerk from Waynesville has "come to California to die"; the Barber in Purdue will eventually follow. Once there Homer becomes a "man *of* the crowd," its Representative Man. He too wants "amour and glamour." And in Faye Greener he believes he's found it. Much of the novel is taken up with Homer's masochistic admiration for Faye's "little performances." He houses her, feeds her, participates in her fantasy of stardom. It is to be a "business arrangement," Faye explains defensively; an "investment," Tod concurs ironically (135). To some extent they are right, though in ways that neither understands, or perhaps understands all too well. Faye's hold on Homer and Tod is analogous to the paralyzed fascination with which the commodity holds its consumers. In West's misogynist construction she is the consummate commodity, the "nautched joint" around which the novel revolves.

If the commodity draws its being surreptitiously from its adoring consumers, the actress goes further, collapsing any distinction between commodity and being altogether. As would-be actress, Faye quite literally fashions herself into a commodity, becoming identical with it. Her periodic bouts as a prostitute for Miss Jenning confirm her commodity status. As for her much-promised "amour," it is always delayed, a version of the "old teaser routine." It is just as well. Though "she was supposed to look inviting . . . the invitation wasn't to pleasure." Her "sword-like legs" (68) raise the stakes, revealing the horrific import behind the fetishistic nature of the commodity: castration.

There is, however, a limit even to Homer's gargantuan capacity for bathetic admiration. When Faye drunkenly takes a lover, she loses her status as spectacle and becomes instead a "dirty black hen." (The obscenity of the image derives as much from her loss of aura as from her promiscuity.) This deflation of fantasy precipitates a crisis for Homer. Homer cannot accept Tod's dismissal of Faye as *mere* excrement—"Good riddance to bad rubbish" (168). That is to say Homer cannot simply frown in the dirty mirror and walk away as though nothing had happened. The consequences of this demystification are more devastating, more volatile.

When yet another performer, Adore, taunts Homer by throwing rocks at him, Homer erupts into violence. The incident begins "innocently" enough. Adore has tied a string to an open purse in the hope of baiting a hapless passerby into reaching for it. This childhood cheat is a recapitulation of the games of confidence that characterize the designs of nearly every performance in *The Day of the Locust*. When the open purse fails to elicit a response, Adore makes the fraud more obvious by "stepping across" the proscenium arch with an unmistakable aggressiveness. The stone Homer receives in the face effectively mirrors the kick Harry receives from Sister Ling; but instead of sorting actor and audience into their respective spheres, the act cinches them in a perverse and knotted relation.

As long as Adore remains within the magic circle delimited by the proscenium arch, his audience can continue to indulge in the fiction of a world somehow above and beyond that of its own making. But the stone from Adore's hand makes it all too apparent that the proscenium arch is, at the very least, permeable. The thrashing Homer administers to the child actor puts an end to this fictional boundary altogether. The scandal that has been suppressed throughout *The Day of the Locust* can no longer be ignored. The audience is at last forced to confront the dead space of a reified world it created but no longer recognizes.

The results are not limited to laughter. Waiting in passive adore-ation for the arrival of the celebrities at Khan's Pleasure Dome, the crowd is galvanized into action. Actor and audience, exhibitionist and voyeur, masochist and sadist—held in exquisite tension by the proscenium arch—now become hopelessly intertwined. Enthralled by the spectacle of its own self-destruction, the crowd indulges in sadomasochistic violence that can only go under the name apocalypse—the climax so long forbidden.

EPILOGUE

It is important to understand just what is happening in these apocalyptic, last pages of *The Day of the Locust*.[20] This is the final exfoliation of a logic we have been tracing from the outset, beginning with *Balso Snell*. Moreover, West's treatment of these events evinces a keen insight into the very American circumstances under which fascism is likely to emerge.

One reading of these events might harken back to the connection between West and Bataille developed in Chapter 2. For Bataille, the demands of social activity under capitalism are such that "all individual effort, in order to be valid, must be reducible to fundamental necessities of production and conservation."[21] While essential to the survival of society, this coercion of human effort into forms of activity that *conserve* life leaves little room for other modes of expression that Bataille considers equally essential, i.e., a pleasure in "*nonproductive expenditure.*" Bataille's vision of expenditure, however, is not satisfied in the kind of expenditure incurred through commodity consumption (a perversion of the "need to destroy"); it is, in fact, radically opposed to it. For Bataille expenditure contravenes the "fundamental necessities of production and conservation" through the transgression of the rational and discontinuous structures upon which day-to-day activity depends. As such it seeks to restore access to a lost unity.

Recall that for Bataille this Dionysian impulse gives rise to an "immense travail of recklessness, discharge, and upheaval" to which he gives the name *potlatch*. Potlatch is the ceremonial festival in which North American Indians periodically "destroy" whatever property they have accumulated. The essential feature of this expenditure involves loss. The greater that loss the more satisfying it is presumed to be. Bataille cites examples of such unproductive expenditures as "luxury, mourning, war, cults, the construction of sumptuary monuments, games, spectacles, arts, perverse sexual activity (i.e., deflected from genital finality)."22 But these traditional modes of expenditure have become atrophied under the pressures of class struggle, leaving only the *potlatch* of revolution itself as the sole means of expression.

It is tempting to frame the outpouring of violence in the final pages of *The Day of the Locust* in just these terms: the final realization of the elusive and monstrous *archontes* that West has pursued from the beginning of his career. One might find confirmation for this reading in Tod's execution of "The Burning of Los Angeles," the painting he has been working on throughout the novel. Tod's description of it approximates the festive air of Bataille's potlatch: "He was going to show the city burning at high noon, so that the flames would have to compete with the desert sun and thereby appear less fearful, more like bright flags flying from roofs and windows than a terrible holocaust. He wanted the city to have quite a gala air as it burned, to appear almost gay. And the people who set it on fire would be a holiday crowd" (118).

West, however, has problematized this reading of the riot by situating it outside the events of the novel. Tod's vision of "The Burning of Los Angeles" remains confined to the idealized space of art, prompting doubts about whether it too partakes in the sham idealism that has victimized the rioting crowd. The gay destruction depicted in "The Burning of Los Angeles" exceeds West's own grasp. Here as elsewhere, the moments of greatest destruction transpire without the spirit of the "holiday crowd" and hence without any notion of matter as an *active* principle.23

The actual riot in front of Khan's Pleasure Dome is a far cry from the expenditure depicted in "The Burning of Los Angeles." Denied the privileged interval aesthetic distance affords, Tod is thrown pell-mell into the rioting crowd where he bears witness to a quite different scene. Its most salient feature is an utter lack of gaiety. At the eye of this hurricane Tod discovers a vicious banality.

> Another spasm passed through the mob and he was carried toward the curb. . . . This rush also ended in a dead spot. . . . Near him was a stout woman with a man pressing hard against her from in front. . . . She paid no attention to him and went on talking to the woman at her side. "The first thing I knew," Tod heard her say, "There was a rush and I was in the middle. 'Yeah.' Somebody hollered, 'Here comes Gary Cooper,' and then wham!"
>
> "That ain't it," said a little man wearing a cloth cap and pullover sweater. "This is a riot you're in."

"Yeah," said a third woman. . . . "A pervert attacked a child."
"He ought to be lynched." Everybody agreed vehemently.
"I come from St. Louis," announced the stout woman, "and we
had one of them pervert fellers in our neighborhood once. He ripped a
girl with a pair of scissors."
"He must have been crazy," said the man in the cap. "What kind of
fun is that?"
Everybody laughed. The stout woman spoke to the man who was
hugging her. "Hey, you," she said. "I ain't no pillow." The man smiled
beatifically but didn't move. She laughed, making no effort to get out
of his embrace. . .
The man in the cap and sweater thought there was another laugh
in his comment about the pervert. "Ripping up a girl with scissors.
That's the wrong tool." He was right. They laughed even louder than
the first time. (183)

Sadistic humor and cheap thrills: this hardly constitutes the exalted
sexuality Bataille's notion of potlatch envisions. West reduces it to all to
banal grotesquerie. If these people "had it in them to destroy civilization," as Tod prophesies, it may not be the result of their "awful, anarchic power" (142); rather, it is just as likely to result from a violence born
of apathy, the dead response to a dead world.

Instead of the cosmic aspiration of sacred violence, what Tod discovers is the sullen fury of the petit bourgeois—the final, violent exfoliation
of what Jean Baudrillard describes as the *ego consumans*. Consumption,
Baudrillard explains, produces no self-consciousness as does the alienation of labor and hence no concomitant solidarity. Rather, the consumer
"stands alone next to millions of solitary individuals." That is because
"consumption is primarily organized as a discourse to oneself." As such
it is individualizing, atomizing, and dehistoricizing. Humored, the solitary consumer may grudgingly indulge himself in a limited gregarious-
ness; betrayed, he becomes an angry man of the crowd.[24]

In West's scenario, this anger leads not to social revolution but to the
fascism of "Dr. Know-All Pierce-All" (184). It is no accident that West describes Dr. Pierce-All's anchorites as possessing "drained-out, feeble bodies and . . . wild, disordered minds" (142). Their physiognomy mirrors
their inward condition. Having yielded its bodily energy to the commodity in an asymmetrical exchange, the *ego consumans* is left without a
body of its own. This loss of the body is devastating. It essentially pro-
hibits access to what one might call the "discourse of the low" and with

it any hope of reconciliation to the "ground of being"—the unity to which *potlatch* aspires.

In the absence of any catharsis, the mind takes revenge on itself with a relentlessness that ends in nihilism. And this nihilism is a prerequisite for fascism. Writing in the late thirties, under the lengthening shadow of fascism, West convincingly articulates a scenario under which that "exotic" ideology might well emerge *within* the American grain.

Madonna's Bustier; or
"The Burning of Los Angeles"

More than half a century after the death of Nathanael West, his name continues to be invoked in an effort to explain some of the more puzzling aspects of our culture. "It's like something out of Nathanael West," a Chicago newscaster opined as he watched live videotape of the burning and looting that took place throughout Los Angeles during the uprisings. Eighteen months later another journalist made a similar observation as she watched Los Angeles go up in flames yet again—this time not as a result of insurrection but at the hands of a bored teenager who started a fire which raged for days through the desiccated canyons of Southern California. During the succession of Bible-sized earthquakes, fires, and floods which have plagued Southern California since then, West's apocalyptic imagination has been cited repeatedly and endowed with the authority of prophecy. Even NBC's Tom Brokaw got into the act, invoking the name of Nathanael West in astonishment as crowds of people lined the freeways of Southern California to witness the surreal, slow-motion chase of O. J. Simpson. Why West? Why now?

The obvious answer is that ever since *The Day of the Locust,* West has been closely tied with Los Angeles, where that novel takes place. As Los Angeles has come to assume a greater place in the national imagination— indeed, to the extent that L.A. has become a crystal ball of sorts in which the rest of the nation reads its own future—West's importance has grown. But that does not explain why an obscure writer from the thirties should speak to us so powerfully today. As we have already seen, West's obscurity in the thirties is at least partially attributable to his own prescience. While many on the left were preoccupied with an anachronistic (and romantic) vision of America as a battleground pitting heroic factory workers against bloated plutocrats, West was quietly chronicling the emergence of a consumer society whose principal actors were not the radicalized masses but a disenchanted and isolated mass man. That is not to say that West did not share the political convictions of those on the communist left, but he never allowed those convictions to obscure his reading of the forces that were making—or rather, remaking—American society during the period. It should be clear by now that much of the drama of his work lies in his attempt to preserve his political convictions in the face of this Brave New World. As we become more and more intimately acquainted with this Brave New World ourselves, Nathanael West has become both a point of reference and an illuminating guide. Indeed, one might say that West's continuing popularity is attributable to the fact that he is one of the most insightful critics of the culture of capitalism and its most recent forms—consumerism, postmodernity, etc.—available in American literature. Before the Frankfurt School's pessimistic account of the culture industry, Guy Debord's "society of the spectacle," and Jean Baudrillard's simulacrum, West offered his own home-grown critique of American society—a critique that seemed to anticipate the insights of all three and root them in the contradictions of our national experience.

No doubt these comments will strike some as extravagant. Permit me to elaborate by returning to one of the most memorable scenes in *The Day of the Locust,* Tod's description of the evening crowd on Vine Street. West writes, "A great many of the people wore sports clothes which were not really sports clothes. Their sweaters, knickers, slacks, blue flannel jackets with brass buttons were fancy dress. The fat lady in the yachting cap was going shopping, not boating; the man in the Norfolk jacket and Tyrolean hat was returning, not from a mountain, but an insurance office; and the girl in slacks and sneaks with a bandanna around her head had just left a switchboard, not a tennis court. Scattered among these masquerades were people of a different type. Their clothing was somber and badly cut, brought from mail-order houses. While the others moved rapidly, darting into stores and cocktail bars, they loitered on the corners or stood with their backs to the shop windows and stared at everyone who passed. When their stare was returned, their eyes filled with hatred."[1]

Nearly forty years before West wrote this passage, the American sociologist Thorstein Veblen took the fashionable clothes he saw on the avenues of New York and Chicago as evidence of "conspicuous consumption" by which a newly moneyed class proclaimed its status. On West's Vine Street consumption is still very much in evidence, but here it obscures more than it reveals. I suggested in the previous chapter that these yachting caps, Tyrolean hats, and bandannas bear no relationship to what they signify: i.e. yachts, mountains, and tennis courts. They are proof only of their owners' capacity to spend money. This is more than just a matter of conspicuous consumption. The world literally begins to dissolve under this new ethos until nothing is left but costumes, performances, actors. In West's hands, Vine Street—and by extension, society itself—has become a masquerade in which social relations are invisible, society itself unreadable. The yachting caps, Tyrolean hats, and bandannas are thus more than mere fancy dress; they herald the emergence of an entirely new social order with a grammar all its own. Whether one chooses to describe that order in terms of a masquerade (as West does), a spectacle (as Debord does), a simulacrum (as Baudrillard does), or simply as postmodernism, the problem is essentially the same. It is impossible to know how to interpret this world, much less act in it—or better yet, on it.

This poses serious consequences for those who cannot afford to participate in this masquerade. On West's Vine Street there is little left for the "mail-order house" crowd to do but watch. Their former status as members of the proletariat gave them an exalted role as the agent of history. But in a consumer society (which embraces haves and have-nots alike) that role no longer exists. Instead, these people have become little more than a group of sullen voyeurs who contemplate the evening crowd of consumer-exhibitionists not so much with ideas of revolution as with the far more reactionary politics of envy and *ressentiment*. In this way West has redefined the nature of social relations in American society, and he has done so with a brevity and deftness so subtle that only now are we beginning to take in the enormous consequences. Class continues to play a dominant role in West's scheme, but from now on class differences will be played out in an entirely different arena defined almost exclusively in terms of actors and their audience, exhibitionists and voyeurs, fancy dress and the mail order-house: the Brave New World of mass culture and consumption. Things will never be quite the same again.

It is not hard to see how the foregoing might illuminate the events in Los Angeles with which I began. West had almost nothing to say about the vexed question of race which was, of course, at the root of the uprisings. (His sole reference to African-Americans can be found in *The Day of the Locust*, where he draws on a derisive stereotype.) But there were other aspects of the uprisings that took on a specific Westian cast—most notably the manner in which they quickly became enmeshed in the politics of representation. From the moment that the beating of Rodney King was captured on videotape, to its ritual reenactment each night on the 6 o'clock news, to its use in the trial of the four police officers accused of using excessive force (and later, charged with civil rights violations), it was clear that the representation of race relations was at least as important as race relations themselves—if not more so. Race has always been one of the most theatricalized elements of American society, but America's theater of cruelty has recently taken on a life of its own, obscuring a densely woven fabric of race relations in a series of spectacular melodramas that have provoked a deadly combination of apocalyptic rage and numbing apathy. This would hardly come as a surprise to West. More than most social critics then or since, he is keenly aware of the extent to which a complex social world has been subsumed in a "daily diet" of "lynchings, murder, sex crimes, explosions, wrecks, love nests, fires, miracles, revolutions, war" provided by the media—making us connoisseurs of our own decay and destruction.[2] Nowhere is this more evident than during the recent uprisings in Los Angeles. Contrary to the radical slogan of the 1960s, those events have made it abundantly clear that the revolution will be televised after all. It appears as though some day in the not-too-distant future we will have the exquisite pleasure of watching our own immolation from the comfort of our living rooms.

West helps us to understand other aspects of the uprisings as well, particularly as they moved from rage into what can only be described as a demented shopping spree. The haunting depiction of "The Burning of Los Angeles" in *The Day of the Locust*—"He wanted the city to have quite a gala air as it burned [and] the people who set it on fire [to] be a holiday crowd"—seemed to anticipate if not prophesize the gala air of the looters as they emerged from burning buildings pushing shopping carts filled with plunder: toiletries, car batteries, stereo components, stuffed animals, milk.[3] Perhaps the most thoroughly Westian moment in all of this—the moment which seemed to reveal the complicated social dynamics of Vine Street most exactly—was the theft of Madonna's bustier from the "Lingerie Museum" in "Frederick's of Hollywood." The theft of Madonna's bustier is to the politics of *ressentiment* what the Communist Manifesto is to the politics of revolution. That is to say, it is the quintessential gesture of *ego consumans,* the revenge of those who buy their clothes from the "mail-order house" against "the stores and cocktail bars" frequented by masqueraders. In the aftermath of the melee, this side of the riots (and here the word riot *is* appropriate) was aptly summed up by a quip that appeared on tee-shirts throughout the city: "My parents went looting and all I got was this lousy tee-shirt."

Not until the O. J. Simpson double-homicide and the bizarre chase scene which followed would that surreal concatenation of eroticism, celebrity, and violence be played out again with such clarity and force. The Simpson trials are in many ways the perfect redaction of the uprisings, their (ostensibly) depoliticized variant. Somehow all the issues raised by the uprisings seem to have been telescoped into what can only be described as a tawdry made-for-television movie, complete with movie stars and their homes, a slew of bad performances, and plenty of commercials. West would have understood, along with Geraldo Rivera, the extent to which this sorry melodrama tells us who we are. Once again, America's most important divisions—race, class, gender—are rehearsed in the form of an elaborate masquerade. Once again we find ourselves on Vine Street watching the masqueraders as they dart into cocktail bars— this time with names like the Riviera Country Club, Mezzaluna, and Starbucks. We note with a mixture of envy and resentment the Bruno Magli shoes, the mansion at Rockingham, the vacations in the Caribbean, the late model sports coup whose license plate—"LTE 4A DTE"—seemed to sum up the sublime insouciance of the whole infamous masquerade.

It is possible that we may come to forgive O. J. Simpson for murder— those of us who believe he did it. Certainly, the crowds which lined the freeways of Southern California—holding signs aloft which read, "Go Juice!"—indicated their inclination to do just that. But we will never forgive Simpson for letting us peek behind the mask, for revealing the emptiness of our own aspirations as a culture. Most of us already suspect the truth. But we must not, cannot, confront that truth directly. That is why O. J. Simpson must keep smiling and we must keep watching. To do otherwise would be to acknowledge that we are, after all, no different from the loiterers on Vine Street who have discovered, as West puts it, that "sunshine isn't enough"; or, to be more accurate, that the whole wild, paradisal promise of consumerism—the promise of easy living in "the land of sunshine and oranges," (otherwise known as "the California lifestyle")—does not offer the satisfactions it proclaims. Few people have exposed the emptiness of that promise more dramatically than O. J. Simpson. Fewer still have explored its radical insufficiency with more insight than Nathanael West.

Notes
Index

Notes

PREFACE

1. Harry Levin compared West's critical negations to the "power of blackness" that distinguished Hawthorne, Melville and Poe (in his magisterial study by the same name) during his visit to the Seminar in American Studies, Harvard University, 1987. The phrase "poet of darkness" comes from a lecture that Harold Bloom delivered at Harvard University in 1989. For an extended meditation on West as a poet of darkness in the "Miltonic-Romantic" mode, see Harold Bloom, *The Breaking of the Vessels* (Chicago: University of Chicago Press, 1982), 21–25. As I said, West is often described as an apocalyptic writer. See especially Leslie Fiedler's commentary on West in his provocative account of the thirties, "The Two Memories: Reflections on Writers and Writing in the Thirties," in *Proletarian Writers of the Thirties,* ed. David Madden (Carbondale: Southern Illinois University Press, 1968), 3–25; and Donald Weber, "West, Pynchon, Mailer, and the Jeremiad Tradition," *South Atlantic Quarterly* 83, no. 3 (Summer 1984): 259–68.

2. West has been described as a surrealist by Edmund Wilson, "The Boys in the Back Room," reprinted in the first and still the most important collection of critical essays on West, *Nathanael West: A Collection of Critical Essays,* ed. Jay Martin (Englewood Cliffs, N.J.: Prentice Hall, 1971), 140; Leslie Fiedler describes him in similar terms in "The Beginning of the Thirties: Depression, Return, and Rebirth," *Waiting for the End* (New York: Dell Press, 1964), 49–50. He is briefly included among writers on the left by Daniel Aaron in his book *Writers on the Left* (New York: Oxford University Press, 1977), 175, 307, 432. Malamud and Heller acknowledge their indebtedness to West in Lloyd Michaels, *A Particular Kind of Joking: Nathanael West and Burlesque* (Ph.D. diss., State University of New York at Buffalo, 1972), 27–28. Lavonne Mueller explores the relationship between Malamud and West more fully in "Malamud and West: Tyranny of the Dream Dump," *Nathanael West: The Cheaters and the Cheated,* ed. David Madden (Deland, Fla.: Everett/Edwards, 1973), 221–34. John Hawkes comments on his literary predecessors in "Notes on the Wild Goose Chase," Symposium: "Fiction Today," *Massachusetts Review* 3 (Summer 1962): 784–88.

3. The phrase "particular kind of joking" is actually a misquotation of the

original, which reads "private and unfunny jokes." The mistake seems to have begun with Richard Gehman, who got both the quote and the addressee of the letter wrong in his introduction to *The Day of the Locust* in 1950. The letter was sent not to George Milburn but to Edmund Wilson on 6 April, 1939. And it has been misquoted ever since. I have followed Norman Podhoretz (who used the misquoted phrase as the title of his essay on West), James F. Light, and others in their "error" because it seems to describe West's distinctive mode of apprehension better than he described it himself. The letter has been reprinted accurately in Jay Martin, *Nathanael West: The Art of His Life* (New York: Carroll and Graf, 1970), 334.

4. As quoted in James F. Light, *Nathanael West: An Interpretive Study* (Evanston, Ill.: Northwestern University Press, 1971), 164.

5. According to Jay Martin, West was a full-time member of the Screenwriters' Guild from the time of his arrival in California in 1933, but he became an active member upon his return in 1936. On 22 May 1939, West was elected studio chairman at Universal for the guild, and six months later he was elected to its executive board (*Art of His Life*, 349). West gives an interesting account of his involvement with the guild in this letter to Edmund Wilson:

> There is a funny situation out here now. The sound men are on strike, and the other unions, camera men etc. are evidently going out with them. We "Writers" (a funny thing out here—when anyone asks you what you are you say "Writer") have a new union and a very radical one, organized by such old "movement" men as Howard, Lawson, Ornitz, Weitzenkorn, Caesar, and practical [sic] every editor of *The Call* since Abraham Cahan's day. But there's no chance of our ever striking—behind the barricades we'll go willingly enough, but organized labor action never. I went to a union meeting where there was some big talk, but at the slightest bit of Producer opposition we'll fold like the tents of the Arabs. The strange thing is that almost all the members of the union admit it themselves. Today when I came to work there were pickets in front of the studio, and it felt queer to walk through them. A writer, one of them shouted, and lip-farted. (25 July, probably 1939, files of Daniel Aaron)

6. West to Malcolm Cowley, 11 May 1939, reprinted in Martin, *Art of His Life,* 335.

7. Daniel Aaron, "Late Thoughts on Nathanael West," reprinted in Martin, *Collection of Critical Essays,* 162.

8. Nathanael West, *Miss Lonelyhearts and The Day of the Locust* (New York: New Directions Press, 1962), 22, 61.

9. Rita Barnard, *The Great Depression and the Culture of Abundance* (New York: Oxford University Press, 1995), 165.

10. See especially Daniel Aaron, "The Truly Monstrous: A Note on Nathanael West," *Partisan Review* 14 (February 1947): 98–106; Aaron, "Writing for Apocalypse," *Hudson Review* 3 (Winter 1951): 634–36; Aaron, "Late Thoughts on Nathanael West," *Massachusetts Review* 6 (Winter-Spring 1965): 307–17 (reprinted in Martin, *Collection of Critical Essays,* 161–70). Norman Podhoretz,

"Nathanael West: A Particular Kind of Joking," in Martin, *Collection of Critical Essays,* 154–60. Leslie Fiedler, *Love and Death in the American Novel* (New York: Dell, 1960), 326–28, 485–91; Fiedler, "Two Memories"; Fiedler, "Master of Dreams: The Jew in a Gentile World," *Partisan Review* 34, no. 3 (Summer 1967): 339–56. See for good measure Isaac Rosenfeld, "Faulkner and Contemporaries," *Partisan Review* 18 (January-February 1951): 106–14.

11. For an interesting discussion of the way in which cold war politics may have affected W. H. Auden's reading of West, see Barnard, *Great Depression,* 168–74.

12. Podhoretz, "Particular Kind of Joking," 154–55.

13. Lionel Trilling, *The Liberal Imagination: Essays on Literature and Society* (New York: Harcourt, Brace, 1950), 56–57.

14. Aaron, "Late Thoughts," 169.

15. Barnard, *Great Depression,* 13. Barnard has two very good chapters on the way mass culture reshaped the social landscape of the 1930s (3–38). See also Warren Susman's commentary in *Culture as History* (New York: Pantheon, 1984), 150–83.

16. The best place to begin reading about this documentary approach is William Stott's magnificent survey of the documentary tradition in *Documentary Expression and Thirties America* (Chicago: University of Chicago Press, 1973).

17. Trilling, *Liberal Imagination,* 4.

18. Here, my investigation has much in common with similar efforts to recover the critical possibilities of an avant-garde tradition that Rosalind Krauss has referred to as "modernism's other." See especially Rosalind Krauss's *The Originality of the Avant-Garde and Other Modernist Myths* (Cambridge: MIT Press, 1988) and her *Optical Unconscious* (Cambridge: MIT Press, 1994); Peter Burger's *Theory of the Avant-Garde* (Minneapolis: University of Minnesota Press, 1984); as well as Hal Foster's *Compulsive Beauty* (Cambridge: MIT Press, 1993).

19. Foster concurs; he argues that because surrealism is "an agonistic modernism within official modernism," it has tended to remain "a blind spot in the [official] Anglo-American view of modernism" (*Compulsive Beauty,* xiii–iv).

20. Dickran Tashjian is one of the few exceptions. He has done more than anyone else to sketch the historical dimensions of the avant-garde tradition in America. See his *Skyscraper Primitives: Dada and the American Avant-Garde, 1910–1925* (Middletown, Conn.: Wesleyan University Press, 1975) and *A Boatload of Madmen: Surrealism and the American Avant-Garde, 1920–1950* (New York: Thames and Hudson, 1995)—both of which I rely on heavily here and throughout this book. My convictions about the critical presence of an avant-garde tradition in America have been bolstered and enlarged significantly by Marjorie Perloff. See *The Dance of the Intellect* (New York: Cambridge University Press, 1985) and *The Poetics of Indeterminacy: Rimbaud to Cage* (Evanston, Ill.: Northwestern University Press, 1981), especially her chapter "The 'French' Decade of William Carlos Williams," 109–54.

21. Roger Shattuck, "Love and Laughter: Surrealism Reappraised," an introduction to Maurice Nadeau, *The History of Surrealism* (Cambridge: Harvard University Press, 1989), 31–32.

22. Andreas Huyssen, *After the Great Divide: Modernism, Mass Culture, Postmodernism* (Bloomington: Indiana University Press, 1986), 6.

23. West, "Some Notes on Miss L," *Collection of Critical Essays,* 66.

24. West, *Miss Lonelyhearts and The Day of the Locust,* 1.

25. This is essentially Jonathan Raban's criticism of West as it is summarized by Barnard in *The Great Depression and the Culture of Abundance,* 142. Raban complains, "West's fictional world is essentially one of objects, of commodities. When people enter it they become transfixed and assimilated into the dime-store jumble of parti-coloured rubbish. . . . If it is surrealism," Raban dismissively concludes, "it is the home-town surrealism of the neighborhood supermarket" (Barnard, 229–30). This is, of course, precisely the point I have been trying to make, albeit from an entirely different point of view. As I argue, West enlarges the anti-aesthetic stance of the avant-garde to include specifically commercial contexts like the dime store and the neighborhood supermarket. In doing so, he adapts the traditional strategies of the avant-garde into a more wide-ranging mode of social criticism. See Jonathan Raban, "A Surfeit of Commodities: The Novels of Nathanael West," in *The American Novel and the Nineteen Twenties,* ed. Malcolm Bradbury (London: Edward Arnold, 1971).

INTRODUCTION: WHO CAN WE SHOOT?
THE CRISIS OF REPRESENTATION IN THE 1930S

1. John Steinbeck, *The Grapes of Wrath* (New York: Penguin Books, 1972), 51–52.

2. Ibid., 65.

3. As quoted in Warren Susman, *Culture as History* (New York: Pantheon, 1984), 193.

4. Arthur Inman, *The Inman Diaries,* ed. Daniel Aaron (Cambridge: Harvard University Press, 1985), 549.

5. Robert Wiebe, *The Search for Order* (New York: Hill and Wang, 1967), xii–xiv.

6. Ibid., 12.

7. Thurman Arnold, "The Crash—and What It Meant," in *The Aspirin Age,* ed. Isabel Leighton (New York: Penguin Books, 1949), 237–38.

8. Daniel Boorstin's reading of the years preceding the Depression supplements Wiebe's argument nicely. Among other things, Boorstin observes that the emerging modern order lacked the heft and density of the preceding one. Traditional associations—the family, church, neighborhood, ethnic groups—were gradually reconstituted into far-flung communities based on nothing more substantial than the logic of statistics (in which "the most ancient and sacred of

human relations—rich and poor, parent and child, husband and wife—were antisepticized into percentages") or the language of consumption (in which people were "affiliated less by what they believed than by what they consumed"). Boorstin has described this disorienting experience as the "defeat of the seen, the nearby, the familiar, by the everywhere community." These new communities were ideally suited to the new order; they "were quick; they were nonideological; they were democratic; they were public and vague, and rapidly shifting." But they could not provide the support that was necessary when Americans were forced to rely on them for more than a poll of public opinion or the purchase of a commodity. *The Americans* (New York: Vintage Books, 1974), 89–90, 166.

9. Alan Brinkley, *Voices of Protest: Huey Long, Father Coughlin, and the Great Depression* (New York: Vintage, 1983), 157.

10. Archibald MacLeish, *Land of the Free* (New York: Harcourt, Brace, 1938), 82.

11. Oscar Ameringer, testimony before the subcommittee of the Committee on Labor, House of Representatives, 72d Congress, 1st session, on H.R. 206, H.R. 6011, H.R. 8088 (Washington: Government Printing Office, 1932), 98–99. As quoted in David Shannon, *The Great Depression* (Englewood Cliffs, N.J.: Prentice-Hall, 1960), 27.

12. Wiebe, *Search for Order*, 97.

13. Ibid., 7.

14. As Alan Brinkley puts it, "To accept that the problem was not an identifiable person or institution but a vast, abstract process would have been to admit that there were no easily discernible explanations or solutions. It would have been to accept that diffuse, incomprehensible forces were governing society. It would have been to invite a sense of futility and hopelessness" (*Voices of Protest*, 157).

15. Steinbeck, *Grapes of Wrath*, 48.

16. Leo Marx's *The Machine in the Garden* (New York: Oxford University Press, 1964) remains the starting point for any investigation into this topic.

17. Steinbeck, *Grapes of Wrath*, 69–71.

18. William Empson, *Some Versions of Pastoral* (New York: New Directions, 1974), 6.

19. As quoted in Terry Smith, *The Making of the Modern: Industry, Art, and Design in America* (Chicago: University of Chicago Press, 1993), 322.

20. Ibid., 315.

21. Even when the signs of modernity are included in the photographs of the FSA—as in Rothstein's photograph of a young, black sharecropper in Gee's Bend peering out her cabin window, beside which hangs an advertisement for the miraculous preservative properties of cellophane—they are there as a foil for the authenticating presence of the "the people." In this case, the girl's strength, probity, and capacity to endure promises her (our) eventual triumph over the worst the Depression has to offer. As Rita Barnard explains it, these photographs "draw the eye away from the realm of spectacular consumption, away from those self-

congratulatory commodities, to the human beings [behind] them. This is, argu-
ably, the classic demystificatory gesture—the classic form of protest—in the [art]
of the thirties" (*The Great Depression and the Culture of Abundance* [New York:
Cambridge University Press, 1995], 139).

22. Lawrence Levine, "The Historian and the Icon: Photography and the History of the American People in the 1930s and 1940s," *Documenting America,
1935–1943* (Berkeley: University of California Press, 1988), 37.

23. This is essentially Richard Hofstadter's argument in *The Age of Reform*
(New York: Vintage, 1955). Among other things, Hofstadter argues that Pop-
ulism tended to fixate on its rural, relatively homogenous, antebellum origins to
the exclusion of all else. At the core of these idealized origins was the yeoman
farmer whose putative independence from the distant marketplace left him free of
the compromises and dependencies required of the urban wage slave. Of course,
this ideal of the yeoman farmer is pure fiction. For all his demurrals, the American farmer has always been a businessman. When times were difficult, however,
the farmer tended to deny his implication in the capitalist system and retreat into
the "role of the injured little yeoman" (47). Hofstadter explains, "the Agrarian
myth encouraged farmers to believe that they were not themselves an organic part
of the whole order of business enterprise and speculation that flourished in the
city . . . but rather the innocent pastoral victims of a conspiracy hatched in the
distance" (35).

CHAPTER 1: AMERICAN SUPERREALISM

1. I am thinking especially of painters like Louis Gugliemi, James Guy, Walter Quirt, and Peter Blume, along with writers like Murray Godwin, Charles
Henri Ford, and, with some qualifications and complications, Djuna Barnes.

2. Dickran Tashjian has some interesting things to say about the way surrealist cultural practices were depoliticized as they were adapted to the American
scene in *A Boatload of Madmen: Surrealism and the American Avant-Garde,
1920–1950* (New York: Thames and Hudson, 1995).

3. Nathanael West, *Miss Lonelyhearts and The Day of the Locust* (New
York: New Directions, 1962), 9, 70; *A Cool Million* (New York: Farrar, Straus
and Giroux, 1970), 163.

4. In a 1939 review of *The Day of the Locust*, Clifton Fadiman described
West as "about the ablest of our surrealist authors." According to Jay Martin the
review irritated West, who responded, "He [Fadiman] is an extremely intelligent
guy and knows what surrealism is and therefore also knows that I am not a surrealist author." Denials like these have tended to stymie critical efforts to understand West within the context of surrealism. West responded the way he did,
Martin speculates, because he feared that Fadiman's "epithet had sunk the book"
with American book buyers. Jay Martin, *Nathanael West: The Art of His Life*
(New York: Carroll and Graf, 1970), 338.

5. Nathanael West, "Through the Hole in the Mundane Millstone," *A Collection of Critical Essays,* ed. Jay Martin (Englewood Cliffs, N.J.: Prentice Hall, 1970), 29. West's contact with surrealism was limited mostly to what he read in journals and books as well as what he saw in galleries. He was probably first introduced to surrealism through journals like *Broom,* the *Little Review,* and *transition.* He also read avidly in the literature of the avant-garde, numbering among his favorite authors many of surrealism's "patron saints" such as those named in the text. And he almost certainly saw the American exhibition of surrealist painting at the Julien Levy Gallery in January 1932.

6. As quoted in Maurice Nadeau, *The History of Surrealism* (Cambridge: Harvard University Press, 1989), 228.

7. In fact, Apollinaire's coy pretense of writing a "woman's column" under the pseudonym of Louise Lalanne may have been at least one source of inspiration for the "mixed" identity of Miss Lonelyhearts, while Jarry's blasphemous satire "The Passion Considered as an Uphill Bicycle Race" is surely the inspiration for *Balso Snell'*s biography of St. Puce ("a flea who was born, lived, and died, beneath the arm of our Lord") as well as for Shrike's own blasphemous allusions to "the Passion in the Luncheonette," the "Agony of the Soda Fountain," and so on, in *Miss Lonelyhearts.* Nathaneal West, *The Dream Life of Balso Snell* (New York: Farrar, Straus and Giroux, 1970), 11; *Miss Lonelyhearts and The Day of the Locust,* 7.

8. As quoted in Hans Richter, *Dada: Art and Anti-Art* (New York: Oxford University Press, 1978), 176.

9. Georges Hugnet offers a good summary of Berlin Dada's aims in "The Dada Spirit in Painting," in *The Dada Painters and Poets,* ed. Robert Motherwell (Cambridge: Harvard University Press, 1988), 141–53.

10. As quoted in Dawn Ades, *Photomontage* (New York: Thames and Hudson, 1986), 42.

11. The relationship between Dada and surrealism is a subject of much debate. Lucy Lippard describes surrealism as "Housebroken Dada" (Introduction, *Dadas on Art* [Englewood Cliffs, N.J.: Prentice-Hall, 1971], 8). Those like Lippard who disdain surrealism do so because they feel that surrealism merely cannibalized the richness of Dada and systematized it. Others, like Roger Shattuck, dispute this assessment, arguing that surrealism was every bit as "wayward and contradictory" as Dada: "Don't let anyone tell you that surrealism took all these high spirits and subdued them, fitted them into a rational synthesis. The situation was very different" ("The D-S Expedition," *The Innocent Eye* [New York: Washington Square Press, 1986], 49). There is no question that, as Robert Motherwell put it, "in proposing [to] undertake psychic researches, investigate automatism . . . and ultimately embrace the politics of the left, [surrealism, or at least Breton's version of surrealism] turned 'the gay blasphemy' of Duchamp and other 'natural' dadas into a world of serious, organized aims" (Introduction, *Dada Painters and Poets,* xxxii). This was not necessarily a bad thing. Surrealism's "systemization"

of some of Dada's most basic premises—chance, incongruous juxtaposition, and the irrational as modes of social criticism—teased out their implications and took them to their logical (and occasionally unsatisfying) conclusions. As far as West is concerned, the tension between "the gay blasphemy" of Dada and the "organized aims" of the left is perhaps the best context in which to understand the tensions that animate his fiction.

12. Nadeau offers a good overview of the key events that defined surrealism's vexed relationship to communism in *The History of Surrealism*, 127–98.

13. The shorter version of the poem, entitled "Christmass Poem," was first published in *Contempo* 3 (21 February 1933): 4. The longer version was never published during West's lifetime, although it has been reprinted since in Martin, *Art of His Life*, 330–31. This poem is usually read as the inspiration behind Tod Hackett's painting "The Burning of Los Angeles" in *The Day of the Locust*. But, as I argue, its real significance lies in West's preliminary attempt to meld surrealism and politics.

14. Early in 1931, upon his return from the Soviet-sponsored Kharkov Conference on revolutionary literature, Louis Aragon published a poem called "Red Front." In it he called for the assassination of the "trained bears of social democracy" and listed some of them by name. The French government took the threats seriously and prosecuted Aragon for an attempt to incite murder, a crime punishable with up to five years in jail. Breton and the surrealists immediately came to his defense, circulating a petition that declared that it was illegitimate to "interpret a poetic text for judiciary ends." Breton's attempt to absolve Aragon of his responsibility for his own words elicited scorn from the more committed members of the communist movement—including Aragon himself!—and contributed to the growing breach between them. Tashjian has a good summary of the affair in *Boatload*, 111–13.

15. The following excerpt from "Red Front" underscores the similarities of the two poems:

> A star is born of earth
> A star today leads toward a burning pyre
> Boudenny's soldiers
> Forward march Boudenny's soldiers
> You are the armed conscience of the Proletariat
> . . .
> Each of your bodies is a falling diamond
> Each of your worms a purifying fire
> The flash of your rifles sends back the ordure
> France first of all
> Spare nothing Boudenny's soldiers
> Each of your cries bears on the glowing Breath
> of the Universal Revolution
> Each time you breathe you propagate Marx and Lenin in the sky
> You are red like the dawn

red like anger
red like blood
. . .
Proletarians of the world unite.

Translated by Maurice Nadeau and reprinted in his *History of Surrealism,* 293–94.

16. Clement Greenberg, "Surrealist Painting," *The Collected Essays and Criticism,* vol. 1: *Perceptions and Judgments, 1939–1944* (Chicago: University of Chicago Press, 1986), 227.

17. Hans Arp quotes these lines from Marcel Janco with approval in "Dada Was Not a Farce," in Motherwell, *Dada Painters and Poets,* 295.

18. Greenberg, "Surrealist Painting," 228. In "Towards a Newer Laocoon," Greenberg's most ambitious (and I must say, breathtaking) attempt to define modern painting's proper "field of activity" (32), he describes Miro, Klee, and Arp as "pseudo- or mock Surrealists . . . whose work, despite its apparent intention [presumably the exploration of the unconscious] has only contributed to the further deployment of abstract painting pure and simple." Greenberg continues, "Indeed, a good many of the artists—if not the majority—who contributed importantly to the development modern painting came to it with the desire to exploit the break with imitative realism for a more powerful expressiveness, but so inexorable was the logic of the development that in the end their work constituted but another step towards abstract art, and a further sterilization of the expressive factors" (*Perceptions and Judgments,* 36–37).

19. Shattuck, *Innocent Eye,* 52.

20. Arp, "Dada Was Not a Farce," 294.

21. Rosalind Krauss, *The Optical Unconscious* (Cambridge: MIT Press, 1994,) 54.

22. Greenberg, "Surrealist Painting," 228.

23. As quoted in Krauss, *Optical Unconscious,* 123.

24. Greenberg, *Surrealist Painting,* 228. Obviously, Greenberg's criticism does not address a good deal of Duchamp's nonrepresentational imagery (nor was it intended to). But the notion of academicism is true to the "spirit" of Duchamp's work.

25. Ibid., 228–29.

26. One finds this hallucinatory/deflationary strategy throughout the work of the "academic" surrealists. The example that immediately comes to mind is Magritte, who renders even the most prosaic objects with "hallucinatory vividness." But he is careful never to allow the flight into the sur-real so highly prized by his contemporaries. His paintings always begin and end in banal settings that serve to "ground" the fantastic in a thoroughly bourgeois context. One can also find the same strategy in the "humdrum" technique that West's Faye Greener unwittingly uses to manufacture her own "fantastic" South Sea tales: "The effect was similar to that obtained by the artists of the Middle Ages, who, when doing

a subject like the raising of Lazarus from the dead or Christ walking on water, were careful to keep all the details intensely realistic. She, like them, seemed to think that fantasy could be made plausible by a humdrum technique" (West, *Miss Lonelyhearts and The Day of the Locust,* 107). Where Faye adopts this humdrum technique in order to make fantasy plausible, West deploys that very same technique in order to devitalize fantasy and subject it to a withering scrutiny.

27. Michel Foucault, *This Is Not a Pipe* (Berkeley: University of California Press, 1982).

28. Hal Foster, *Compulsive Beauty* (Cambridge: MIT Press, 1993), 96.

29. In her illuminating essay "The Photographic Conditions of Surrealism," Rosalind Krauss argues that surrealism can be defined by its insistence that all reality, all nature is reducible to "a kind of writing." But clearly, for the surrealists that Greenberg has in mind, that is a situation to be overcome. See her *The Originality of the Avant-Garde and Other Modernist Myths* (Cambridge: MIT Press, 1988), 87–118, especially 113.

CHAPTER 2. EUCLID'S ASSHOLE:
THE DREAM LIFE OF BALSO SNELL

1. Nathanael West, "The Fake," box 1, Jay Martin Collection, Huntington Library, 8–9.

2. Ibid., 11–12.

3. Although West claimed to have spent two years in Paris, he actually spent less then three months there (from 13 October 1926 until early January 1927), during which he worked on *The Dream Life of Balso Snell.* For more on West's activities in Paris and his response to the expatriates who had preceded him there, see Jay Martin, *Nathanael West: The Art of His Life* (New York: Carroll and Graf, 1970), 78–92.

4. West's work is situated at some distance from the paradigm of high modernism. In fact it is more accurately placed within a tradition that originates with the "avant-garde" and culminates in "postmodernism." Unlike their high modernist counterparts, many of those who participated in this "other" tradition tried to fashion an art that remained open to history—eschewing even the notion of "art" itself. This anti-aesthetic marshaled a powerful cultural critique of the romantic paradigm upon which modernism continued to function—i.e., a dependence on a centered subject, a faith in the capacities of representation, a reliance on organic, determinate forms. In West's hands this critique was readily adapted to a subtle exploration of the impact of the forms of mass culture on subjectivity and everyday life.

5. This sort of "scandal" is a staple of autobiographies and accounts of the period. For an example, see "The Significant Gesture" in Malcolm Cowley's *Exile's Return* (New York: Viking Press, 1985), 164–70.

6. Nathanael West, *The Dream Life of Balso Snell* (New York: Farrar, Straus and Giroux, 1970), 30. All future references to this novel will appear parenthetically within the text.

7. West, "The Fake," 1.

8. Stanley Edgar Hyman, *Nathanael West,* University of Minnesota Pamphlets on American Writers (Minneapolis: University of Minnesota Press, 1962), 15; Daniel Aaron, "The Truly Monstrous: A Note on Nathanael West," *Partisan Review* 14 (February 1947): 100; Edmund Wilson, "The Boys in the Back Room," in *Nathanael West: A Collection of Critical Essays,* ed. Jay Martin (Englewood Cliffs, N.J.: Prentice-Hall, 1971), 140; Malcolm Cowley, as quoted in Gerald Locklin, "*The Dream Life of Balso Snell*: Journey into the Microcosm," in *Nathanael West: The Cheaters and the Cheated,* ed. David Madden (Deland, Fla.: Everett/Edwards, 1973), 23.

9. "The Cheaters and the Cheated" was the working title of *The Day of the Locust.*

10. In teasing out the ideological implications of these complementary concerns, I will have occasion to draw on the work of Georges Bataille and Mikhail Bakntin. I do so not in order to legitimate West by putting him in their "august" company. Rather, their theoretical writings provide me with the opportunity to explain West's approach to a shared set of questions. This approach is particularly illuminating, as we shall see, in those instances where there are important differences between them.

11. The inspiration for the novella may have been James Branch Cabell's *Jurgen,* but as we shall see, West takes an entirely different tack from Cabell's highly mannered aestheticism.

12. Nathanael West, "Through the Hole in the Mundane Millstone," in Martin, *Collection of Critical Essays,* 30.

13. The title of the book may have been inspired by Marcel Duchamp's rejection of Tristan Tzara, who attempted to use Duchamp's name to organize an exhibition of Dada artists in 1921 without the latter's permission. Duchamp sent Tzara a telegram that read simply, "PODE BALL" (the phonetic spelling of *peau de balle* or "balls to you"). Much of *Balso Snell* reads like an extended elaboration on Duchamp's infamous urinal—conducted, appropriately enough, by Balso Snell, who is described by West as an "ambassador from that ingenious people, the inventors and perfecters of the automatic water-closet" (6).

14. American literature would have to wait until Charles Bukowski for a similarly enthusiastic (and ill-conceived?) paean to the human posterior.

15. Roger Shattuck, *The Banquet Years* (New York: Vintage Press, 1968), 35–37.

16. The pun is also highly prized by the surrealists, who saw it as an entrée of sorts into the surreal, the means of transcending the iron cage of rationality embedded in language. But West's punning in *Balso Snell* is less a means of transcending language than of exposing its fundamental arbitrariness. His strategy

has much in common with Jonathan Culler's description of the pun's function as it is described in "The Call of the Phoneme," *On Puns: The Foundation of Letters*, ed. Jonathan Culler (Oxford: Basil Blackwell, 1988), 1–17. Culler writes, "When one thinks of how puns characteristically demonstrate the applicability of a single signifying sequence to two different contexts, with quite different meanings, one can see how puns both evoke prior formulations, with the meanings they have deployed, and demonstrate their instability, the mutability of meaning, the *production of meaning by linguistic motivation*" (14; italics mine).

17. Randall Reid, *The Fiction of Nathanael West* (Chicago: University of Chicago Press, 1967), 19.

18. Georges Bataille, "The 'Old Mole' and the Prefix *Sur* in the Words *Surhomme* and *Surrealist*," *Visions of Excess: Selected Writings, 1927–1939* (Minneapolis: University of Minnesota Press, 1985), 34.

19. Georges Bataille, "The Big Toe," *Visions of Excess*, 20–23.

20. As quoted in Maurice Nadeau, *The History of Surrealism* (Cambridge: Harvard University Press, 1989), 156. Bataille's wild and vitriolic dispute with Breton can be boiled down to the usual differences that separate idealists and materialists. In "The Second Manifesto of Surrealism," Breton condemns Bataille as "an 'excrement-philosopher' who refuses to rise above big toes, mere matter, sheer shit, to raise the low to the high, to proper form and sublimated beauty" (Hal Foster, *Compulsive Beauty* [Cambridge: MIT Press, 1993], 112). Bataille likewise chastises Breton—this time in more measured language—for continuing "to express [his] basic predilection for values *above* the 'world of facts'" despite his rapproachement with communism. In place of surrealism's "banal . . . 'revolt of the Spirit,'" Bataille argues for a "point of departure [that] has nothing to do with the heavens, preferred station of . . . Christian or revolutionary utopias." The real revolution, he reminds Breton, "begins in the bowels of the earth, as in the materialist bowels of the proletarians" ("'Old Mole,'" 33, 35). It is possible that this antagonism between Bataille and Breton is what West had in mind when he wrote his blurb for the dust jacket of *Balso Snell* in which he attempts to distinguish between various surrealisms.

21. Alan Stoekl, Introduction, *Visions of Excess*, xv. For more on this, see Bataille's "The Critique of the Foundations of the Hegelian Dialectic," ibid., 105–15.

22. Georges Bataille, "Base Materialism and Gnosticism," *Visions of Excess*, 47.

23. On the surface, at least, the linguistic virtuosity of West's negations in *Balso Snell* would appear to possess an autonomous power that one might describe in terms of *archontes*. But as Randall Reid, one of West's most astute critics, correctly surmises, West's "talent was hardly volcanic. . . . His success depends upon the cool precision of each phrase, not on an exuberant display of energy" (*Fiction of Nathanael West*, 37).

Nowhere are West's differences from Bataille more clearly drawn than in this statement from John Raskolnikov Gilson, a would-be Gnostic who is tortured by his failure to turn matter into an active principle: "If I could only turn irritation into pain; could push the whole thing into insanity and so escape. I am able to turn irritation into active pain for only a few seconds, but the pain soon subsides and the monotonous rhythm of irritation returns" (28). West would agree.

24. Bataille, "'Old Mole,'" 33.

25. West to Edmund Wilson, 6 April 1939, private files of Daniel Aaron.

26. Mikhail Bakhtin also offers a warning that bears directly on this subject:

> If the positive and negative poles of becoming (death-birth) are torn apart and opposed to each other in various diffuse images, they lose their direct relation to the whole and are deprived of their ambivalence. They then retain the merely negative aspect, and that which they represent (defecation, urination) acquires a trivial meaning, our own contemporary meaning of these words. (*Rabelais and His World* [Bloomington: Indiana University Press, 1984], 150)

In *Balso Snell* the "positive and negative poles" are irrevocably sundered. As a result there is no sense of wholeness of which they are a part, no dialectical "ambivalence" out of which each constructs it opposite.

27. Peter Stallybrass and Allon White, *The Politics and Poetics of Transgression* (Ithaca, N.Y.: Cornell University Press, 1986), 113. Stallybrass and White go on to explore the construction of this privileged discourse still further. They argue that "A recurrent pattern emerges: the 'top' attempts to reject and eliminate the 'bottom' for reasons of prestige and status, only to discover, not only that it is in some way frequently dependent upon that low-Other . . . but also that the top *includes* that low symbolically, as a primary eroticized constituent of its own fantasy life. The result is a mobile conflictual fusion of power, fear and desire in the construction of subjectivity: a psychological dependence upon precisely those Others which are being rigorously opposed and excluded at the social level. It is for this reason that what is *socially* peripheral is so frequently *symbolically* central" (5).

28. To be sure, the relationship between the body and any psychic or social topography is a complex one in which distinctions made in one domain are continually structured, legitimated, and dissolved by reference to the symbolic hierarchy that operates in the others. But this highly charged, multifarious dialectic among seemingly disparate symbolic domains is, in fact, the means by which a culture quite literally "thinks itself" (Stallybrass and White, *Politics and Poetics of Transgression,* 3). Not only does West understand this but it serves as the foundation for his social criticism.

29. See Leslie Fiedler, *Love and Death in the American Novel* (New York: Dell, 1960), especially 485–90; Fiedler, "The Two Memories: Reflections on Writers and Writing in the Thirties," reprinted in *Proletarian Writers of the Thirties,* ed. David Madden (Carbondale: Southern Illinois University Press, 1968), especially 8–9, 18; Harold Bloom, *The Breaking of the Vessels* (Chicago: University of Chicago Press, 1982), especially 21–25.

30. Nathanael West, *Miss Lonelyhearts and The Day of the Locust* (New York: New Directions, 1962), 132.

31. Mikhail Bakhtin, *Problems of Dostoevski's Poetics* (Minneapolis: University of Minnesota Press, 1984), 63.

32. West, "Through the Hole in the Mundane Millstone," 30.

33. Mikhail Bakhtin, *The Dialogic Imagination* (Austin: University of Texas Press, 1971), 293.

34. Ibid., 326.

35. In *Les Pas perdus* Breton makes a similar observation: "If every work of art is a forgery it is not only because the man who composes it cannot possibly be sincere. In addition to the constraints of art, ordinary language is 'the worst of conventions' because it imposes upon us the use of formulas and verbal associations which do not belong to us, which embody next to nothing of our true natures; the very meanings of words are fixed and unchangeable only because of an abuse of power by the collectivity. . . ." As quoted in *The Dada Painters and Poets,* ed. Robert Motherwell (Cambridge: Harvard University Press, 1988), xxxv.

36. Bakhtin, *Rabelais and His World*, 11.

CHAPTER 3. "LOUSY WITH PURE / REEKING WITH STARK":
CONTACT

1. E. E. Cummings, "Let's Start a Magazine," *Contact,* 2d ser., 1, no. 1 (February 1932): 10. Cummings' poem, quoted in the epigraph, was one of four published in the opening pages of *Contact*'s first issue in the thirties. The second poem in that series parodies the magazine's ambitions in a more elliptical and playful manner:

```
                              r-p-o-p-h-e-s-s-a-g-r
                        who
a)s w(e loo)k
upnowgath
                           PPEGORHRASS
                              eringint (o-
aThe): 1
                    ea
                  !p:
S                                                                              a
                            r)
rI vInG                                      .gRrEaPsPhOs)
                                               to
rea(be)rran (com)gi(e)ngly
      ,grasshopper;
```

        ("r-p-o-p-h-e-s-s-a-g-r," "Let's Start a Magazine," 11)

The poem, to "quote" Cummings' penultimate line, is "rearrange(d) becomingly" in a game of verbal and typographic play whose symbol is the grasshopper. The colons, parentheses, and other forms of punctuation are there for pure show—making a mockery of the meaning-making operations they purport to parse into grammatical units. One can (if one must) rearrange the letters in this poem in order to paraphrase it thus: Grasshopper, who as we look up now, gathering into the . . . leaps, arriving to rearrange becomingly. But it is the becoming rearrangement of alphabet and sense that most interests Cummings. And that rearrangement has a rather pointed message for the editors of *Contact.*

The message is based on the parable of the grasshopper and the ant invoked by the poem. In that admonitory little story it is the ant's willingness to labor while the grasshopper plays that ultimately enables it to survive the winter. The grasshopper, lacking such foresight, goes begging. But here Cummings reverses the values and celebrates the indifference and *joie de vivre* of the grasshopper. Given the context in which the poem appears, it is hard not to conclude that Cummings intended the poem as a sly parody of the magazine's ambitions. While the "worker" ants of proletarian fiction perform the tedious labor of social criticism, Cummings asserts in grand fashion his right to go on playing.

2. Dickran Tashjian, *William Carlos Williams and the American Scene, 1920–1940* (Berkeley: University of California Press, 1978), 24, 27. Tashjian goes on to argue that this spirit of "contact" animated much of the domestic cultural scene of the American avant-garde: from Stieglitz's early photographs, to Duchamp's readymades, to the Precisionists, to the objectivists, to the poetry of William Carlos Williams himself.

3. Williams and McAlmon were adamant in their rejection of "past art" as a "hangover from previous generations no better equipped to ascertain value than are we" ("Opening Comment," *Contact,* original ser., 1, no.1 [December 1920]: 1). They were equally adamant in their rejection of all "imported thought": "Americans are still too prone to admire and to copy the very thing which should not be copied, the thing which is French or Irish alone, the thing which is the result of special local conditions of thought and circumstance" ("Further Announcement," *Contact,* original ser., 1, no. 1 [December 1920]: 10).

4. William Carlos Williams, "Yours, O Youth," *Contact,* original ser., 1, no. 3 (n.d.): 14. Williams' discussion of the significance of "contact" was carried on throughout the life of the magazine. But his most succinct meditation takes place in the essay cited above.

5. Williams and McAlmon "Opening Comment," 1.

6. William Carlos Williams, "Final Comment," *Contact,* original ser., 1, no. 2 (January 1921): last page.

7. Williams and McAlmon, "Further Announcement," 10.

8. Jay Martin, *Nathanael West: The Art of His Life* (New York: Carroll and Graf, 1970), 144.

9. West's faith in the little magazine as a forum for experimental writing was

amply demonstrated in a letter he and Julian Shapiro sent to a column entitled "Book Marks for Today," in the New York World Telegram (20 October 1931), 23 (reprinted in William White, Nathanael West: A Comprehensive Bibliography [Kent, Ohio: Kent State University Press, 1975], 131). One of the most distinctive aspects of Contact was its commitment to the tradition of the little magazine. Each number contains an extensive bibliography (compiled by David Moss) devoted to the publishing history of the little magazine. In a short commentary entitled "The Advance Guard Magazine," Williams offers his own idiosyncratic overview of that history, which concludes by saying that "the 'small magazine' must in its many phases be taken as one expression" (Contact, 2d ser., 1, no. 1 [February 1932]: 89).

10. It could also be argued that Contact was to prove crucial in the gestation of Williams' Paterson as well.

11. West to William Carlos Williams, October 1931, box 1, Jay Martin Collection, Huntington Library.

12. West to William Carlos Williams, November-December 1931, box 1, Jay Martin Collection, Huntington Library. The date of this letter is unclear, but the events to which it refers place it in November or December of 1931.

13. West to William Carlos Williams, June 1932, box 1, Jay Martin Collection, Huntington Library.

14. Williams may have had reservations of his own about Sheeler's appropriateness. In the late thirties he confided to Constance Rourke that Sheeler's reliance on the impersonal effects of photography often resulted in an empty realism (Tashjian, William Carlos Williams and the American Scene, 81). For more on the ideological implications of Sheeler's aesthetic, see Terry Smith, The Making of the Modern (Chicago: University of Chicago Press, 1993), 93–136.

15. West to William Carlos Williams, June 1932, box 1, Jay Martin Collection, Huntington Library.

16. For more on the importance of cover design in defining the tone, themes, and aspirations of the little magazine—as well as some wonderful illustrations—see Cary Nelson, Repression and Recovery: Modern American Poetry and the Politics of Cultural Memory, 1910–1945 (Madison: University of Wisconsin Press, 1989), 181–233.

17. In a commentary entitled "The Advance Guard Magazine," Williams picks up his running battle with T. S. Eliot where he left off. Taking the latter's appointment to a teaching position at Harvard as an occasion for comment, Williams expresses his concern over the increasingly "professorial" and "system[atic]" (read bookish) approach to American letters. After criticizing Eliot's Criterion (88), he goes on to chide the other journals of high modernism for a variety of sins—citing the "unreasoned exclusiveness" of the Hound and Horn (89), the scattershot or "everywhere" approach of Poetry (88), the Eurocentric bias of the Dial (89). This diatribe not only lacks the fire of its predecessors, it is placed at the end (rather than the beginning) of Contact's first number, indicating its diminished importance in the raison d'être of the magazine.

18. William Carlos Williams, "Comment," *Contact,* 2d ser., 1, no. 1 (February 1932): 1, 8.

19. Mike Gold, "Proletarian Realism," *Mike Gold: A Literary Anthology* (New York: International Publishers, 1972), 206–7.

20. Richard Pells, *Radical Visions and American Dreams* (Middletown, Conn.: Wesleyan University Press, 1973), 181.

21. Literary histories of proletarian literature and the fierce debates it spawned abound. Perhaps the best place to begin is with Daniel Aaron's *Writers on the Left* (New York: Oxford University Press, 1977) and Richard Pells's *Radical Visions and American Dreams.* Walter Rideout's *The Radical Novel in the United States* (New York: Hill and Wang, 1966) is somewhat dated but still useful. James Gilbert's *Writers and Partisans* (New York: Columbia University Press, 1992) fills in some of the gaps in the above-mentioned studies, most notably in his sympathetic discussion of *Partisan Review.* Gilbert's study finds its Janus-faced opposite in Barbara Foley's *Radical Representations* (Durham, N.C.: Duke University Press, 1993). Foley's exhaustive analysis is marred by her tendentious determination to "treat 'anti-Communist,' 'anti-Marxist,' and 'anti-Stalinist' as interchangeable" terms (7). Cary Nelson's *Repression and Recovery* contains an extensive and provocative discussion of proletarian poetry (a genre of writing largely neglected by the rest). Nelson's study is easily the richest and most provocative examination of proletarian literature available. Paula Rabinowitz, *Labor and Desire: Women's Revolutionary Fiction in Depression America* (Chapel Hill: University of North Carolina Press, 1992), provides a useful corrective to a heretofore male-centered discussion. David Madden's critical anthology, *Proletarian Writers of the Thirties* (Carbondale: Southern Illinois University Press, 1968), offers uneven but generally helpful essays on specific proletarian writers (like Robert Cantwell, Jack Conroy, Daniel Fuchs, and Dalton Trumbo). "The Roots of Radicals," by Marcus Klein, has some interesting things to say about Nathanael West. But the best essay in the volume by far is Leslie Fiedler's memoir, "The Two Memories: Reflections on Writers and Writing in the Thirties." Finally, William Stott's *Documentary Expression and Thirties America* (Chicago: University of Chicago Press, 1986) provides a good counterweight to the tendency to read the "socially concerned" writing of the thirties exclusively in terms of a leftist aesthetics and agenda.

22. Williams, "Comment," 1.

23. The bulk of the material published in this first issue is, in fact, reminiscent of *Seven Arts,* particularly insofar as it is devoted to the relationship between high art and commercial culture. Thus, for example, S. J. Perelman offers a satire of the latter in his *faux* movie proposal, entitled, "Scenario." And Ben Hecht makes his allegiances clear in "Ballad of the Talkies": "Squawking hams / will go the way of last year's snows / . . . While Gallant Thespis thumbs his nose." Only Diego Rivera is willing to side (at least to a point) with commercial culture. In "Mickey Mouse and American Art," he compares cartoons ("the standardization of the drawing of details, the infinite variety of groupings") to Egyptian friezes, Grecian

earthenware, and the folk art of Mexico. "The animated cartoons," he argues, are "of the purest and most definitive graphic style, of the greatest efficacy as social products, drawings joyous and simple that make the masses of tired men and women rest, make the children laugh until they are ready for sleep. . . . The aesthete," he concludes, "will find that MICKEY MOUSE was one of the genuine heroes of American Art in the first half of the 20th Century in the calendar anterior to the world revolution." *Contact,* 2d ser., 1, no. 1 (February 1932): 36, 37–39.

24. The following is a table of contents for the three numbers of *Contact* under discussion:

February 1932

Editor's Introduction	William Carlos Williams
Four Poems by Cummings	E. E. Cummings
My Country 'Tis of Thee	Charles Reznikoff
Ballad of the Talkies	Ben Hecht
Mickey Mouse and American Art	Diego Rivera
Poems	Louis Zukofsky
Scenario	S. J. Perelman
Idiot of Love	Parker Tyler
The Colored Girls of Passenack	William Carlos Williams
Miss Lonelyhearts and the Lamb	Nathanael West
It's All Very Complicated	Robert McAlmon
The Advance Guard Magazine	William Carlos Williams
Bibliography of the Little Magazine	David Moss

May 1932

Mary	Nathan Asch
Two Chapters from Miss Lonelyhearts	Nathanael West
Return of the Native	Marsden Hartley
Over the Green Mountains	Erskine Caldwell
Two Poems	William Carlos Williams
Mexican Interval	Robert McAlmon
Fire at the Catholic Church	Julian Shapiro
Circus	Evan Shipman
Paseo	Charles Kendall O'Neill
Wine and Water	Eugene Joffe
Succumbing	Paul Eaton Reeve
Sitting in the Sun	David Cornel De Jong
Collect to the Virgin	Nancy Cunard
My Country 'Tis of Thee	Charles Reznikoff
Comment	William Carlos Williams
Bibliography of the Little Magazine	David Moss

October 1932

A Painter Tries to Articulate	Hilaire Hiler
Entered as a Second Class Matter	S. J. Perelman
For Bill Bird	William Carlos Williams
Two Poems	Carl Rakosi
Once in a Sedan	Julian L. Shapiro
Chance Encounter	Charles C. Topping
Two Poems	Yvor Winters
Miss Lonelyhearts on a Field Trip	Nathanael West
Second Beach, Newport	Carl Bostelmann
Mama's Little Girl	Erskine Caldwell
Suicide	William Closson Emory
Two Poems	Louis Zukofsky
Jo-Jo	James T. Farrell
Farewell to Alamos	Robert McAlmon
Rush Hour	Eugene Joffe
Voice Out of Cornish	Fred Maxham
Charley Weiman	John Herrmann
Comment	William Carlos Williams
Some Notes on Violence	Nathanael West
Bibliography	David Moss

25. Philip Rahv, "Notes on the Decline of Naturalism," *Literature and the Sixth Sense* (New York: Houghton Mifflin, 1970), 84–85.

26. Lionel Trilling, "Reality in America," *The Liberal Imagination* (New York: Viking Press, 1950), 4, 13. Trilling directed a similar criticism at Farrell, whom he charged with a failure to move beyond the surface of modern life. In Farrell's novels, he wrote, the "over-expansion of detail . . . pass[es] for complexity" (as quoted in Aaron, *Writers on the Left*, 432).

27. Rahv, "Notes on the Decline of Naturalism," 86.

28. I have no wish to resurrect Rahv and Trilling's hostility toward a politically engaged literature on behalf of what eventually became canonized (largely through their own efforts) as an apolitical modernism. But I do wish to recuperate an argument whose merits, it seems to me, have been obscured by the onslaught of criticism directed at the editors of *Partisan Review* in recent years. The chief merit of that argument lies in its insistence on the importance of literary form in the apprehension of an increasingly complex social reality. For Rahv and Trilling that means a preference for James, Kafka, and Dostoevski. For me that means an interest in Nathanael West and the historical avant-garde—a tradition that is at odds with both the modernism of *Partisan Review* and the more overtly engaged literature of the radical left.

29. Nathanael West, "Some Notes on Miss L," in *Nathanael West: A Collec-*

tion of Critical Essays, ed. Jay Martin (Englewood Cliffs, N.J.: Prentice-Hall, 1971), 66.

30. Frank Norris, "A Plea for Romantic Fiction," The Responsibilities of the Novelist And Other Literary Essays (New York: Greenwood Press, 1968), 214.

31. Nathan Asch, "Mary," *Contact,* 2d ser., 1, no. 2 (May 1932): 10.

32. James T. Farrell, "Jo-Jo," *Contact,* 2d ser., 1, no. 3 (October 1932): 77.

33. If this sort of reductiveness falls well short of the critical standards espoused by modernist aesthetics, the exclusive focus on the so-called "brute facts" of existence deviates from the standards of the radical left as well. Under the guidelines of the latter—laid down by Mike Gold, Granville Hicks, and others—suffering, isolation, and betrayal cannot be allowed to stand without risking a corresponding pessimism about the possibilities for amelioration. Sincere efforts to portray the harsh circumstances of the disenfranchised cannot, must not, result in the existentializing of suffering, lest the result be political quietism. This was one of the heresies to which the proletarian literature of the day was most susceptible and for which it was carefully scrutinized by its partisans.

There is no shortage of this sort of heresy in the pages of *Contact.* In "Mary," for example, the narrator's long search for the "real" Texas culminates in his encounter with the raped "country" heroine, who is down-at-the-heels, starved, drifting. Her desperate condition is taken as an emblem of "truth," against which the narrator measures the "false" pretensions of modern cities like Dallas (characterized as having "blocks and blocks of houses all more or less alike [with] Buicks and Chevrolets standing before [them]" [9]). The limitations of this static, polarized opposition as a construction of reality are obvious enough. But from the viewpoint of the left, the most troublesome feature of this construction is the absence of any dialectical alternative. Hence, Mary's desperate circumstances (or, for that matter, Jo-Jo's) come to constitute reality itself, thereby eliminating the potential for agency. In this case, at least, Asch succumbs not just to "bad" literature, but to "bad" politics as well.

34. William Carlos Williams, "The Canada Lily," *Contact,* 2d ser., 1, no. 2 (May 1932): 38. Wallace Stevens suggested as much in his preface to Williams' *Collected Poems, 1921–1931.* There, Stevens argues that Williams' romance with the "real" (or what he called the "anti-poetic") is in fact a form of sentimentality: "To a man with a sentimental side the anti-poetic is that truth, that reality to which all of us are forever fleeing" (as quoted in Tashjian, *William Carlos Williams and the American Scene,* 144).

35. Williams ultimately submitted this sketch to Nancy Cunard's anthology of black culture called *Negro* (1934). What more enlightened readers made of the sketch, one can only guess.

36. William Carlos Williams, "The Colored Girls of Passenack—Old and New," *Contact,* 2d ser., 1, no. 1 (February 1932): 57, 58, 61. Other examples abound. In another vignette from the memoir, Williams writes,

I've seen tremendous furnaces of emotional power in certain colored women un-
matched in any white. . . . Once I went to call on a patient in a nearby suburb.
As the door opened to my ring, a magnificent bronze figure taller than I and
fairly vibrant with a sullen attentiveness stood before me. She said not a word
but stood there till I told her who I was. Then she let me in, turned her back and
walked into the kitchen. But the force of her—something, her mental alertness
coupled with her erectness, muscular power, youth, seriousness—her actuality—
made me want to create a new race on the spot. I had never seen anything like
it. (61)

Elsewhere, in a poem called "A Negro Woman," Williams transforms the black
female into yet another metaphor for the "real." This time, instead of infusing reality with mystery and potency, she becomes the figure for its *lumpen* qualities
("the bulk / of her thighs / causing her to waddle / as she walks), qualities that are
ultimately redeemed by the "upright marigolds" that she holds in her hand (*Selected Poems* [New York: New Directions, 1976], 156).

37. Dickran Tashjian characterizes Williams' approach to reality in terms of a
"complex empiricism" (*William Carlos Williams and the American Scene*, 18).
J. Hillis Miller's essay on Williams in *Poets of Reality* (Cambridge: Harvard University Press, 1965) is more subtle, and probably more accurate. Miller argues
that Williams' "theory of poetry . . . rejects both the mirror and the lamp, both
the classical theory of art as imitation and the romantic theory of art as transformation" (309–10). In Williams' work, Miller continues, there is a "strange lack
of tension": "the opposition between the inner world of the subject and the outer
world of things" ceases to exist. Instead, things exist in a "space both subjective
and objective, a region of co-presence" (288). This has profound implications for
the poet's use of language. Williams does not think of words as representing
things. Rather, as Miller explains, "For him things are already possessed before
being named" (299). Thus, instead of merely copying nature, Williams views the
poem as "an extension of the processes of the earth, 'not realism but reality
itself'" (310).

In his subsequent essay on Williams in *The Linguistic Moment* (Princeton:
Princeton University Press, 1985), Miller partially revises, or rather complicates,
this earlier estimation. He argues that Williams' hunger for presence is stymied in
Spring and All (and in some of his other poems) by his own recognition of the
"linguistic moment" in his work, which "disrupts or dislocates the perceptual or
phenomenological vocabulary within which [Williams] for the most part remains
caught" (375).

38. Williams, "Comment," *Contact,* 2d ser., 1, no. 2 (May 1932): 109.

39. Nathanael West, "Miss Lonelyhearts on a Field Trip," *Contact,* 2d ser., 1,
no. 3 (October 1932): 51.

40. William Carlos Williams, "Marianne Moore," *Imaginations* (New York:
New Directions, 1970), 317.

41. Nathanael West, *The Dream Life of Balso Snell* (New York: Farrar, Straus and Giroux., 1970), 14.

42. This is actually a description of Tod's personality in *The Day of the Locust* (New York: New Directions, 1962), 60.

43. West to William Carlos Williams, March 1932, box 1, Jay Martin Collection, Huntington Library.

44. West to William Carlos Williams, April 1932, box 1, Jay Martin Collection, Huntington Library.

45. Nathanael West and William Carlos Williams, "Epigram," *Contact,* 2d ser., 1, no. 1 (February 1932): title page.

46. Hugh Sykes Davies, "American Periodicals," *Criterion* 45, no. 11 (July 1932): 772–73.

47. Nathanael West, "Some Notes on Violence," *Contact,* 2d ser., 1, no. 3 (October 1932): 132. Reprinted in Martin, *Collection of Critical Essays,* 50.

48. Leslie Fiedler, *Love and Death in the American Novel* (New York: Dell, 1960), 484.

49. West, *Balso Snell,* 36.

50. Nathanael West, *Miss Lonelyhearts and The Day of the Locust* (New York: New Directions, 1962), 18.

51. William Carlos Williams, "Sordid? Good God!" in Martin, *Collection of Critical Essays,* 71. Williams goes on to add, "If this is so, why then so is *Macbeth* sordid, so *Crime and Punishment,* so nearly the whole of Greek tragedy. And so's your old man. Blah" (71).

52. West, "Some Notes on Miss L," 66–67. See for example the hash that John Raskolnikov Gilson makes of his attempt to offer a psychological account of his motivation for murder in *The Dream Life of Balso Snell.* Instead of explaining his motives he prefers to rummage through a reliquary of case studies that include not only Freud's Dora but Dostoevski's Raskolnikov and Shakespeare's Iago.

53. West, "Some Notes on Violence," 132–33.

54. Edmund Wilson makes a similar claim in "The Boys in the Back Room," his memoir on Hollywood writers: "The America of the murders and rapes which fill the Los Angeles papers is only the obverse side of the America of the inanities of the movies" (in Martin, *Collection of Critical Essays,* 142). West's virtue as a writer was to make the two sides of that coin indistinguishable.

55. What is true of imagery and event is true for the novel as a whole. Arguing that "Lyric novels can be written according to Poe's definition of a lyric poem," West urges American writers to follow suit:

> Forget the epic, the master work. In America fortunes do not accumulate, the soil does not grow, families have no history. Leave slow growth to the book reviewers, you only have time to explode. Remember William Carlos Williams' description of the pioneer women who shot their children against the wilderness like cannonballs. Do the same with your novels. ("Some Notes on Miss L," 66)

56. Nathanael West, "Through the Hole in the Mundane Millstone," In Martin, *Collection of Critical Essays*, 29–30. Nor, for that matter, did William Carlos Williams give up his own "French phase." Instead, West and Williams merely sought a more appropriate use for their avant-garde experiments. For West that meant *Miss Lonelyhearts*; for Williams, *Paterson*. Ultimately, however, it was West—both in his manifesto and in his fiction—who led the way.

57. As quoted in Martin, *Art of His Life*, 149.

58. West to William Carlos Williams, December 1932, box 1, Jay Martin Collection, Huntington Library.

59. William Carlos Williams, "A New American Writer," in Martin, *Collection of Critical Essays*, 48–49.

CHAPTER 4. THE PEOPLE TALK: *MISS LONELYHEARTS*

1. Arthur Inman, something of a Miss Lonelyhearts himself, kept a diary composed of painstaking interviews with people he called "talkers" solicited through classified ads in the newspaper. For an example of an exchange that could have just as easily appeared in a letter to Miss Lonelyhearts, see Arthur Inman, *The Inman Diaries*, ed. Daniel Aaron (Cambridge: Harvard University Press, 1985), 552.

2. As Terry Smith puts it, "The image of the industrial worker . . . was *displaced* by the increasing attention paid to another kind and place of work—agricultural labor. In the popular memory, the industrial worker appeared at the ghostly peripheries of recollection. Center stage was occupied by the conscience-piercing visages and empty landscapes of the farm worker, embattled into destitution" (*The Making of the Modern: Industry, Art, and Design in America* [Chicago: University of Chicago Press, 1993], 293).

3. The designation "the people" was a subject of much debate on the left during the thirties. The communists tended to prefer "the masses" to "the people"—or better yet, "the proletariat." But sympathetic critics like Kenneth Burke urged them to forgo such terminology in favor of "the people." The term "the people," Burke argued, "'was closer to our folkways,'" because it was "suggestive of 'the ultimate classless feature which the revolution could bring about,' and 'richer as a symbol of allegiance.' Words like 'worker' or 'proletarian,'" he insisted, "[were] negative symbols emphasizing the 'temporary antagonism,' [that] tended to exclude the very elements the Communist propagandist hoped to recruit." Others, like Joseph Freeman, reacted strongly against that idea, arguing that the "substitution of 'people' for 'worker' . . . was 'historically associated with demagoguery of the most vicious sort.'" As quoted in Daniel Aaron, *Writers on the Left* (New York: Oxford University Press, 1977), 291.

4. This passage, from Carl Sandburg's *The People, Yes* ([New York: Harcourt Brace, 1936]) is typical of the rhetoric of the day:

The people will live on.
The learning and blundering people will live on.
They will be tricked and sold and again sold
And go back to the nourishing earth for rootholds,
    The people so peculiar in renewal and comeback
    You can't laugh off their capacity to take it.
The mammoth rests between his cyclonic dramas. (284)

5. At least two critics of the thirties have argued that the American left made a strategic mistake by romanticizing an anachronistic folk culture instead of giving a qualified embrace to mass culture. See William Phillips, "What Happened in the '30's," *Commentary* 34 (September 1962): 204–12; Robert Warshow, "The Legacy of the '30's," reprinted in *The Immediate Experience* (New York: Doubleday Anchor, 1962).

6. Andreas Huyssen, *After the Great Divide: Modernism, Mass Culture, Postmodernism* (Bloomington: Indiana University Press, 1986), 44–62.

7. Patrick Brantlinger, *Bread and Circuses: Theories of Mass Culture as Social Decay* (Ithaca, N.Y.: Cornell University Press, 1983), 17.

8. See Vachel Lindsay, *The Art of the Moving Picture* (New York: Liveright, 1970), and Gilbert Seldes, *The Seven Lively Arts* (New York: Sagamore Press, 1957).

9. Nathanael West, *Miss Lonelyhearts and The Day of the Locust* (New York: New Directions Press, 1962), 22. All subsequent citations to *Miss Lonelyhearts* will appear in the text.

10. Once again, Sandburg's book-length poem captures the spirit of what West was writing *against.* Sandburg describes his ambitions for *The People, Yes* in the epigraph:

Being several stories and psalms nobody
would want to laugh at

interspersed with memoranda variations
worth a second look

along with sayings and yarns traveling on
grief and laughter

running sometimes as a fugitive air in the
classic manner

breaking into jig time and tap dancing
nohow classical

and further broken by plain and irregular
sounds and echoes from

the roar and whirl of street crowds, work
gangs, sidewalk clamor,

with interludes of midnight cool blue and
inviolable stars
over the phantom frames of skyscrapers.

Raymond Williams argues that under the guise of preserving folk culture, "uncritical, abstracting literary anthropologies" (like Sandburg's) tend to take a rich and quite specific tradition and transform it into "an unlocalized, unhistorical past." *The Country and the City* (New York: Oxford University Press, 1973), 258.

11. Mike Gold, Editorial, *New Masses*, August 1928, 2.

12. Walter Benjamin, "Art in the Age of Mechanical Reproduction," *Illuminations*, ed. Hannah Arendt (New York: Schocken Books, 1969), 232.

13. Bertolt Brecht, "The Radio as an Apparatus of Communication," *Brecht on Theater* (New York: Hill and Wang, 1986), 52.

14. Jean Baudrillard, "The Masses: The Implosion of the Social in the Media," *Selected Writings* (Stanford: Stanford University Press, 1988), 207–8.

15. The curative powers of the pastoral remain, apparently, beyond the reach of Miss Lonelyhearts or anybody else. Nowhere is this more evident than in the "little park" to which Miss Lonelyhearts retreats on several occasions (4, 19, 27). Here, there is no longer any pretense regarding the possibilities of redemption. Instead, nature reveals itself as thoroughly inorganic, reified—no different from the city that "menaced the little park from all sides" (27). The "orgy of stone breaking" (27) that created the city's skyscrapers is of a piece with the stone obelisk commemorating the Mexican American War at the center of the park. Both testify to the alienation of nature: the former manifests the dissipation of physical energy in stone, while the latter "celebrates" the transformation of the pastoral ideal into the imperialist ideology of Manifest Destiny. These "erections" to a displaced nature, West tells us, "seemed red and swollen in the dying sun, as though [they] were about to spout a load of granite seed" (19)—making them a parody of rejuvenation.

16. For a related consideration of the relationship between pain, language, and politics, see Elaine Scarry, *The Body in Pain* (New York: Oxford University Press, 1985), and David B. Morris, *The Culture of Pain* (Berkeley: University of California Press, 1993).

17. Baudrillard, "Masses," 208.

18. *Advice to the Lovelorn*, Reader's Report, Twentieth Century Fox studio files, 4/26/33, 2–4. This reader's report along with the treatment and subsequent drafts of *Advice to the Lovelorn* was loaned to me by Twentieth Century Fox Studios.

19. This is essentially the argument that Lary May makes in *Screening Out the Past* (Chicago: University of Chicago Press, 1983).

20. A "treatment" is a blueprint in which the plotline and themes are worked out *sans* dialogue. Once the producers and studio executives have approved it, the screenwriter is free to "develop" the treatment into a full-blown screenplay. Praskins' Treatment was followed by three subsequent drafts (dated 6/24/33, 7/8/33, 7/13/33) under the title of "Miss Lonelyhearts." There is also a "Revised

Final" draft dated 9/29/33, together with some additional revised pages dated three days earlier. All this can be found in the Twentieth Century Fox file of *Advice to the Lovelorn* along with miscellaneous materials (e.g., a reader's report on *Miss Lonelyhearts,* as well as Conference Notes dated 6/26/33). Subsequent references to the Treatment and First Draft will be cited in the text.

21. Lee Tracy—something of a poor man's Spencer Tracy—made a name for himself as the fast-talking Hildy Johnson in the Broadway version of *The Front Page* (1930), and he went on to play many similar roles thereafter. The choice of Lee Tracy for the lead in *Advice to the Lovelorn* says much about the sort of "tough guy" movie Zanuck had in mind.

22. West himself considered mingling these two personas in a single character in earlier drafts of his novel, but later dropped the idea.

23. "Used to be a boy cupid," his office boy observes, both times with a "dead pan" (First Draft, 9, 25). The boy's characteristic deadpan is, of course, another link to *Miss Lonelyhearts,* but it is deployed for humor rather than to suggest the terrible effort required to stave off recognition of pain or loss.

24. It is conceivable that his predicament might represent a displacement of those very pressures. But the whole affair is treated so casually that it is difficult to pursue this line of argument very far.

25. May, *Screening out the Past,* 53–55.

26. Quoting from the Production Code of 1930, Robert Sklar describes this as the "formula of 'compensating moral value': if 'bad' acts are committed, they must be counteracted by punishment and retribution, or reform and regeneration, of the sinful one. '*Evil and good are never to be confused* throughout the presentation,' the code said. The guilty must be punished; the audience must not be allowed to sympathize with crime or sin." *Movie Made America* (New York: Vintage Press, 1975), 174.

27. *Advice to the Lovelorn,* Conference Notes, Twentieth Century Fox studio files, 6/26/33, 3.

28. The rest of the review reads like this:

> It is true that *Sanctuary* was as low as literature could reach, but at least one can say this about it: it was done artistically and only adult minds could comprehend the meaning conveyed. The case of *Miss Lonelyhearts,* however, differs in that it is written in a language that an eight year old boy or girl will understand.
>
> The worst feature of this book, however, lies not in its vulgarity but in the fact that it uses as the main characters a columnist and a newspaper editor, presenting both in the worst of colors. The editor is painted as a dirty dog, and the columnist bereft of the slightest trace of decency.
>
> Since I know how sensitive newspaper people are, I felt that if this book were produced and the exhibitors innocently bought and showed the picture, the harm that would be done to exhibitor interests would be incalculable; for the newspaper people might accuse also the exhibitors of being a party to this defamation of newspaper folk carried on systematically by the moving picture

producers. Several times the producers have promised the newspaper people that they would refrain from presenting the newspaper profession in a bad light, and their word was accepted. Imagine how the newspaper men will feel if this book were to be put into a picture without an effort on our part to stop it. (*Harrison's Reports*, 26 August 1933, 134, 136)

This was a sensitive time in the relations between movies and the public, and Harrison apparently believed that he had a mission to save the movies from the stigma of West's novel. He sent letters to all the leading dailies and newspaper associations asking them to protest the production of the film. Most important, he urged exhibitors to request that NRA director Hugh S. Johnson declare the standard production practices of blind selling and block booking unfair, since such pictures as this one could thus be forced upon unwilling or unwary exhibitors by the studios. Jay Martin, *Nathanael West: The Art of His Life* (New York: Carroll and Graf, 1970), 208.

Clearly, Harrison's moral zeal in this regard was at least partly motivated by a desire to hype his journal. In a separate notice entitled "Subscribe to the Forecaster," Harrison adds, "The production of *Miss Lonelyhearts* proves that you cannot be too watchful as to the sort of material the producers put into pictures. And the only way by which you can keep informed of these expositions of bad taste is to subscribe to Harrison's Forecaster" (26 August 1933, 136).

Outraged by the attack on his novel, West wrote to his publisher—Harcourt, Brace—about the possibility of legal recourse. He got this response: "Certainly you couldn't sue Mr. Harrison on the grounds that his review was definitely hurting the sales of the book because there have been too few sales during the past two months. In fact, I imagine that his tirade will probably help sell a few copies of the book" (letter to Nathanael West, 7 September, 1933, box 1, Jay Martin Collection, Huntington Library). Harcourt, Brace proceeded to capitalize on the situation with a press release that quoted just enough of Harrison's "tirade" to titillate a prospective audience with the promise of obscenity. It then went on to dress up that obscenity as "art" with authoritative accolades from several noteworthy writers. Apparently, you can have your cake and eat it too.

This exchange over *Miss Lonelyhearts* is illuminating for the way it chronicles the fate of West's text once it was released into the marketplace where its defenders and detractors alike engaged in games of confidence that had little or nothing to do with the novel itself.

29. Leonard Praskins, *Advice to the Lovelorn*, revised pages, Twentieth Century Fox studio files, 9/26/33, 33.

30. As quoted in Martin, *Art of His Life*, 209.

CHAPTER 5. THE FOLKLORE OF CAPITALISM: *A COOL MILLION*

1. As quoted in Jay Martin, *Nathanael West: The Art of His Life* (New York: Carroll and Graf, 1970), 248–49). West worked on "American Chauve

Souris" with the New York producer-director John Houseman, whom he met through the Perelmans. After working casually with Houseman for two months, West had achieved a loose structure that satisfied them. For a brief period, more than one producer seemed sufficiently interested so that some thought was given to casting; West suggested the humorist Irvin Cobb for the role of the master of ceremonies. By the end of June, however, nothing had developed. All the commercial producers to whom the outline was submitted at last turned it down, and West himself lost interest. "Within a few years," Houseman writes, "every single item [in West's proposal] had been used and abused—first by the folk singers and later by the show business exploitation of the same themes and subjects" (Martin, 249).

2. Miles Orvell has suggested to me that "American Chauve Souris" may not be as antithetical to the satiric spirit of *A Cool Million* as I have argued here. He takes the title of the revue—*chauve-souris* (French for bat, which is itself slang for prostitute)—as a sly acknowledgment of the revue's prostitution of history despite its stated intentions to the contrary. Comments, ASA panel, "Marketing Authenticity in Depression America: Folklore, Privilege and Cultural Difference," American Studies Association, Pittsburgh 1995.

3. Warren Susman, "The Culture of the Thirties," *Culture as History* (New York: Pantheon, 1984), 153–54.

4. For more on this, see Jackson Lears, *No Place of Grace* (New York: Pantheon, 1981), and *The Invention of Tradition,* ed. Eric Hobsbawm and Terrence Ranger (Cambridge: Cambridge University Press, 1983).

5. Certainly there was no single ideological orientation behind this phenomenon. Interest in the folkways of the United States attracted conservatives like the Southern Agrarians or Midwestern regionalist painters like Grant Wood and Thomas Hart Benton in addition to romantic socialists and left-leaning fellow travelers like William Carlos Williams and Nathanael West himself. About the only group that did not take an active interest in American folkways per se was the American Communist Party. The Party was constrained by a resolutely internationalist outlook that preferred to see culture break down along class lines rather than along national or regional boundaries that were perceived as dangerously chauvinistic. The Communist Party did relent somewhat during the years of the Popular Front under the slogan "Communism Is Twentieth-Century Americanism." (The results were predictable enough, and even downright ludicrous, with Washington and Jefferson touted as protocommunists).

6. Susman argues that ever since Van Wyck Brooks's call for a "usable past" in 1918, there has been a general agreement among intellectuals—particularly during the thirties—"that an intelligent reading of the past might make possible man's intelligent direction over the future course of history" ("History and the American Intellectual: The Uses of the Past," *Culture as History,* 19).

7. As quoted, ibid., 19.

8. Nathanael West, *A Cool Million* (Farrar, Straus and Giroux, 1970), 68. Subsequent citations from this volume will appear in the text.

9. Martin, *Art of His Life*, 230. For more on the uses and abuses of folk culture as a salve for the ills of modernity, see Miles Orvell, *The Real Thing: Imitation and Authenticity in American Culture* (Chapel Hill: University of North Carolina Press, 1989), and Terry Smith, *The Making of the Modern: Industry, Art and Design in America* (Chicago: University of Chicago Press, 1993).

10. Roland Barthes, "Striptease," *Mythologies* (New York: Hill and Wang, 1980), 85.

11. There are several good histories of the Gospel of Success. Among them, Kenneth Lynn, *The Dream of Success: A Study of the Modern American Imagination* (Boston: Little, Brown, 1955); John Cawelti, *Apostles of the Self-Made Man* (Chicago: University of Chicago Press, 1965); Richard Weiss, *The American Myth of Success: From Horatio Alger to Norman Vincent Peale* (Urbana: University of Illinois Press, 1988); Donald Meyer, *The Positive Thinkers* (New York: Pantheon, 1965).

12. Nathanael West, *A Cool Million: A Screen Story*, Columbia Studios Story Department, September 1940.

13. It is perhaps no accident that the fiction of Horatio Alger—the great popular romance of individualism and social mobility—should reach the peak of its popularity at the precise moment when the suzerainty of the large-scale corporation appeared to be most complete. At a time when individualism seemed to have disappeared, "never to return," Alger's fiction constructed a consoling fable that elided history in order to allow for the continuance of America's most sacred mythology. His homely advice to his young readers to "try and trust" was the popular analogue to the Progressive crusade against the monopolistic practices of the large-scale corporation during the years between the Sherman Antitrust Act (1890) and the Clayton Antitrust Act (1914)—the very years that constitute the heyday of Alger's popularity.

14. Matthew Josephson, *The Robber Barons* (New York: Random House, 1962), 47.

15. Cawelti, *Apostles of the Self-Made Man*, 109.

16. Nathanael West, *Miss Lonelyhearts and The Day of the Locust* (New York: New Directions, 1962), 31.

17. Hal Foster, *Compulsive Beauty* (Cambridge: MIT Press, 1993), 126. For an extended commentary on the critical uses to which these exquisite corpses were put, along with some intriguing photographs, see 125–53.

18. In the same way steel is made to look like cheese, human beings are made to look like slaves. In both instances, "nature"—in the case of the latter, "human nature"—is transformed into something it is not for the purposes of exchange. Thus, Quakers are branded like cattle, Negroes are enslaved, and children are turned into wage laborers.

19. The immediate source of inspiration for Whipple and the program of his

National Revolutionary Party (otherwise known as the "Leather Shirts") is not, as one might expect, Huey Long or Father Coughlin but William Dudley Pelley, the leader of a fascist organization called the Silver Shirts. If Calvin Coolidge's inane optimism offers a model for the sunnier side of Whipple as the apostle of success, Pelley's gospel of hate emerges ominously with failure. Pelley might seem, at first glance, an eccentric source of inspiration. Unlike Coolidge, or for that matter Long, he is not immediately recognizable as within the American grain. For one thing, he was too enamored of the "fervent Hitlers and gesticulating fascists" upon whom he openly modeled himself. Indeed, Pelley insisted that the inspiration for his Silver Shirts came to him during an out-of-body experience (he claimed to have died for seven minutes) in which the oracle told him that "when a certain young house-painter comes to the head of the German people, then do you take that as your time symbol [sic] for bringing the work of the Christian Militia into the open" (as quoted in Martin, *Art of His Life*, 233). He did so in 1933, and thereafter his mission as he saw it was to lead a mass movement against anti-Christian conspirators in order to recast the social order. That new social order was, however, very much *in* the American grain. Inspired by Edward Bellamy's *Looking Backward*, Bernard Baruch's War Industries Board, and Roosevelt's National Recovery Act (the latter two of which he vehemently scorned), Pelley advocated a corporate state that would be constructed along technocratic lines, with a planned economy carefully controlled by experts. The fruits of that new social order would be used to create a commonwealth in which only "100 per cent Americans" would be allowed to hold stock.

20. In the early thirties Pelley received a great deal of press. Besides Spivak's article "Silver Shirts among the Gold," *New Masses* 11, no. 2 (10 April, 1934), there were a number of others: Arthur Graham, "Crazy like a Fox: Pelley of the Silver Shirts," *New Republic* 79 (18 April, 1934): 264–66; John Smertenko, "Hitlerism Comes to America," *Harpers* 167 (November 1933): 660–70.

21. Harry Cohn, it should be noted in passing, was another admirer of Mussolini. In 1933 Columbia released a documentary feature called *Mussolini Speaks,* which combined excerpts from Mussolini's speeches with film clips illustrating his accomplishments. Il Duce was so pleased with the film that he invited Harry Cohn to Rome to receive an award. Cohn was immensely flattered by the occasion, and he kept a picture of Mussolini over his desk until it was no longer politic to do so. It was not so much Mussolini's corporate state, but the style of the great dictator that most impressed him. (Cohn's methods were already notoriously dictatorial; they became more so as his power increased.) When he returned to the United States, Cohn had his office designed to imitate the same vast proportions that had overwhelmed him during his visit with Mussolini: "By the time I arrived at his desk, I was whipped," Cohn said, already anticipating its potential for intimidation back in Hollywood (Bob Thomas, *King Cohn* [New York: McGraw-Hill, 1990], 102).

22. Martin, *Art of His Life*, 245.

23. Ibid., 380.

24. Two of those four writers—Nathanael West and Boris Ingster—were a team. They produced a fourteen-page "adaptation" entitled "*A Cool Million: A Screen Story.*" It is undated, although Jay Martin places it during September of 1940 (*Art of His Life,* 379–80). The project was then assigned to Sidney Buchman, who wrote what is labeled as a "Treatment." It is further described as a "first draft" and dated 2 November, 1940. It is forty-four pages long. This treatment was followed by an incomplete draft of a screenplay (labeled "A COOL MILLION: Screenplay" by Sidney Buchman) of thirty pages. The project then languished for three or four years until it was assigned to Wilfred Pettitt. He wrote two drafts. The date on the first one (labeled "First Draft") is partially obscured, but it could be as early as January 1943. It is forty-seven pages in length. The second draft (labeled "Second Draft") is dated 18 January, 1944. It is forty pages long. The two drafts are virtually identical. The difference in page length is attributable to a difference in format. If Pettitt wrote the first draft in January of 1943, he may have simply asked for a clean draft (the original had lots of handwritten changes in the margins) to be drawn up when he returned to it in January of 1944. So far as I know, there were no other drafts or writers associated with the project. I did not have access to production notes and memoranda.

25. Martin, *Art of His Life,* 380.

26. Even though the screenplay deviated substantially from *A Cool Million,* West and Ingster sold it as an "adaptation" because adaptations of published novels received higher fees. West told Ingster they were safe in the deception since "no one would read the book to check" (Martin, *Art of His Life,* 370). He was right; Columbia paid $10,000 for it.

27. Boris Ingster had come to Hollywood with Sergei Eisenstein to make *Thunder over Mexico* (which was never produced). He stayed on after Eisenstein left and established a reputation for himself as a deft hand at plotting narratives. Before he began his collaboration with West he was best known as the screenwriter of two successful ice-skating pictures starring Sonja Henie (*Thin Ice* and *Happy Landing*). Because English was not his first language, Ingster preferred to write as part of a team. According to Martin, "Ingster had read *Miss Lonelyhearts* and *The Day of the Locust* and set out to become friends with West." The relationship appeared to be a fruitful one for both of them. West wrote to his sister, Laura, "Boris has enough energy to drive a steam shovel. . . . Although he doesn't write English himself, he knows what he wants in that language and aside from the tedium I must say that he really knows a hell of a lot about the business" (*Art of His Life,* 366). Besides the adaptation of *A Cool Million,* West and Ingster collaborated on several other projects: *Before the Fact* (the film that Hitchcock was later to make as *Suspicion*), *Amateur Angel,* and *A Bird in the Hand.* Ingster later went on to considerable success as the producer of one of the most popular television shows of the sixties: *The Man from UNCLE.*

28. West and Ingster, "*A Cool Million,*" 11.

29. The screwball comedy was certainly one source of inspiration, but Mark Twain's short story "The Million Pound Bank Note" may have been another. The two stories are remarkably similar—so similar, in fact, that to speak of Twain's short story as the "inspiration" for West's adaptation may be too generous.

30. As film historian Thomas Schatz explains, this screwiness demonstrates that these class-crossed lovers "share the same ideals of . . . direct and honest human interaction and a healthy disregard for depersonalizing social restrictions." *Hollywood Genres* (New York: Random House, 1981), 152.

31. Capra and Riskin's *Mr. Deeds Goes to Town* provides the prototype for this sort of pastoral resolution. As Andrew Bergman explains, "In *Deeds,* he [Capra] was concerned with constructing a nearly all-embracing unity by having his village type force the urbanites to accept his values. The film ran the 'back to the earth' formula in reverse; rather than advocating return to the land, Capra attempted to bring the values of the country back to the city." "Frank Capra and Screwball Comedy," reprinted in *Film Theory and Criticism,* ed. Gerald Mast (New York: Oxford University Press, 1974), 772.

32. Instead of situating this adaptation in Capra's trilogy of *Deeds-Smith-Doe,* one might just as easily find a place for it in Buchman's own social trilogy, the first two installments of which are *Theodora Goes Wild* and *Mr. Smith Goes to Washington.* In the absence of *A Cool Million* (which was never produced), the last place in that trilogy was ultimately filled by Buchman's *The Talk of the Town* (1942). For a brief but insightful commentary on Buchman's work, see Richard Corliss, *Talking Pictures* (New York: Penguin, 1974), 275–83.

33. Where West and Ingster were content to end their story with the bank's discovery that the missing money is really just the result of a clerical error, Buchman insists on seeing Joey have his day in court—literally and figuratively.

34. Parenthetical references are to Buchman's "Treatment."

35. The Hays Commission was established in 1923 in response to the censorship battles that raged throughout the twenties. It is another manifestation of the antimodern, populist sentiment chronicled throughout this chapter. In 1921 it offered the "Thirteen Points," the first in a series of official moral codes which were meant to serve as guidelines for filmmakers. In 1927 this was followed by "The Don'ts and Be Carefuls," which was in turn superseded by the notorious "Motion Picture Production Code of 1930."

36. "The Motion Picture Production Code of 1930," reprinted in *The Movies in Our Midst,* ed. Gerald Mast (Chicago: University of Chicago Press, 1982), 324.

37. Ibid., 324.

38. Martin, *Art of His Life,* 380. According to Martin, West challenged Buchman to "go back to the novel" if he wanted social significance.

39. "Motion Picture Production Code of 1930," 331.

40. Ibid., 324.

41. Thomas, *King Cohn,* 301. This failure to name names did not earn Buchman a contempt charge as it did so many others. Buchman's lawyer circumvented

the committee by pointing out that they lacked the necessary quorum to issue such a charge, and Buchman was allowed to go unmolested. According to Thomas, "Buchman was furious that his attorney would use the tactic, and he later waived the lack of quorum, thus placing himself open to a citation for contempt of Congress" (301). Buchman was subpoenaed again, but this time he refused to appear. Instead, he filed a motion to have the subpoena thrown out, arguing that he had already appeared before the committee in good faith. He was cited for contempt and fined $150 in addition to receiving a one-year suspended sentence. For more on the circumstances surrounding Buchman's testimony in particular and the HUAC hearings in general, see Victor Navasky, *Naming Names* (New York: Viking Press, 1980).

42. Harry Cohn—never one to let an investment languish—took one more crack at *A Cool Million* in 1943–44. This time journeyman Wilfred Pettitt was asked to see what he could do with Buchman's treatment and aborted script. Pettitt came up with a forty-page adaptation of his own, which contains the same basic plotline that West and Ingster had originated, as well as most of Buchman's elaborations. But Pettitt was largely untroubled by the concerns that prompted much of Buchman's temporizing and hesitation. Instead, he was frankly concerned with reestablishing the viability of the Alger myth. But instead of attempting to accomplish this through the reconciliation of rural and urban values, Pettitt conceived of the problem as temporal in nature. Horatio Alger—like Miss Lonelyhearts' advice column—was simply in need of an update. This allowed Pettitt to shed much of the baggage that gave Buchman so much trouble. In order to update Alger, Pettitt needed to concoct a scenario in which Joey can abandon the anachronistic elements of Alger's credo without necessarily losing sight of its fundamental values. This, as we have already seen, is easier said than done. If Pettitt's criticism were too harsh, it would risk undermining Alger's values altogether, and if it were too gentle, it would not perform the cultural work necessary to imbue those values with an updated and more congenial form. Whatever drama Pettitt's treatment possesses lies in this delicate negotiation.

Pettitt began by caricaturing the "Victorian stiltedness" (First Draft, 1) of the Alger mythology with its "aversion to such frivolities as movies and dances and smooches in the shadow of the haystack" (2). Joey's application of Alger's creed is at once seen as too literal, and his disappointment in the world's failure to live up to that creed is misplaced: "Angela tells him that it isn't the world that's out of whack. It's Joey. The world always does crazy things to people who haven't learned how to laugh at it, or with it. And things will keep happening to Joey until he stops being such a stuffed shirt" (28).

Angela manages to dismiss the Alger hero in a single epithet: He is a "stuffed shirt." In place of Alger's high, moral self-seriousness, she urges him to adopt a sense of play. This, she tells Joey, will enable him to "laugh at or [more importantly] *with*" the world—by which she means that he must learn to turn its craziness to his own advantage. Learning to laugh at the craziness of the world, however, does not mean forsaking value altogether. Pettitt recognized that in order to "play the game," Joey may be required on occasion to exchange his "Yankee honesty" for "Yankee sharpness." But Pettitt was careful to distinguish his "legitimate" manipulation of appearances from the more "dishonest" manipulations of "the crooks and the wise guys" (31). On those occasions when Joey *is* tempted to "step over the line" (by resorting to "bribery" [32]), Angela is there to remind him of the difference between laughter and cynicism.

Joey is ultimately rewarded for his honesty as well as his laughter with "offers of employment from heads of corporations all over the country." Moreover, he eventually comes to realize that "there *are* successful people who respect, and who live by, the homely virtues; that America is still the land of opportunity, even though at times her demeanor may appear to be a little cockeyed" (39). This is exactly the balance that this project had been seeking ever since its inception in Hollywood. Unfortunately, it is a resolution that is imposed *on* the text rather than achieved *through* it. Alger is vindicated, but only after his moral creed has been taken away from the "stuffed shirts" in Oatsville and placed in the hands of more flexible practitioners in New York City—who are laughing, as it were, all the way to the bank.

CHAPTER 6. THE CLICHÉS ARE HAVING A BALL:
THE DAY OF THE LOCUST

1. "It is strange," Nathanael West once observed, "but the movies are always trying to forget 'the barber.' Even Mack Sennett tried *once* to forget him. He lost several hundred thousand dollars, then took another look at the sign hanging on the wall of his scenario department. 'Remember: The extent of intelligence of the average public mind is eleven years. Moving pictures should be made accordingly.'" "Soft Soap for the Barber," reprinted in *Nathanael West: A Comprehensive Bibliography,* ed. William White (Kent, Ohio: Kent State University Press, 1975), 171.

2. J. K. Huysmans, *A Rebours* (New York: Penguin, 1986), 37.

3. Ibid., 208–9.

4. Ibid., 29.

5. Mikhail Bakhtin, *Rabelais and His World* (Bloomington: Indiana University Press, 1984), 52.

6. Umberto Eco, "*Casablanca,* or The Clichés Are Having a Ball," reprinted in *On Signs,* ed. Marshall Blonsky (Baltimore: Johns Hopkins University Press, 1985), 38. What Eco says about *Casablanca* might be extended to the world West's characters move through: "When the choice of the tried and true is limited, the result is a trite or mass-produced film, or simply kitsch. But when the tried and true repertoire is used wholesale, the result is an architecture like Gaudi's *Sagrada Familia* in Barcelona" (36).

7. Nathanael West, *Miss Lonelyhearts and The Day of the Locust* (New

York: New Directions, 1962), 139. Subsequent citations from *The Day of the Locusts* will appear in the text.

8. West, *Miss Lonelyhearts and The Day of the Locust,* 11.

9. Ibid., 22.

10. Nathanael West, *The Dream Life of Balso Snell* (New York: Farrar, Straus and Giroux, 1970), 47.

11. For more on the sadomasochistic dynamics of the "gaze," see the conflicting testimony of Laura Mulvey's "Visual Pleasure and Narrative Cinema" and Gaylyn Studlar's "Masochism and the Perverse Pleasures of the Cinema." Mulvey's influential article argues for the sadistic dimension of the specifically male gaze as it implicates the objectified female in a set of narrative operations ultimately designed to denigrate her. The latter essay offers an interesting counterargument to that claim by arguing for the power of the female image—released from narrative forms—to overpower its audience. In Studlar's formulation the sadistic gaze of the voyeur is transformed into an exquisite form of masochism. Both essays are reprinted in *Movies and Methods,* vol. 2, ed. Bill Nichols (Berkeley: University of California Press, 1985), 303–14, 602–21.

12. René Girard, *Deceit, Desire, and the Novel* (Baltimore: Johns Hopkins University Press, 1965), 39, 73.

13. Walter Benjamin, *Illuminations,* ed. Hannah Arendt (New York: Schocken Books, 1969), pp. 155–200, 217–252.

14. Girard, *Deceit, Desire, and the Novel,* 90.

15. Karl Marx, *Capital,* ed. Frederick Engels, translated from the third German edition (1883) by Samuel Moore, vol. 1 (New York: International Publishers, 1967), 73.

16. W. J. T. Mitchell, *Iconology* (Chicago: University of Chicago Press, 1986), 195.

17. West, *Dream Life of Balso Snell,* 3.

18. Norman O. Brown, *Life against Death* (Middletown, Conn.: Wesleyan University Press, 1965), 179–307.

19. West, *Dream Life of Balso Snell,* 139. This alienation of the life of the body cannot be accomplished with any degree of permanence. Indeed, the wholesale confusion of inorganic things with Being ultimately contributes to what might be described as a "return of the repressed." West allegorizes this in animal terms. Each Westian character comes with his/her appropriate animal totem: Abe Kusich is figured as a series of dogs: a "growling puppy" (66), a "terrier in a harness" (150), a "dog with a foxtail in his ear" (167). (Not even Freud's exalted "id" escapes Westian bathos, here demoted to the status of a domesticated house pet.) Faye begins the novel as a "game bird" [108] and ends ignominiously as a "dirty black hen" (147). Homer's hands are figured as "a pair of strange aquatic animals" (82), and he himself is described as a "turtle." But his totem is clearly the predatory lizard that he will become by the end of the novel. Just as the human is constantly lapsing into the animal, the animal itself is not allowed to stand as a

fixed counter. *Tragopan,* the horse that Abe recommends to Tod, is Greek for "pheasant" (65). Abe's fighting cock is described at various points as a snake (151), a goose (152), a cat (155), and a worm (152). Thus, nature reveals itself as protean, a seething cauldron of thwarted energies that exist just beneath the surface, always waiting to erupt. These animal epithets give *The Day of the Locust* something of the quality of an inverted Aesopian fable. Instead of anthropomorphizing nature, West alienates the human in a series of animal masks that function to dramatize the repressive nature of consumer society.

20. Rita Barnard argues that there is a "curious sense of relief that accompanies this outburst of violence." In her thoughtful reading of this final scene, the riot is depicted as "the moment when the pent-up oppositional forces of the outmoded, the excluded, and the superannuated are explosively released" (164). As my own argument suggests, I am inclined to think that Barnard's attempt to wrest a "positive moment" from West's *Kulturpessimismus* is "no more than . . . wishful thinking"—a possibility that she herself acknowledges in *The Great Depression and the Culture of Abundance* (New York: Cambridge University Press, 1995), 186).

21. Georges Bataille, "The Notion of Expenditure," *Visions of Excess* (Minneapolis: University of Minnesota Press, 1985), 117.

22. Ibid., 118.

23. "The Burning of Los Angeles" has received a great deal of comment of late. Rita Barnard reads the painting more positively than I do: i.e., as a "dialectical image" that celebrates the destruction of Los Angeles as the "precondition for an as yet unimaginable redemption" (186–87). Thomas Strychacz, on the other hand, sees the painting as oscillating between Tod's attempt to resist the "unauthentic culture" of Hollywood and his recognition that art cannot provide the "way out" he seeks (*Modernism, Mass Culture, and Professionalism* [New York: Cambridge University Press, 1993], 196–99).

24. Jean Baudrillard, "Consumer Society," *Selected Writings* (Stanford: Stanford University Press, 1988), 54.

POSTSCRIPT: MADONNA'S BUSTIER

1. Nathanael West, *Miss Lonelyhearts and The Day of the Locust* (New York: New Directions, 1962), 60.

2. Ibid., 178.

3. Ibid., 118.

Index

Aaron, Daniel, xi, xiv, xv, xvi
Adorno, Theodor, xix, 69
Advice columns, 69, 71–87; hegemonic strategies of, 71–73
Agee, James, 67
Agrarianism, 9, 10, 52
Alger, Horatio, 94–99, 101, 106, 108, 110–11, 167n13, 171n42
"American Chauve Souris" (West), 88–89, 94, 101, 165n1
American Dream, American Way, Gospel of Success, 10, 94, 96–97, 98, 101
American Humor (Rourke), 90
American Writers' Congress, xii
Anger, Kenneth, 105
Anti-aesthetic, xvii, xix, 42, 148n4
Antimodernism, 10, 90
Anti-Nazi League: West's involvement in, xii
Anti-Semitism, 104
Apocalypse, 34–35, 62, 128, 132, 135
Appel, Benjamin, 67
Appollinaire, Guillaume, 16, 145n7
Aragon, Louis, xviii, 17, 18, 22, 146n14
Arensberg Circle, xviii
Armory Show, xviii
Arnold, Matthew, 89
Arnold, Thurman, 5
Arp, Jean, 19
Asch, Nathan, 55, 56
Avante-garde, xviii–xix, 64–65, 148n4; accidentalism as a strategy of, 15; and its critique of art, xviii–xix; and the substitution of artifice for nature, 113–118; and the problem of authority, 26–27, 41–43; automatism as a strategy of, 18–20, 101; its relation to and rebellion

from bourgeoisie, 21, 24–29, 77; and games of confidence, 23, 42; and the collapse of critical distance, 25, 27; death of, xx; deflation as a strategy of, 21, 101; in *The Dream Life of Balso Snell*, 28–43; excrementalism as a strategy of, xix, 28–43; and experimentalism, 65; exquisite corpses as a motif in, xix, 23–26, 99–101; in "The Fake," 23–26; hallucination as a strategy of, 21, 147n26; inversion as a strategy of, 42, 73; and kitsch, xix; madness as a strategy of, 26, 36; in relation to modernism, 148n4; plagiarism as a strategy of, 96, 104; readymade as a strategy of, xix, 20, 42, 114, 116; and the problem of representation, 23–26; and the cultivation of scandal, 24–26, 77; status in United States, xviii; West's affinities with, xix. *See Also* Dada; Surrealism

Bakhtin, Mikhail, 38–39, 42, 71, 114
Barnard, Rita, xi, xiv, 143n21, 174n20, 174n23
Barnes, Djuna, xviii
Barthes, Roland, 93
"Base Materialism and Gnosticism" (Bataille), 34
Bataille, Georges, 33–37, 76, 128–30, 150n20
Baudelaire, Charles, 36, 119
Baudrillard, Jean, 70–71, 73, 76, 119, 130, 133–34
Benjamin, Walter, xi, 70, 71, 122
Berlin, Irving, 76
"Big Toe, The" (Bataille), 33

175

Gershwin, George, 88
Girard, René, 122
Glass Menagerie (Williams), 4
Gnosticism, 34–35, 37
Godwin, Murray, 50
Gold, Mike, 51–53, 65, 68, 70
Gone with the Wind (Mitchell), 90
Grapes of Wrath, The (Steinbeck), 3, 6–9, 53, 69; Ma Joad, xii–xiii, 69
Great Depression and the Culture of Abundance, The (Barnard), xi
Green, Paul, 88
Greenberg, Clement, 18–22, 147*n*18
Grosz, George, 17

Hanson, Howard, 88
Harrison's Reports, 85–6, 164*n*28
Hartley, Marsden, 49
Hawkes, John, xi
Hays Commission, 109–10, 170*n*35
H. D. (Hilda Doolittle), 49
Hearst, Randolph, 92
Heartfield, John, 17, 22
Hegel, G. W. F., 34
Heller, Joseph, xi
Hemingway, Ernest, 50
Herbst, Josephine, 50
High/Low polarity, xix–xx, 28–43, 58, 76, 82, 97, 99, 130; Bakhtin on, 151*n*26; Bataille on, 33–34, 36–37; and the construction of bourgeois subjectivity, 36–37
Hi Nelly (film), 77
His Girl Friday (film), 77
Hoch, Hannah, 17
Hofstadter, Richard, 144*n*23
Holiday (film), 106
Hollywood, xii, xvi, xix–xx, 37–38, 42, 69, 76, 84, 93, 105, 112–15; and *The Day of the Locust*, 113–31; and mass man, 69, 113
Hollywood Babylon (Anger), 105
Hope, Bob, 105
Horoscopes, 69
Humor in West's fiction, xix, 16, 97, 99, 114–15, 121, 125, 130; as bathos, xix; in the form of deadpan, 16, 72–73; as dirty jokes, 29–30; as Dadaist *geste*, 25;

as grotesquerie, 114, 117; as hysterical laughter, 27; indebted to Jarry's slapstick and scatological humor, 16, 29; as parody, 26, 72, 103, 125; in the form of puns, 26, 29–30, 40, 72, 149*n*16; as sophomoric humor, 27–30; in the form of a vaudeville routine, 97; West's inability to write "big things" without laughing, xii; West's "particular kind of joking," xi–xiii, xv, 15, 139*n*3; compared to Heartfield, 17; as universal vs. political satires, xvi
Huysmans, J. K., 32, 113–14
Huyssen, Andreas, xviii
Hysteria, 27, 36, 73, 98, 118

I Am a Fugitive from a Chain Gang (film), 6
Idealism in West's fiction: as compared to Bataille, 33–34, 36; and discourse, 38–43; and *The Dream Life of Balso Snell*, 26–29, 33–34, 38–39; noses, circles and triangles as metaphors for, 26–38, 100; and the singular/plural polarity, 28
Ideology, xv, xx, 37, 38, 39, 43, 84, 101; and the structure of reality, 58; and the "cultural work" of adapting a screenplay, 77–78; and discourse, 39, 43; and dreams, 19, 20, 38; and entertainment, 78; and innocence, 10–11, 42, 63, 99, 115–16, 121, 127; and *Miss Lonelyhearts*, 73, 77, 84; and obscenity, xii–xiii, 115–16; and pain, 74–76, 99; and proletarian literature, 52; and the excesses of the 1930s, xv; and True Love, 74, 77, 79, 82–84, 115; and the structure of reality, 58; and suffering, 55–56, 99–100; and West's depoliticization by *Partisan Review*, xv–xvi; and West's refusal of metamorphosis, 38
Il Mare (magazine), 66
Ingster, Boris, 105, 107, 109, 169*n*27
Inman, Arthur, 4, 67, 161*n*1
Inman Diaries, The (Inman), 67
It Happened One Night (film), 106

James, William, 31
Jarry, Alfred, 16, 29, 145*n*7

The Wisconsin Project on American Writers

Frank Lentricchia, General Editor